# VIRTUOSITY OF THE
# NINETEENTH CENTURY

# VIRTUOSITY OF THE NINETEENTH CENTURY

*Performing Music and Language in Heine, Liszt, and Baudelaire*

*Susan Bernstein*

STANFORD UNIVERSITY PRESS

STANFORD, CALIFORNIA

Stanford University Press
Stanford, California

© 1998 by the Board of Trustees of the
Leland Stanford Junior University

Printed in the United States of America
CIP data appear at the end of the book

# Acknowledgments

Research for this book was supported in part by a Henry Merritt Wriston Fellowship from Brown University and a research stipend from the Deutscher Akademischer Austauschdienst. I am grateful to these sources, as well as to the Herzogin Anna Amalia Bibliothek, Weimar, and the Stiftung Weimarer Klassik for allowing me access to their resources. I am especially grateful for the patience and helpfulness of the librarians at the Music Library of the Peabody Conservatory, Baltimore, and at the Orwig Music Library at Brown University.

Deepest thanks to the many friends and colleagues whose encouragement and intellectual engagement with this project I could not have done without: Carolyn Dean, Kevin McLaughlin, Karen Newman, Jeffrey Wallen, Samuel Weber, and Susan White. The manuscript was also helped by the careful readings and comments of a reading group at Brown University: Christina Crosby, Mary Anne Doane, Coppelia Kahn, and Ellen Rooney. I thank my colleagues at Brown University, especially in the Department of Comparative Literature, for their support of my work.

I thank my parents, Lionel and Jodie Bernstein, and my sister Molly Bernstein. I am grateful to Dae Kwang Sunim and my Dharma family in the Kwan Um School of Zen. I extend special thanks to Spencer Billings Nineberg.

I owe special gratitude to Helen Tartar of Stanford University Press, whose dedication to this project was absolutely crucial. Thanks also to Nathan MacBrien, who saw the book through production, for his careful and conscientious work on the text. For corrections and camaraderie in the final hours, warm thanks to Denise Davis.

Finally, I would like to thank those teachers and colleagues whose interventions made this book possible in the most pointed sense: Neil Hertz, Carol Jacobs, Peter Fenves, Avital Ronell, Philippe Lacoue-Labarthe, and, most of all, Werner Hamacher.

# Contents

# Note to the Reader

References to works in the Bibliography are indicated by volume and page in the text. The following editions and abbreviations are used for frequently cited works:

*Augsburger Allgemeine Zeitung.* (*AZ*)

Baudelaire, Charles. *Oeuvres complètes*. 2 vols. Ed. Claude Pichois. Paris: Bibliothèque de la Pléiade, 1975. (*OC*)

Heine, Heinrich. *Sämtliche Schriften*. 6 vols. Ed. Klaus Briegleb. Munich: Carl Hanser Verlag, 1978. (*SS*)

———. *The Romantic School and Other Essays*. Ed. Jost Hermand and Robert C. Holub. New York: Continuum, 1985. (*RS*)

———. *The Works of Heinrich Heine*. 12 vols. Trans. Charles Godfrey Leland. New York: Dutton, 1906. (*Works*)

Liszt, Franz. *Gesammelte Schriften*. 6 vols. Ed. Lina Ramann. Leipzig: Breitkopf und Härtel, 1881. (*GS*)

Wagner, Richard. *Dichtungen und Schriften*. 10 vols. Ed. Dieter Borchmeyer. Frankfurt am Main: Insel Verlag, 1983. (*DS*)

———. *Gesammelte Schriften und Dichtungen*. 10 vols. Leipzig: Fritsch, 1897. (*GS*)

———. *Richard Wagner's Prose Works*. 8 vols. Trans. W. A. Ellis. New York: Broude Brothers, 1966. (*WPW*)

For readers' convenience, references to existing English translations have been provided when possible. These have been consulted and incorporated wherever possible, and modified as necessary. All other translations are my own. When two citations are given, the first refers to the original-language source, the second, to the translation.

# VIRTUOSITY OF THE NINETEENTH CENTURY

# Introduction

Probably more than any other art, music poses a problem for descriptive language. Some advocate a formalistic approach to speaking about music, while others go to the opposite extreme, allowing music to be the vehicle for any and all emotional content. In this passage from *Either/Or*, Kierkegaard describes this problem in terms of the heterogeneity of thought and music:

> The chief difficulty . . . was that, whereas I wanted to demonstrate by way of thought that the elemental originality of the sensuous is music's essential theme [*genstand*], this still can be demonstrated properly only by music, just as I myself also came to a knowledge of it through music. The difficulty with which the subsequent discussion must struggle is more particularly this: since that which music expresses, the theme under discussion here, is essentially the proper theme of music, music expresses it much better than language is capable of doing, which shows up very poorly alongside it.[1]

According to this passage, music disseminates itself. In resounding, it reveals and communicates its essence. Language, in contrast, makes a "poor showing," for it only points to this relationship that remains absent as music. The conflict between the conceptual mediation of language and the immediacy associated with music makes possible an experience of the limit of language's capacity to signify something other than itself. This limit can only appear because something has been positioned outside or beyond it. In *Premises: Essays on Philosophy and Literature from Kant to Celan*, Werner Hamacher exposes this spatial tension in terms of the operation of language itself, which opens the dual functions of referentiality and thematization: "The imperative of flight into referentiality is an imperative of language. It commands . . . the abandonment of the uncertain basis of language in order to seek in a supposedly nonlinguistic domain the stable ground for its capacity for truth. . . . But access to this domain outside of language can only be attained, problematically, by means of language, because this outside can be encountered in language only as a 'theme.'"[2]

This outside, the "theme" of thematization that Kierkegaard calls music here, has often been hypostatized and carried off as the ineffable language of sentiment, the outpouring of the nonverbal or of "the preverbal," unhampered by the codes of patriarchal society or rationality. What eludes Kierkegaard's text is not "music itself" but a certain indivisible relationship between subject and expression, or theme and predicate: "that which music expresses, the theme under discussion here, is essentially the proper theme of music." The deficiency of language Kierkegaard invokes lies in the presupposition of propositional "propriety." Music only exceeds language because it has a "proper" theme, defined as an *object* (*genstand*) that is not accessible to language. But music's own theme comes forth contiguously with its movement, not in a propositional relationship that divides subject and object. Kierkegaard points not simply to an "other" to language but perhaps to another kind of language governed by a nonoppositional and inseparable relationship between subject and predicate.

The intimation of this "other" grammar suggests that music turns toward language as a critique of language's binarisms: subject and predicate, inside and outside, origin and expression, center and extension. "If," writes John Cage, "at this point, one says, 'Yes! I do not discriminate between intention and nonintention,' the splits, subject-object, art-life, etc. disappear, an identification has been made with the material" (*Silence*, 14). Famously, Cage worked to render obsolete the difference between music and nonmusic, sound and silence, that is, those other sounds not intended to be heard, the so-called silence of coughs in the audience or passing trucks. Cage describes sound in a way that does not contradict Kierkegaard's characterization of music's immediacy, but nor does it engage exclusivity or opposition:

> *A sound does not view itself as thought, as ought, as needing another sound for its elucidation, as etc.; it has not time for any consideration — it is occupied with the performance of its characteristics: before it has died away it must have made perfectly*

*exact its frequency, its loudness, its length, its overtone structure, the precise morphology of these and of itself.*

*Urgent, unique, uninformed about history and theory, beyond the imagination, central to a sphere without surface, its becoming is unimpeded, energetically broadcast. There is no escape from its action. It does not exist as one of a series of discrete steps, but as transmission in all directions from the field's center. . . .*

*A sound accomplishes nothing; without it life would not last out the instant.* (14)

Cage asks us to think and experience textured differences rather than oppositions. Sound begins as neither identity with nor difference from language but rather as the sheer force of broadcasting, of transmission and extension. Sound performs its predicates.

The problem of talking about music, entrenched as it is in issues of performance, repetition, broadcasting, transmission, and vibration, mirrors a problem of language more generally, a difficulty in speaking about language's *own* performance. Throughout its occidental history, music consistently brings language up against its own limit, a limit that can form a blind spot or redirect us to think differently. The double valence around the topic of music is itself historical. The relation between music and language changes in reciprocity with linguistic, semiotic, and musical theories. The cosmological Pythagorean model defined music as the very principle of order holding together the universe. Music was the key to both epistemology and ontology; the mathematical expression of its laws demonstrated the regulation of being and opened access to it. Greek harmony signified the restricted art of sound, the science of proportions it embodies, and the correspondence between the two levels. The "harmony of the spheres" demonstrates the pervasion even of astral bodies by the single set of musical proportions governing the tones of the lyre as well.[3] Music has traditionally acted as a metaphysical metaphor, allowing the passage back and forth between matter and ideality. Plato describes the allegory of the cave as a "prelude" to the truth it is meant to convey.[4] The same structure echoes in Leibniz's preestablished harmony, a principle that allows experience to be brought into conformity with a transcendent ground.[5]

The close association of music and mathematics has allowed a facile oversimplification that I have repeated in this brief historical sketch. To begin with, it suggests that the rationalistic mathematical concept of music is independent of historical and ideological factors. But any discussion of music soon displays its biases and prejudices, even when based on mathematics; Plato's condemnation of certain musical modes is only the most well known and perhaps among the least subtle. Descartes, for example, in his little-known *Traité sur la musique* (Treatise on music), condemns the interval of the fourth for reasons that do not seem strictly mathematical. The fourth, writes Descartes, has no proper place in music; "for it is rendered thoroughly disagreeable, as if one were presented with the shadow for the body, or the image for the thing itself" (*Oeuvres* 5: 465–66). Embedded in a nontempered system, Descartes hears the resonance of the fourth with the seventh as an encroachment on the integrity of the fifth, the dominant interval. But this hearing is not simply hearing, nor is it a neutral assessment of mathematical relations; it is a moralizing aesthetic judgment based on the ontological ordering of being and simulation, thing and image.

As models of cosmological transparency fall apart and music's divine office becomes unclear, questions about its possible meaning become more pressing.[6] In Europe, the eighteenth century is especially marked by new inquiries into the nature and origin of language that tend to include music. Rousseau is generally considered a landmark figure in these linguistic considerations of music. Refusing Rameau's mathematically and experimentally grounded theory of harmony, Rousseau refigures music in the image of language, proclaiming it to be the originary language of the heart.[7] Though this function may be a privilege, at the same time music loses considerable force, no longer extending as the science of the cosmos encompassing all the arts inspired by the Muses. Music now operates not as a metaphysical metaphor but as a metaphor for language itself or a metaphoric language that can express a hidden interior, a region of sensibility that eludes the clear contours of conceptual description. For Rousseau, the musical metaphor leads inward, not upward. It points to its own figurative performance, not to a transcendent ground or principle. Rousseau is surely not to be taken as an expert on music; but he was one of the first writers to stamp music with a linguistic character and to establish the complicity of music and metaphor.

For Kant, the mathematical aspect of music does not contribute to the purely sensual pleasure that can be derived from it, a pleasure he describes as a kind of mechanical irritation. In Kant's view, because music resides fully in its resounding body, it is the lowest of the arts.[8] But others join Rousseau in praising music's ability to figure subjectivity. E. T. A. Hoffmann calls it the most Romantic of all the arts.[9] Hegel ranks music second only to poetry, placing it at the center of the Romantic arts. For Hegel, music represents pure abstract subjectivity. Importantly, this art form is necessarily a movement in time, a movement of bare communication, a vibrating that is interiorized through the "theoretical" sense of hearing.[10] Music is a minimal mirror of subjectivity as a form of expressive communication in time (*Ästhetik* 2: 277).

This brief introductory narrative may appear to follow a continuous history of music. The points I have drawn forth, however, are not meant to show development or continuity of the art of music.[11] Instead, they illustrate how evaluations and definitions of music are articulated in relation to implicit notions about language, knowledge, and being. While some factors in this set of relations may be constant in many Western texts, any discussion of music is also historically specific. This book focuses on a set of questions about performance, interpretation, language, and music, limited primarily to the first half of the nineteenth century. Music is perhaps a false friend in bringing together the subjective ineffability of Romanticism on the one hand, and, on the other, the critical force of performance. In its Romantic heritage, music continues to mystify the critical edge it presents.[12] With the growing prestige of music in the nineteenth century, musical virtuosity emerges as a specific sociohistorical phenomenon.[13] Music comes to the fore as the ideological place of expressivity, while lyric poetry loses expressive currency; at the same time, journalism and the print industry grow at enormous rates. This book examines how the definition of music as the "ineffable" art that exceeds language—a definition that becomes commonplace through Romanticism—allows music and musical figures of speech to expose a more general problem of communicative media that is both structural and historical. Metaphors involving music, virtuosity, and musical instruments consistently occupy key positions in critiques concerned with the historicity of subjectivity and language. Just as the Romantic legacy of music has largely fallen into oblivion, the history of music that makes these metaphors possible has generally been obscured.

The isolation of musicology, owing largely to its daunting technical difficulties, along with its institutionally entrenched formalism, is a common plaint of virtually all recent texts working to open the border between music and cultural studies. The work of Rose Rosengard Subotnik stands out as one of the few successful syntheses of musical and cultural analysis. Other musicologists, such as Carolyn Abbate and Susan McClary, have begun to provide models for how to talk about music in connection with contemporary literary, aesthetic, and cultural theory. No doubt anyone writing on music works in the shadow of Theodor Adorno, though the question of how to work with his theories and interpretations of music is not a simple one. The intersections of music and philosophy have informed my interests here more specifically as I have encountered them in the work of Philippe Lacoue-Labarthe and Jean-Luc Nancy. In *Le Sujet de la philosophie* and *Musica ficta*, Lacoue-Labarthe explores the borders of music and subjectivity to illuminate the finitude implied by the functions of repetition, the unconscious, and memory. These works first brought me to ask why musical figures of speech like *resonance* and *syncopation* have a critical force in theoretical discourse and how this force might be related to the history of music and to the history of writing about music.

This book takes up a specific point of intersection between music and literature that forms the constellation of virtuosity, its shadows, figures, and meta-phors in works of Heinrich Heine, Franz Liszt, and Charles Baudelaire. Chap-ter 1, "Virtuosity and Journalism," presents the changes in the printing industry and publishing in the eighteenth and nineteenth centuries that inform this book as a whole. This printing milieu is the historical background upon which the similar patterns linking virtuosity and journalism appear, both considered to be fallen or debased facets of music and poetry. An analysis of Heine's journalism (with a focus on *Lutetia*) connects virtuosity and musical metaphors to the paradoxically threefold journalistic project: to report an "objective truth," to produce a viable commodity, and to "smuggle" in a subjectively filtered sense of the era. The negative attitudes toward journalistic writing and virtuoso perfor-mance reveal that both are threatening to the position of a stable identity and the priority of meaning. Attacks on both journalism and virtuosity can, in part, be attributed to the sense of danger to authority.

Chapter 2, "The Musical Alibi," confronts the relation between language and music. It explores how music was defined historically as an "other" to language; but this definition actually emerges through a displacement of linguistic prob-lems: alienation, the commodification and instrumentalization of language, hy-perconventionalism, and a general loss of a foundation for meaning. The role of music and musical figures of speech in recent semiological work shows that this displacement, which idealizes music as a mode of expression that can evade nor-mative constraints, is part of the legacy of Romanticism that is still operative in assumptions about music today. Music functions as the semiologists' "Golden Age," capable of unifying message and meaning. In contrast, I put forth an al-ternative that seeks to understand the "musical" in both language and music as a process expanding in time and space that requires no foundational unity. This musical character plays an important part in the critique of metaphysics em-phasizing the historicity of articulation and performance and the materiality of subjectivity in language.

Chapter 3, "Instruments of Virtuosity," analyzes Heine's music criticism in his letters *Über die französische Bühne* (On the French stage, 1837–40) and *Lu-tetia: Berichte über Politik, Kunst und Volksleben* (Lutetia: Reports on politics, art and popular life, published weekly, 1840–43, and in book form in 1854). These texts show oscillations of the roles Heine distributes to Giacomo Meyerbeer, Frédéric Chopin, and Franz Liszt, and contradictions in Heine's evaluations of them. Heine's reception of music mirrors his own relationship to language; the descriptions of musicians enact the tropes he explicitly attributes to them. Chopin is allied with composition and poetic metaphor, while Liszt is defined in terms of performance and the metonymic "prose" of its material social con-ditions. Heine's own instrumental use of language functions as an ironic critique of instrumentality without claiming an ability to escape the conditions it describes. In this way, Heine's language aligns him with the virtuoso. At the same time, Heine cannot quite give up the poetic ideal that brings him into fictionalized dialogue and identification with Chopin. This duality is legible, too, in Heine's outspoken ambivalence and anxiety around the power and autonomy of musical instruments.

Chapter 4, "Virtuosity, Rhapsody, and Romantic Philology," connects the structural issue of the relation between rule and instantiation to the problems of authorship and delivery and musical composition and performance. A discussion of philology brings out comparisons with the "delivering" arts of the virtuoso and the ancient Greek rhapsode (F. Schlegel and Nietzsche). In the eighteenth- and nineteenth-century theory of the epic, the work of the philologist, the rhapsode, and the virtuoso converges as a reproductive gathering that forges and transmits cultural tradition. Deliberations on the "Homer question" are duplicated in nineteenth-century debates about the relation between musical composition and performance. The competition between composition and execution is especially strong in the relationship between Wagner and Liszt. While Wagner's privileging of composition follows a logocentric model of authorship, Liszt consistently disturbs this hierarchy, installing instead a model of contiguity, that is, placing *side by side*. As a figure of contiguity, Liszt works as a performer, distributor, and disseminator rather than as an author. The often indiscriminate juxtaposition of heterogeneous elements (what some call "the bad" and "the good") in Liszt's music has been one of the main reasons that his work has been devalued. In contrast, Béla Bartók's writings on Liszt urge the acceptance of flaws and uneven quality as part of what constitutes the openness of possibility in history and tradition. Bartók contrasts this with Wagner's "perfection," which leaves no space for a future or a response. A discussion of Liszt's book *Des Bohémiens et de leur musique* (On the Gypsies and their music)[14] shows Liszt's explicit identification of the modern virtuoso, exemplified by Gypsy musicians, with the ancient rhapsode. The disciplines of philology and folklore come together in Liszt's albeit very undisciplined effort to display a popular and extracultural origin to his own *Hungarian Rhapsodies*, often criticized as tasteless showpieces meant only to display the performer's talent. In *Des Bohémiens et de leur musique*, Liszt performs a curious idealization of the Gypsies as a people with no fixed place or property and no writing who live *side by side* with the rest of European culture. Liszt defines music here as the "narrationless epic" of the Gypsies. The Gypsies are not simply idealized as a "natural," "naive," or "originary" culture. Rather, Liszt defines them as lacking proper identity, like the virtuosi and the rhapsodes. Liszt clearly identifies with this culture he invents; but in his very position as a gatherer and author, he contradicts his own premise.

Liszt's position as an author thus invalidates itself in another case of his compulsive inconsistency.

Chapter 5, "Liszt's Bad Style," presents Liszt's life as the story of his production through style and advertising. The extramusical qualities attributed to Liszt evoked much disgust in some of his contemporaries, an effect that has continued through his reception up to the present. This rejection of Liszt is based on the dread of his personal incoherence and the spectacle of instability. Liszt displays how identity is produced as *consistency* and *(con)text* rather than as an authoritative and authorial unity. These issues are played out in an analysis of Liszt's book *F. Chopin*. Liszt's writing has generally been severely criticized as uninteresting, verbose, and digressive. At the same time, there is a serious uncertainty about his authorship, since no manuscripts in his hand survive. His two female partners are generally considered to have been his ghostwriters. Such interpretations try to protect Liszt as a creative center. The ambivalence of virtuosity is then split and displaced onto Marie d'Agoult, who represents "good style," and the Princess von Sayn-Wittgenstein, the incarnation of "bad style." In any event, Liszt is not "properly" the author of his own writing—only another consequence of his generally improper relationship to language, a strange relationship that is also supported biographically.

Chapters 6 and 7 focus on Baudelaire's essay "Richard Wagner et *Tannhäuser* à Paris" (Richard Wagner and *Tannhäuser* in Paris). Chapter 6, "Poetic Originality and Musical Debt: Paradoxes of Translation," focuses on the aporia between reference and signification that distinguishes the relationship between literature and music. A reading of Paul Valéry's essay "La Situation de Baudelaire" (The place of Baudelaire) shows how it both describes and repeats the aporia in Baudelaire's Wagner text. The Baudelaire essay emerges from its journalistic context through a peculiar strategy of collection, reading, copying, and editing that brings out the philological side of Baudelaire's poetics. A close reading of this technique shows how Liszt appears at important performative junctures in the essay and enacts gestures reflecting Baudelaire's writing strategy.

Wagner's role as a representative of the authorial position is stressed in Chapter 7, "Rivalry Among the Arts and Professional Limitations." In contrasting Wagner and Liszt, Baudelaire establishes a double voice that endorses the centrality of a creative subject yet undermines it through the gesturing narrative of his presentation. This equivocality permits interesting comparisons, with important divergences, between Wagner's theory of the *Gesamtkunstwerk* and Baudelaire's aesthetics of correspondence. Chapter 8, "Music, Painting, and Writing in Baudelaire's *Petits poëmes en prose*," concludes with readings of several of Baudelaire's prose poems, showing the oscillation between points of illusory transcendence and the prosaic expanse subtending them. These paradoxes thus produce, again, the aporias of virtuosity and its embeddedness in finitude. Finally, Baudelaire's address to Liszt in the prose poem "Le Thyrse" brings together poet and virtuoso in a text alternating between lyric transcendence through apostrophe and the newspaper style of juxtaposition, foregrounding both musical instruments and the printing press. With and through Liszt and Thomas de Quincey, Baudelaire can both identify with and withdraw from the self-contradictions of "bad style."

In the course of this book, the broad historical view of the journalistic world is brought together with a more formalist interest in the operations of prosopopoeia and predication. For it is these, finally, that are at stake in the many struggles for control, articulated in this nineteenth-century musical talk, over the power of animation and the power to say what is.

# I. Virtuosity and Journalism

In *Kreisleriana*, E. T. A. Hoffmann writes of music: "It is the most romantic of all the arts, one might almost say the only one that is genuinely romantic. . . . Music reveals to man an unknown realm, a world that has nothing in common with the external world of the senses that surrounds him" (26/96). In the eighteenth century, Rousseau established music as the figurative language of the heart; Hegel later canonized the Romantic confinement of music as the art of pure, though empty, interiority. Hoffmann thus places himself in the midst of the Romantic alliance of music and metaphysical subjectivity. As lyric poetry begins to lose its expressive currency, music is idealized as the ineffable art that exceeds the normative constraints and commonplaces of language. In the Romantic formulation, music compensates for an increasing erosion of reliable and effective expression. The reason for this erosion, however, lies not in a flawed lyricism but rather in a general destabilization of language directly related to massive developments of journalistic discourse following the invention and refinement of print. By the nineteenth century, journalism was deplored as the source of corruption while music was heralded as a place of escape from its powers.[1]

Yet journalistic technology and musical magic are not opposed; both are apparitions of the instrumentalization of language and the waning dream of communicative expression. Hoffmann's irony points constantly to the interconnectedness of expression and mechanism in his tales of music and automation, showing an obsession with a difference that simply does not stand still.[2] This fluctuating difference opens up a network of nineteenth-century preoccupations with music and poetry and their concealed and disavowed grounding in a common language of technology, journalism, and exchange. Thematizations of music and musical figures of speech expose the tension between the instrumentalization of language often allied with journalism and the idealized expressive function that comes to be reserved for poetry and above all for music. Journalism comes under attack as the discourse governed by inauthentic and debased standards and is made to bear all the negative predicates of self-interested instrumentality. In music as in language, suspicion about transient modes of communication emerges in historical tandem with the rise of commercialism; newspapers and concerts are coapparitions of the fall of publication by subscription and court-subsidized private music production.[3] The virtuoso emerges as a counterpart to the journalist, displaying the same evanescence and instability of purpose. The virtuosi provide the cultural reporter with subject matter, while the virtuoso's success is a function of journalistic advertising and good press coverage.

Virtuosity, accompanied by musical qualities and instruments, appears with remarkable consistency in this critique of journalism. Virtuosity and its accoutrements form a consistent constellation in nineteenth-century writing that allows the articulation of a profound ambivalence revealing deep anxieties about language. It is obstinately grounded in materiality and singularity. The virtuoso performance can never be dissociated from the time and space of its occurrence; it takes place in a foundational relationship to its instrument and is constituted by the physical contact with the stage, the audience, and the ambiance. The figure of the virtuoso emerges through the material details of clothing, personal appearance and charisma, name, fame, and money. Virtuosity is uniquely precise in describing the loathed worldliness and self-interested superficiality of journalistic writing. At the same time, champions of virtuosity claim that its technical mastery transcends the limitations of the technical, that its prestige consists in this ability to allow music to rise above its material instruments and merge with poetic ideality. This projection of poetic ideals onto music continues even through twentieth-century semiotics and theories of representation. Musical terminology resounds consistently in theoretical analyses of linguistic performativity concerned with the historicity and finitude of a subjectivity grounded in language.

The virtuoso is a sociohistorical figure that emerges within the confines of a specific history of music, of the economics and politics of entertainment and spectacle, and of journalism. In the modern European languages, the terms *vir-tuoso* and *virtuosity* date from the Italian cinquecento. At that time, the terms stressed the sense of "possessing virtue" (from the Latin *virtus*)—force and valor—in an art, science, or skill, including war. The second sense of "efficacy in producing particular effects," though itself not value laden, tends toward the disparaging tone of "mere" skill that is less than art. The Italian word *virtuoso* included nonprofessional connoisseurs, people of "varied culture" and good taste. In the seventeenth century, the Italian terms entered French, German, and English, emphasizing at first the same quality of expertise. In the seventeenth century, according to the *Oxford English Dictionary*'s indications of the earliest usage, "virtuosity" signified the "manliness" (from the Latin *vir*) of extraordinary ability and connoisseurship in the arts and sciences; the shift toward dilettantism began around the same time. In France and Germany, the main areas of concern in this book, the word *virtuose* began to appear in the mid-seventeenth century, with the same general sense of great skill in any number of areas, including even alchemy, along with the arts and sciences. Here, too, the term was not especially related to music until a century later. The terms *virtuoso* and *virtuosity* first came to refer specifically to music in the eighteenth century, in particular to the special "devotion to . . . technique in playing and singing." (Grimm, Littré, and the *Grand Robert* associate the meaning of virtuosity as musical expertise with the nineteenth and twentieth centuries. Interestingly, the English and German dictionaries stress the reversibility of expertise into empty dilettantism and the display of technical skill for its own sake, while the French and Italian dictionaries barely mention this more threatening side of virtuosity.[4] Historical change in the dual evaluation of virtuosity, turning from cheerful mastery to deceptive mockery, can be seen in the short interval between Mozart (1756–91), the virtuoso universally hailed as genius and prodigy, and Paganini (1782–1840), the first really professional virtuoso, a technician made popular in part by rumors of possession by the devil evident in his uncanny mastery of his instrument. Paganini was known as a cramped and diseased person, suffering from tuberculosis, cancer of the larynx that reduced his voice to a hoarse whisper, and various skin diseases, among a host of other illnesses. This diseased image is indelibly connected with his status as technician, while Mozart, of course, remains forever the fresh-faced creative genius of Milos Forman's film.

The appearance of terms relating to music, instruments, and virtuosity in discussions of language does not indicate a simple borrowing or transference of terms from one referential sphere to another, nor do these terms support an analogy between musical and linguistic rhetoric. The history of the relation between language and music, especially in music criticism or writing "about" music, has focused either on parallels, analogies, and disparities or on an absolute difference between music and the language that attempts to describe, explain, or define it.[5] These discussions, whether they privilege one medium over the other or argue for a metaphoric commensurability between language and music, inevitably reach a limit at the permanent dissociation between the internally determined conditions and limitations of language on the one hand and "music itself," idealized as a pure object, on the other. The preservation of "music itself" as that remnant or excess that always evades language has a specific history that is a function of an uneasiness and instability around the troubled status of language, displayed with increasing acuity in the nineteenth century in the mistrust of journalistic prose. While the characteristics of journalism endanger the haven of lyric transcendence, its safety is transposed to the region of music. In *Unsung Voices*, an insightful study of the relationship between music and language, musicologist Carolyn Abbate describes the privileging of music in just this way with regard to Nietzsche: "Nietzsche's are large claims for music, typically nineteenth-century claims. Music is granted security of meaning, transcendent force, even a prelapsarian virtue" (16). Nietzsche, Abbate argues, belongs in this respect to a history beginning with Rousseau and continuing all the way to Paul de Man, a history that must maintain the status of music as *not* a language (18).

Though Abbate develops important strategies for approaching the relation of language and music, she still maintains the fundamental difference between them as a difference between subject and object, language and theme, that continues to pose this relation as an insoluble problem. She writes:

> Far from being a refuge from worldly questions of meaning . . . seemingly without any discursive sense, it [music] cries out the problems inherent in critical reading and in interpretation as unfaithful translation. For interpreting music involves a terrible and unsage leap between object and exegesis, from sound that seems to signify nothing . . . to words that claim discursive sense. . . . What is lost in the jump is what we all fear: what remains unsaid. (xv)

This division between language and music assumes a stable difference between subject and object that, in the Kantian manner, cannot be crossed successfully. But the terminology of virtuosity—its bodies, instruments, hands, and economy—is not organized in a subject-object relation. Virtuosity permeates equally discourses and practices of both music and language. There cannot really be any question about whether journalistic language adequately names its "object," for the operation of musical figures in the critique of journalism already renders the function of reference unreliable. Journalistic virtuosity is precisely the failure of reference, for it does not faithfully report about its world. But nor does it oppose reference by presenting itself as an idealized "other" language of transcendent expression. Instead, virtuosity both produces and exposes the mundane and material conditions of production—need, greed, egotism, and calculation—common to both the journalistic page and the virtuoso's face.

The figure of the journalist evokes an entire set of familiar nineteenth-century concerns: political disillusionment, lack of commitment, pleasure and profit seeking, the alienation and isolation of the individual. Balzac's presentation of the protagonist Lucien in *Illusions perdues* is organized around these same problems, interestingly articulated through the constellation of poetry, journalism, and music. With visions of poetic immortality, Lucien has gone to Paris, leaving his sister Eve Séchard and her poor printer husband in Angoulême to continue the family business, an outdated printing concern. The provincial Séchards devote themselves to supporting Lucien's poetic project, providing him with funds and encouragement. But once in Paris, Lucien's ambitions are swayed by the power, parties, and profits of journalism, which bit by bit erode his poetic pretensions. Eve finally loses her illusions about Lucien when she receives a letter about him from his friend D'Arthez:

> He's lazy, like all men of poetic temperament, and thinks he's clever enough to juggle difficulties away instead of overcoming them. He'll be courageous and cowardly by turns. . . . Lucien is a harp whose strings become taut or slack according to variations of the weather. . . . We all of us felt hurt because Lucien admired intrigue and literary knavery more than the courage and the honourable conduct of those who advised him to accept combat instead of filching success, to leap into the ring instead of taking a job as a trumpeter in the band. (4: 907 / *Lost Illusions*, 511)

Lucien, lacking the staying power to transform his "poetic temperament" into a work of true merit, has exchanged the heroic position in the ring for the sideshow of journalism. The changeable character D'Arthez describes opts for personal gain and the superficial glories of the spectacular. Just as the strings of the harp respond physically to the weather, Lucien and his actions are subject to bodily influences, material needs and desires, self-interest, and sensation. The juggler—the journalist—stands outside the ring of genuine action with a trumpet announcing the event from which he remains detached and disengaged.

In Balzac's novel, the journalist typifies a more general erosion of values intimately related to the innovations in printing technology. Lucien rises in journalism directly at the expense of the anachronistic printer, his brother-in-law David Séchard, who continues to run Lucien's father's failing print shop. The general corruption of the press in the first decades of the nineteenth century, too, emerges with the vast increase of journals, newspapers, and with simply the sheer number of printed pages in circulation. In Paris, Girardin and Dutacq revolutionized the writing market in 1836, founding a plethora of newspapers based, for the first time, on funding through advertisement rather than subscription (*La Presse*, *Le Siècle*, and so forth).[6] These papers included the *feuilleton*, where reviews, art criticism, and various "belles lettres" were published.[7] This escalation of print means an increase in the number of information sources as well as a generalized information *acceleration* — an ever-rising ratio between distance and velocity. This acceleration characterizes both journalistic production and its consumption. The overwhelming quality of this acceleration is, of course, one of the most prominent characteristics of the virtuoso, whose technique often aims more at speed than at quality, mistaking speed for skill, difficulty for expression.

As life speeds up, everything gets shorter. In *Flugblatt und Zeitung* (Flyer and newspaper), a witty text from 1922, Dr. Karl Schottenloher sums it up: "Brevity is the origin and end of all non-book reproduced communications" (16). The flighty pages of journalism, Schottenloher says, should be short, cheap, and easy to read. This brevity, however, is expansive. The preface to the *Pfennigmagazin* (Penny magazine, published since 1833) reads: "Immeasurable is the realm of knowledge; it embraces the whole world; past and present, heaven and earth, land and sea. Our efforts should all be bent on bringing all of this before the friendly reader" (quoted in Raabe, 115). Speed, number, and expanse likewise converge in the successes of Girardin, who, within a few weeks, had established several journals at half the price to consumers, with circulations in the "tens of thousands." In Germany, the production of all printed matter increased 300 percent, rising from 775 in 1740 to 2,569 in 1800. Printing speed increased with the introduction of fast presses, replacing the Stanhope. In Prussia, the number of fast presses grew by over 150 percent between 1819 and 1852, allowing for fast and cheap production of both periodicals and "classics."[8]

Sensationalism, plagiarism, manipulation, and falsification are standard stylistic traits of the expanding competitive market for printed matter. In this milieu, Lucien's initial poetic ideals are deflated and absorbed into an economically and materially determined world. His literary production is guided by finite bodily situatedness, not by universal ideas or emotions. Lucien is compared to a harp, a physical object, a technically constructed mechanism reacting to the material conditions determining the sounds it will emit. The exposure of the origin of linguistic production in a *mere* instrument is the real scandal of journalism, for it underscores the material origin of meaning. The *musical* instrument plays a unique role in this metaphoric configuration. For the musical instrument, when well tuned, can also emit the lyric strains that obscure the instrument's stringed frame, its "prosaic" basis and intimate dependency on—the weather. The musical instrument, in its own ambivalence, is a hinge that not only exposes the material foundation of language but also conceals it in the mystified reception of music that allies it with lyric ideality.

The prominence of the musical instrument in the above passage from Balzac is systemic and in no way accidental. Balzac's text exposes the sinews of the musical instrument, and with them, the worldly conditions of the journalist's manipulation of language.[9] The ideal of poetic integrity decomposes in the context of the corrupt practices of journalism. This decomposition is allied with a mutability and instability of character typical of both the journalistic page, destined for the reader in whose hands cheap newsprint very quickly falls apart, and the journalistic writer. These conditions have largely informed the ambivalent reception, since his own day, of Heinrich Heine—a writer so closely associated with nineteenth-century journalism that Karl Kraus writes of him: "Without Heine no *feuilleton*" (*Heine und die Folgen*, 7). Heine emigrated to Paris in 1831, not long after the time when *Illusions perdues* takes place. Both poet and journalist, Heine must have traveled many of the paths traced out by Balzac's fictional Lucien. Heine's fellow German-Jewish immigrant in Paris, Ludwig Börne, describes Heine in terms that repeat the same configuration and oppositions among poetry, journalism, and musical instruments:

> He seemed like a withered leaf [*Blatt*] driven about by the wind until, finally, it becomes heavy with the earth's dirt, remains lying on the ground and itself turns to rot. Heine hung his love-harp over his shoulder and arrived in Paris with his strings sprung; the power of poetry abandoned him so that, as a German poet, he can now only be held for dead. He wrote about German literature in French papers [*Blättern*], and he tried to make us believe that he was concerned . . . with something universal and serious, or something patriotic. . . . Heine's final deed is the prosaic understanding of this world in Paris, a thinking with no solidity. (quoted in Briegleb, 158)

As Heine shifts from poet to journalistic prose writer, the broken strings of the harp protrude. The unstable Heine condemned by Börne is like a leaf (*Blatt*: leaf or page) blown about in the wind, corrupt and decomposing. The impropriety of this changeable and exchangeable existence is insinuated by the disturbing proximity between this *Blatt* and the French *Blättern*: the poet falls, his strings show, when he leaves the homeland to wander abroad, exchanging the act of producing German poetry for merely spreading rumors about it in foreign papers. The move and exchange also coincide with an act of self-interest which, Börne claims, conceals itself, passing itself off as something general and nationally grounded.[10] Börne, too, associates a certain unreliability of Heine's language with the mutability of role-playing for the purposes of public spectacle and personal profit.

Börne's moralizing disapprobation of Heine's instability of character, directed at his writing, extends to Heine's lifestyle as well. Though he completed a law degree, Heine was uninterested in pursuing a career in law. In his biography *Heinrich Heine*, Jeffrey Sammons writes: "During the several years after receiving his degree, Heine's external affairs are marked by drift . . . [he became] increasingly a ward of his family" (115). For much of his life, Heine received financial support from his wealthy Uncle Salomon (25), though he was never willing to subsidize Heine's literary career. Sammons describes the financial difficulties of freelance writing in Heine's time, mixing in some of Heine's personal characteristics:

> The self-employed writer was a relatively new phenomenon in society at that time, and with rare exceptions it was a skimpy existence at best. Heine was persistent in his vocation; at the same time he had little capacity or inclination for conventional work. His desultory searches for employment were so devised . . . as to guarantee failure. Indeed, apart from the ill-starred early adventures in the world of commerce, Heine held a paying position for only six months of his life. His capacity for self-denial was not very well developed either. (27)

Though more sympathetic than Börne's, Sammons's tone implies the same disapproval of Heine's lack of staying power, the transience of the drifter or good-for-nothing. As Georg Lukács points out, "Petty bourgeois moralizers among Heine's biographers reproach him with levity and extravagance" ("Heinrich Heine als nationaler Dichter," 90).

Lack of political commitment and stable position, the dependence on others, self-interest, nonproductivity, role-playing, changeability, living abroad, and writing in the newspapers are traits that go together; Heine indeed appears to have much in common with Lucien Chardon. But these characteristics, veritable commonplaces of the disillusioned nineteenth-century dandy, drifter, or bourgeois loiterer, relay finally to an irresponsibility or unreliability of language that has always rendered Heine suspect. This unreliability, however, is a product of discursive and market conditions in which distribution and dissemination have utterly outstripped writing, spanning even "heaven and earth." Discursive irresponsibility is structural and cannot be reduced to an individual's psychological flaws. The effort to do so—whether Börne's, Sammons's, or perhaps even Balzac's—precisely denies the exposed unreliability of language and hopes to quarantine and resolve it as the work of psychological individuals: exceptions and aberrants. Heine's open display of an unstable and "improper" relationship to language—a language exhibiting the reversibility of instrument and figure, matter and meaning—has surely contributed to his difficult and ambivalent reception.

In contrast to the "petty bourgeois" critics, Lukács describes Heine's instability in sociopolitical terms instead of in terms of an individual's career choices. As the title of Lukács's essay implies, "Heinrich Heine als nationaler Dichter" (Heinrich Heine as national poet), Lukács does not consider Heine's failure to identify with a group as idiosyncratic deviance. On the contrary, he interprets Heine's isolation as representative of general historical conditions. Lukács classifies Heine's work, like his life, as a "transitional border-line phenomenon" (124), an instability adequately reflecting objective contradictions of the historical world. Heine's writing, for Lukács, provides insight into "those contradictions that tear apart his thought and his life into irresolvable dissonances" (97). The musical term *dissonance* describes a specifically historical existence, binding the subject "Heine" to material conditions, just as Balzac's harp remains subject to the weather. If the *dissonance* of Heine's irony cannot be sublated into a stable term, nevertheless it remains in dialectical relation to *harmony*, just as Heine's particular marginality, for Lukács, is grounded in the general principle of alienation.[11] This relation provides a guideline that makes possible the interpretation of contradictions in Heine's writing. "For Heine," Lukács explains, "irony becomes a principle for destroying bourgeois illusions of a supposedly harmonious reality" (127).

In Lukács's figurative use of the musical terms *dissonance* and *harmony*, the instrument's strings are not showing. These terms allow Heine's particularity to be integrated into a general interpretive schema. Individual utterances are understood not as individual but as the expression of a historical totality, a world. Lukács quotes Friedrich Hebbel, describing this translation of the world into expression: "The important German poet Friedrich Hebbel, Heine's contemporary, characterizes his art nicely: 'In lyric poetry, Heine found a form in which the most desperate tones, the expression of a world gripped in convulsions, shrilly resounding together, could be made to waft forth again as delightful music'" (131). The poet is seen as one who brings together and transforms the tones of the world into an audible result, combining them into a unified and organized composition that can be perceived and harmoniously interpreted. At the same time, this schema opens the possibility that there is something in those strains that cannot be integrated into the sense of the world they transmit, a remnant that, in the several passages quoted above, has the shape of a musical instrument. The protrusion of musical figures of speech indicates an adherence to specificity and singularity that cannot be recuperated within a generality. This resistance to totalization dwells in the technical manipulation and operation of a material instrument.

The singular autonomy of the hand that plucks, strums, strikes, or writes *re-mains*, and thus potentially obstructs, the hand's integration into "Spirit" or a meaningful totality. In relation to Heine, Lukács interprets this kind of ob-struction as "the danger of manner [*Manier*] that always exists for any subjec-tive style carried out seriously. . . . Even his 'private tactics,' his exaggeratedly personal mode of polemics, his striving to attain a wide effect and a popular ex-pression at any cost, would have to tend in the direction of manner" (138). Manner (*Manier*) points to an individual handling of language. The moment of subjective excess in "manner" is marked by the protrusion of the hand (*manus*, manner, manipulation), again suggesting a bodily obstacle parallel to the mate-riality of the musical instrument and technical detail. Personalized tactics, like individual rhythm, timing, or tact, reveal a measured language, a calculated lan-guage that can be put in the service of self-interest to obtain personal fame, sen-sational effect, and popularity. For Lukács, then, manner evokes the constant danger of an inauthentic relation to language because it presents a use or us-ability of language that dissociates it from the interiority of a subject:

> Heine hovers always before the danger that his genuine deep lyrical feeling [*sein echtes, tiefes lyrisches Gefühl*] may reverse into a mannered sentimentality. . . . But the ironic sublation [*Aufhebung*] of feeling is only a deep and therefore justified irony when the feeling was a genuine one [*ein echtes*] in the poet himself. The witty resolution of an inauthentic sentimentality remains an empty witticism. (138–39)

The possibility that Heine's language is merely put together and not really ex-pressive indicates a point at which idiosyncrasy would simply be deviance and could not be integrated into a totalizing interpretive schema. In Börne's criti-cism of Heine, this treacherous point is emblematized by the figure of the harp player. In Balzac's text, the conglomerate juggler-trumpet-player-harp takes up the same spot: the crucially sensitive and vulnerable point at which the poet's traditional accessory—the lyre or harp—plays a constitutive, and not an ac-companying, role and in fact exhibits its own power to produce and transmit sense.

In contrast, Lukács's harmonious musical metaphors conceal the instrumen-talists behind the composer. Lukács's shift into a figurative register deletes the literal realm of music altogether. His orchestration of history erases any vestige of the individual performers, their technical skill and manual contact with phys-ical instruments upon which the totalization of the conceptual orchestration de-pends. Orchestras must depend on activities that are not ideally productive of music: the performing virtuosi that materially produce, reproduce, transmit, sound, and resound. The technical aspect of manipulation, implied in "manner," presents the greatest threat of all to the ideal of an expressive language and the illusion of organic unity. Describing Heine's polemic with contemporary poets, especially Platen, Lukács attributes to Heine precisely the hatred of virtuosity, hoping to consolidate the concepts of expression, poetry, nativity, and organicism. He ventriloquizes Heine, bringing out his

> critique of [Platen's poetry's] lack of popular quality, of the non-spontaneity of its poetic form. He ridicules Platen's "metrical mastery." He is in principle an enemy of that artificial virtuosity [*gekünstelten Virtuosität*] with which Platen tries to force Classical meter onto the German language. Heine sees this as a false tendency in principle, as a tendency that contradicts the essence of the German language, of German verse. The greater the virtuosity, the greater the damage this developmental tendency brings to German verse. (135)

Similarly, Lukács claims that Heine envisions an "authentic and deep political poetry in which the tendency [*Tendenz*] grows organically out of the material and is not glued to the content in an abstract prosaic way" (137). The virtuoso, a manipulator of artificial techniques independent of expression, simultaneously exploits and exposes this prosaic glue. The artifice of prose, when used "properly," on the other hand, "ought to" retreat behind the organic unity of poetry. "The stylistic battle," Lukács writes,

> of the great writers of the nineteenth century is about the overcoming of the capitalistic prose of life, an overcoming that is constantly open to the dangers of Romantic white-washing. . . . Stylistic success depends on the degree to which it is possible for the writers to grasp, with a correct world-view, the elements of that disappearing poetry of life, and to integrate this poetry as a correctly grasped and therefore poetically legitimate component, into the whole picture. (141)

The capitalistic prose of life has been translated, through successful style, into the *poetry of life*: those elements that can be caught up by literature and integrated within the unity and wholeness of a portrait. Accusing Heine of egotism, Börne, too, points precisely to his lack of organic unity: "His world-view falls apart into bits and pieces" (quoted in Briegleb, 159). This remark foreshadows a more recent critic's description of Heine's journalistic prose, characterized as "a series of riddles, of mystifying innuendos, a mere rhapsodic hodgepodge of whims, moods and reflections" (Weigand, quoted in Preisendanz, 30–31).

It is hard to know whether it is really Heine, and not much more Lukács and later critics, who deplores virtuosity. The virtuoso stands between musical instruments in the critique of journalistic writing and their other face in the musical metaphors relating part to whole in Lukács's text, for example. Virtuosity is the ambiguous ground that makes it possible for Lukács to read epic veracity in Heine's writing, while others find there a mere rhapsodic hodgepodge. Both virtuoso and journalist are amalgamated and heterogeneous figures, touching and handling material instruments even as they are effaced. Both destabilize the clear distinction between means and ends, technique and sense, medium and communication.

Heine's journalist texts, written during the early burgeoning of journalism, are often considered fundamentally innovative.[12] The novelty seems to be located in his efforts to produce an enduring image of the transience of history; the "subjectivity" of his style, critics often note, serves to display a subject changing and moving in time.[13] The uneven style of *Lutetia*, a compilation of articles written in Paris between 1840 and 1843, for example, fluctuates among personal opinions, anecdotes, gossip, and, one is tempted to say, anything that occurred to Heine at the moment he was writing. The well-known German critic Wolfgang Preisendanz, for example, considers the significance of style to be the innovative, even revolutionary, aspect of Heine's journalism in general. While Preisendanz, with others, evaluates this style positively as a technique for displaying the particularity of a subject in time, the digressions and arabesques this method generates cannot always be so comfortably recuperated. In *Heinrich Heines Musikkritiken* (Heinrich Heine's music criticism), Michael Mann, the critic who has focused most thoroughly on Heine's musical writings, allies the tendency toward the anecdotal digression with general practices of journalism. Because the music critic is an amateur, his texts are propelled by a need for stylistic flamboyance: "The guiding demand for pleasant and witty expression, often combined with very little technical knowledge, inevitably leads to a flattening and a lack of objectivity in criticism: dwelling on external representations of people and side-tracks into indiscretions are the order of the day" (16). Lukács associates this need for popularity, this demand for the appeal of the expression, with the danger of manner—but perhaps this need and this danger are constitutive of the journalistic sphere in general. While Mann attempts to limit his study to Heine's critical texts—those describing a definite and real event—and excludes "the passages that lose themselves in musical reveries" (13), biographical research shows that Heine was not actually present at many of the performances he describes, some of which are fictional conglomerates that never took place at all. Despite his dilettantism, Heine's writings on music have been extremely influential, and he is still quoted in historical accounts today.[14]

Thus, the stylistic freedom of Heine's texts is also a product of general journalistic practices, including fiction and plagiarism presented as "information," the object of real, immediate experience. Nineteenth-century journalistic style often deliberately distorts. While something historical is still transmitted in this falsification, it does not lie in the direct transmission of experience; it does not follow a mimetic representational model. The historicity implied by the significance of *Schreibart*—manner of writing—cannot simply be read off of style, for this significance is not constituted by the singularity of "expression" alone but equally by the general pragmatic constraints of journalism: the amateur status of the critic, the need to earn money, and the demand for texts of a certain appeal, shape, and size produced within definite time limits.

Musical expertise provides no antidote to the problems of journalism that influence and shape writing about music, extending even into the sphere of music history "proper." Richard Wagner describes his own participation in journalistic falsification, naming Heine as his model:

> To fill the columns of the *Abendzeitung* [Evening paper], I adopted the shameful practice of patching together whatever I was told in the evenings, based on newspaper stories and restaurant conversations, by *Anders* and *Lehrs*, who themselves never had any experiences worth telling about, and seasoning all this in the piquant style made popular in recent journalism by Heine.
> (*Mein Leben* 1: 237 / *My Life*, 198)

For Wagner, too, journalistic writing is determined by the need to fill up space and is satisfied to be an aggregate of pieces of language related neither to a referent nor to a subject.

The difficulties posed by Heine's digressiveness typically evoke critical concern both about the restitution of meaning to particularly politically charged passages and about the unity and reliability of the subject "Heine" more generally. These classic exegetical problems revolve around and reinforce an oppositional conflict between the value-laden terms *active* and *passive*, *creative* or *productive*, and "merely" *reproductive* or *imitative*. "Expression" and "technology" tend to run in a course parallel to these sets of mutually exclusive oppositions. Expression is supposed to reveal intention and interiority, while technology is disparaged as the manipulation of a material instrument that exceeds expression. The quarrel between "literature" and "journalism" follows the same pattern. Literature is supposed to be restricted to expression. What is called journalistic foregrounds the technological aspect of writing; it assumes a particular historical subject in bodily contact with its means of communication and spans the various activities of producing a text—from the physical juxtaposition of words on a page to the deployment of grammar to the selection and arrangement of rhetorical figures. In this schema it is hard to say where the printer's "composition" differs from that of the "author." Perhaps the printer's composition—the juxtapositioning of metal type in the wooden frame on the press—

must be understood as a metaphoric double of what comes to be called the "ideal" composition of the poet or musical composer.

"Composition" locates and maintains a constant possibility of confusion between these doubles. To allay the anxiety this confusion provokes, the two ends of this opposition tend to be all the more forcefully articulated when the difference between them is endangered. The division of labor between composition and the physical activities of writing establishes a border between the two professions—a division parallel to the separation of musical composition and execution or performance. With the institutionalization of the border between composition and writing, the technological aspect of writing can be judged to be calculated, mediated, and manipulated, not inspirational or spontaneous.[15] Poetry and prose have traditionally been organized in terms of the same polarity, understood as distinct functions of language allied with Roman Jakobsen's categories of metaphor (substitution, point of contact between *langue* and *parole*) and metonymy (relationships of contiguity).[16] The vertical pole of expression involves individual production in a specific usage or realization, while technology merely puts together or repeats given forms or utterances that have already been produced.

Even as they become generalized metaphors for modes of production, the terms *poetry* and *prose* remain linguistic. Although irreducible to empirical genres, they remain oriented toward normative literary forms. The privileging of the poetic *remains* logocentric, as does the dismissive reduction to "mere prose" of all that exceeds the poetic. "Mere prose," on the one hand, restricts and circumscribes a domain opposed to the linguistic ideals of poetry. Prose, on the other hand, while it remains literary, reaches to a limit of conceptual control over exposition, expanding and opening onto conditions of instrumentality and technology. These conditions of finitude are not limited to language understood in the restricted sense of a communication of meaning, intention, or expression. Prose, like virtuosity, has two sides: its artifice and its art.

The ambiguity of prose that Heine names the "art of prose" ends the opposition between poetry as artful expression and prose as artificial technique. Indeed, Heine and his work defy generic circumscription.[17] Heine's lyric poetry probably has the most secure place in the literary canon, though his texts, of course, span a remarkable range, including travel memoirs, fiction, historical and aesthetic commentary, and political writing in both poetry and prose. His corpus meanders through phases and periods, poetry and prose, and varying personal and partisan alliances altering with historical events. Heine's variety makes it impossible to contain him within any standard category of literary criticism, precisely because he stands for an untenability of the oppositions that make possible such categorization. Heine poses a difficulty for criticism legible in a pained and ambivalent reception. "His very name is an irritation," writes Theodor W. Adorno in the essay "Die Wunde Heine" ("Heine the Wound"), the title of which testifies to Heine's problematic relation to literary tradition.

Heine irritates the philological habit of seeking unity in an authorial subject, "the work," and in a unified historical world and period. One might simply reject these categories as obsolete, as many readers would do today. But more interesting is how Heine himself already participates in and articulates the dilemma about the tenability of such categories. Heine's reflections on his own style in the preface to *Lutetia* (probably the work most cited to illustrate the innovative character and "subjectivity" of his style), for example, bring out the split character of his authorship. In 1854, Heine published the letters he had written from Paris in the early 1840s for the *Augsburger Allgemeine Zeitung* (*AZ*). The collection was entitled *Lutetia: Berichte über Politik, Kunst und Volksleben* (Reports on politics, art and popular life), and a French translation was published soon after. In the preface to the French edition (1855), Heine draws attention especially to the temporal intervals in the production of this text, emphasizing that the book spans a double temporality of "writing" on the one hand and of collection and editing on the other. The individual entries, published once a week over a period of four years, extend through Heine's day-to-day life, communicating with whatever events and other publications he happens to encounter. As a series of *feuilleton* articles sent home to Germany to describe the Parisian scene, *Lutetia* first existed within a temporal and spatial distribution that cannot be approximated by the present-day reader. The articles marked a weekly present, inscribed in the printed dates of a newspaper—marks appearing in space where the paper was distributed and held in the hands of readers. In contrast, the book can be purveyed as a whole. Heine wants to suggest that the collection has been put together from a quiet and calm position, a cool and collected contemplative site exempt from the turbulence of the times characteristic of the first writing.

In publishing *Lutetia* in book form, Heine participates in the philological desire for the authority and unity of a productive subject. And it is, of course, extreme habit to read these texts in book form, available in several collected works, each with its own *Lesearten*, technical variations, representations of historical circumstances, and editorial alterations. The philological apparatus—meant to include variety but actually a convenience imposing unity—provides an indelible book frame to Heine's journalistic entries. This collecting itself focuses attention on "Heine," deleting the surrounding text of the *AZ* along with the arbitrary and vanished circumstances of its published apparition and readership.

With no delusions of historical reconstruction, it is interesting to consider Heine's text in the context of the pages on which they were printed. The anonymous entries in the *Augsburger Allgemeine Zeitung* are divided first geographically under consistent headings: "France," "Germany," "North America," and so on. Several ciphered entries are included under these rubrics, along with paraphrases from various foreign papers. The Gothic type is small and thick; the page is emphatically dense, the ciphers marking authorship minute. Considerable optical concentration is called for to distinguish between entries and ciphers; however, general categories appear in heavy print and seem to swallow the crammed columns below them.

In issue 145 on May 25, 1841, for example, Heine's individual report "Mignet - Cousin - Guizot" is surrounded by plenty of material invoking anxiety about the stability of presence and identity. A paraphrase from the *Revue des deux mondes* reports on an uprising in the Ottoman empire, lamenting the lack of any European power's ability to contain this region within "civilization" and indeed regretting Europe's failure to be itself: "Over time, only Europe would be able to do this—that is, a united and upright Europe, Europe if it were what it is not, what it is unable to be" (*AZ*, 1156). A lengthy contribution considers why German colonization has failed, noting the tendency of "hard-working" German emigrants to disappear into the new land. This article displays a distress about the inability of German identity to maintain and propagate itself: "Germany could pour out its heart's blood for centuries without founding a new Germany in another part of the world. . . . So it is high time that Germany begin to spread out and lay the basis for new German peoples" (*AZ*, 1154). There is a description of ruins in Mexico and a proclamation entitled "The Public Press on Asiatic Conditions," which announces in no uncertain terms: "In general, one can take it as a rule that all news in the Indian papers about western Asia, if it hasn't come through Tapezunt and Constantinople, through Damascus and Syria, either is based on misunderstanding or is simply invented" (*AZ*, 1156).

In the midst of these dense third-person paraphrases and reports of political disruption, instability of national identities, ruins, unreliability of the press, and only a few advertisements (for ship and train travel, some lexicons, and various business announcements), it is not surprising that Heine's first-person style obtrudes. In the context of the page, though, this stylistic character can be understood in relation to its contiguous surroundings rather than as an innovative invention of a subject. If the deviation is part of the rule, the lively presence of Heine's reports can be no more reliable than the defunct information from Asia. The *I* of his entries, too, is subject to drowning in thick print, geographical dispersion, and typographical division linked with disappearing identities and advertisements drawing in greater and greater distances to be traveled at ever increasing speeds. This is literally the case; in this issue, both a Danube ship line and the Rhine Railway are advertised with some of the very few pictures in the paper: a ship and a train (*AZ*, 1159).

Heine's collection and publication of *Lutetia* in book form seeks to gain control over this sense of unchecked spreading, decay, and lack of differentiation. Heine is trying to pull himself together. While the journalistic entries were published anonymously in bits and pieces, in book form they are gathered together under the authorial name of "Heine." Heine bestows the unity of the book and of the proper name, he explains, in order to restore what was mutilated through censorship and journalistic editing:

> Namely, since these letters appeared in the aforementioned newspaper in complete anonymity and underwent considerable alterations, I was afraid that they would be published after my death in this dubious form, or even perhaps be amalgamated with foreign additions [*mit fremden Zusätzen*] under my name. In order to avoid any such posthumous mishap I have preferred to prepare an authentic edition of these letters myself . . . thus at least vindicating the reputation of my style during my lifetime.[18]

The correction and unification of style is overseen by a mastering gaze seeking to create a proper image associated with the proper name. Above all, unity of style requires excision of "amalgamated foreign additions," a phrase that describes the whole character of the *Allgemeine Zeitung* just as aptly as any particular disfigurations of Heine's texts themselves. Although Heine thus reclaims the integrity of his style through revision, he nevertheless refuses responsibility for his text precisely at the level of "style":

> I accept complete responsibility for the truth of what I said, but not for the manner in which I said these things. Anyone who sticks to the mere word [*das bloße Wort*] will find it easy to pick out a number of contradictions and frivolities and even a lack of honest intention in my reports. But anyone who comprehends the spirit of my communications will see everywhere the strictest unity of opinions, an unwavering love for the cause of humanity, and a perseverance in my democratic principles. (*SS* 5: 230 / *RS*, 297–98)

In flatly contradicting his repossession of style asserted at the beginning of the preface, this statement reenacts the lack of consistency it describes. At the same time, Heine urges a figurative reading, going beyond "the mere word," *das bloße Wort*, that will somehow hold together the disparity between page 227 and page 230 and resolve the contradiction. The many self-contradictions of Heine's texts and the problems they pose for interpretation are well known, especially for those seeking to determine Heine's political position. These contradictions are often interpreted as an encoding in response to externally imposed constraints of censorship. This view implies that a unity of intention can be restored beneath stylistic contradictions and ambiguities. In *Writing Through Repression*, Michael Levine points out how the processes of translation and restoration, largely informing the study of the effects of censorship on literature, serve to protect the integrity of the authorial position.[19] The isolation of censorship as an external force safeguards the polarity between external (and thus "inessential") influence and internal originality.

Heine claims, in the prefaces, that a figurative reading will synthesize the dispersed aspects of his texts and render forth the image of a unified and consistent subject identified with the utterance of truth: the "spirit" (*Geist*) of the "communications." But this allegorical schema cannot be reduced to the special conditions of censorship; in fact, it prescribes a more general process of reading compelled by all excursions into printed matter. For without the transgression of "the mere word," *das bloße Wort*—taken *à la lettre*, a literal mark—nothing can be read at all. The inconsistencies and obscurities of Heine's texts cannot always be traced to particular political configurations.

The reduction of stylistic devices to external censorship, as Levine has argued, reinforces the distinction between language as a "mere signifying instrument" on the one hand and as authentic expression on the other—that "inner core" of true and unified intention that would remain once the external distortions were removed. The editor of *Lutetia* has an interest in perpetuating this notion in order to establish the authority of his text as well as his own character. But the political censorship to which Heine's journalism is subject is not the sole cause but rather one of many results of a more general dissemination in time and space of the *I* posed in and by writing. The extension within time and space of writing itself sets limitations and obstacles to the idealized intimacy of expressive communication. The delimitation of these conditions to specific political contingencies makes possible the ideal that, in other circumstances, the detours and distortions of writing could still be bypassed. Heine's remarks help to preserve this ideal, attributing his texts' flaws and incomprehensibilities to these political conditions, presented more generally as problems of time and space. Heine appeals: "I count on the reader's sense of fairness in considering the difficulties of time and place with which I had to struggle when I first published these letters" (*SS*, 230 / *RS*, 297). Linguistic expression itself compels the digression and errance into time and space; even in the following passage, written safely and uncensored in the preface, Heine uses a figurative disguise:

> The difficulties of place which I just mentioned were those of censorship; the censorship exercised by the editorial board of the *Gen. News.* [*AZ*] was even more restrictive than that of the Bavarian authorities. I often had to decorate

the ship of my thoughts with flags whose emblems were not exactly the right expression [*rechte Ausdruck*] of my convictions. But the journalistic pirate could have little concern for the color of the rags hanging from the mast of his vessel, the rags with which the winds played their airy games. I only thought of the precious cargo that I had on board and wanted to smuggle into the harbor of public opinion. (*SS* 5: 230 / *RS*, 298)

Heine finds no *rechte Ausdruck*, no "right expression," no direct and nonfigurative terms with which to state that the written text is not the right expression. The necessary detour of language into articulation already forces the figurative reading of the letter, a reading that functions as a revision or correction of error. The above passage suggests that an interpretive, nonliteral reading enacts a reapproximation of the expression to its sense. Yet Heine's interpretive hint is given as and by figurative language—by the very allegorical structure it instructs us to read. These statements, which make a claim for a unity of conception and the authorial control of its figures, are themselves in need of interpretation; the authorial subject has already handed itself over to the chance movement of the wind and the indeterminate materiality of color. One cannot assume that the speaker of this passage, who uses language in the same figurative way he describes, possesses a fundamentally different relationship to language that would authorize an unproblematic and unambiguous decipherment of this very instruction.

The ship works as a metaphor for language in motion, for the journalistic writer (*I*) moving in time and space, publishing weekly and attaining a mass geographical distribution, crossing national boundaries, street corners, café tables. This ship is marked by the varying colors of its articulation, the particular utterances of an *I* extended and dispersed through the text. Through playful articulation, a particular self or point of view is smuggled into the generality of public discourse—a private self is published. But these utterances cannot be conflated with the immediate experience of an *I*; Heine himself confesses that he exploits them to smuggle in something else. This something else (a certain unique individuality or untranslatability that, in what follows, we shall find associated with music), can be identified neither with the ship as a unified subject subtending a discourse nor with the particular utterances marking it. This *I* is not captain of his ship or master of his fate, but only smuggled goods.

The relationship to language held up for display—of the journalistic pirate to its arbitrary colors—installs an edge of excess in those flags. They are not expressive symbols; rather, they are emblems, decoys from the content smuggled along, thanks to the diversion of the colorful flippancy of the flags, the decoys of style, color, tone, and articulation that cannot be reduced to a transmitted sense but without which there could be no transmission at all. The subjective cargo thus oscillates between the frame of its publication, which brings it into public port, and the marks of the particular utterances by which it is announced; but it can be identified with neither. This "subjectivity," which can only be understood as a self-differentiating movement, cannot be reconstituted or held fast as something prior to and separate from its textual articulations.

In the preface to the French edition, Heine writes: "I accept complete responsibility for the truth of what I said, but not for the manner [*die Art und Weise*] in which I said these things" (*SS* 5: 230 / *RS*, 297). Here he allies himself with the totality of what he has said—its "truth"—but refuses responsibility for the locality of his utterances (attributing irregularities to censorship), though at the same time he claims to have rescued the beauty of his style by excising foreign additions. The "truth" seems to be associated with the revised, edited, and translated—thus retroactive—whole. In the letter of dedication preceding the German edition, Heine describes the process of revision primarily as one of completion:

> Of many of these [letters] I had made rough sketches, which . . . aided me in restoring suppressed or altered passages. . . . So with these, as well as with messages which I had sent without having made a preparatory sketch, I filled the gaps and improved the alterations as well as I could from memory, and where I found passages in which the style seemed strange [*fremdartig*] and the sense still stranger, I endeavoured to rescue artistic honour and the beautiful form by annihilating the suspicious places altogether. (*SS* 5: 235–36 / *Works* 8: 19)

But in this same preface to the German edition, written one year earlier than the French preface, Heine locates the authenticity of the text not in the whole but in the brokenness—the points of idiosyncratic incision—of the parts. Here he claims that the additional writing of revision and collection is merely a remedy for censorship and has touched nothing essential. Instead, the authenticity of the date, the "color of time," and the truth of the picture are registered in the *performance* of the first writing:

> But this expunging in places where the insane red pencil had raged most freely only concerned inessential matters, and in no wise the judgments of things and people, which indeed might often be erroneous, yet which should be very faithfully reproduced, lest the original colour of the time be lost. And by adding to the work a goodly collection of as yet unpublished reports—which had not been submitted to any censorship—without any change whatsoever, I was able to supply by an artistic arrangement [*Zusammenstellung*] of all these monographs a whole which forms the faithful portrait [*das getreue Gemälde*] of a period which was as important as it was interesting. (*SS* 5: 236 / *Works* 8: 19)

The portrait derives its fidelity from the production of judgments in the first writing. These individual acts, through which judgments fell and sentences were formed, remain timebound; they indicate points of incision into history in which the generality of language has been realized in articulation, breaks in the totality of existing utterances by the production of new ones.[20] The *ursprüngliche Zeitfarbe*, the "original colour of the time," emanates from these acts, embedded in an indeterminate multiplicity of historical conditions in contiguity with a body. This "producedness" is their truth.[21]

The first-person narrative simulates the originary production of language suggested here, insinuating a direct relation of the *I* to the world. It would seem that the "faithful portrait" derives both its color and its authenticity from the first performance it reproduces. For the sake of this veracity, Heine underplays the editorial collecting; the unity added later is nothing but a simple act of termination and spatial aggregation. Casting these prosaic and mundane terms structuring the retroactive assemblage of the work in this inessential light, Heine wants to suggest that his editing is "merely reproductive." The "merely reproductive" aspect of writing allows expression to be transmitted or the veritable witness to be reported.

I say that the use of the first person *simulates* a certain kind of immediacy that in fact cannot hold. For while the articulated judgments bear witness to their performative production, their repeatability has detached them from their temporal context. The reproduction of judgments undertaken by the editorial *I* is not identical to their production, for they will have been altered by the pages on which they have been placed. The editorial hand, which bestows the "beautiful form," does not "merely" reproduce an immediately expressive *I*. The editor's additions, resulting in the whole, themselves constitute an amalgamation "with foreign additions" (*mit fremden Zusätzen*); but now, from the present of the preface, the daily *I* has become foreign (*wo Stil und Sinn . . . fremdartig vorkommen*). While the *I* strives to articulate the presence of a subject at home in its world, with every stroke of the pen and tick of the clock, it becomes foreign. The *I* reasserted in the shaping hand of the editor or collector appears in its turn to be at home in its present; the revisions and collections, which lend unity, thus attempt to domesticate the foreignness of its own prior extension. But what is there to suggest that the editorial *I* is more trustworthy than the narrating *I*, which itself has undoubtedly already been edited, organized, and composed? In claiming to add nothing but spatialization, the editor hands its sovereignty and authority over to the *I* it reproduces.

The disjunction of the articulated *I* is played out in the oppositions between poetry and prose, production and reproduction, and expression and technique. Heine also thematizes these oppositions in terms of nationality. His remarks on

Platen (quoted by Lukács above) juxtapose the artificial forms of classical meter with the natural expressivity of German verse. Similarly, he considers German poetic meter to be "natural" compared to the adopted formality, the "naturalized" citizenship, of French meter.[22] Heine makes us forget that German meter, too, is calculated and conventional. Thus, the denial of the instrumentality of poetic language—the forgetting of poetic technique—is associated with the lyric of the homeland. The German poet preserves an illusion of natural language, just as the editor preserves the expressive authority of the narrating *I* he collects.

The still collectedness and domestic comfort on native ground that Heine attributes to lyric poetry contrast sharply with the geographical wandering and constant exposure to foreign control associated with journalistic writing. Heine's reflections on journalistic writing do not hide, but in fact outline, the instrumentality of its linguistic medium. In journalistic prose, Heine says, the instrument is above all the fact, a form prescribed by the medium: "Knowing the traditions of the *Gen. News.*, I know, for example, that it always sets itself the task not only of bringing all facts of the time in the most expedient fashion to the attention of the public, but also of making a complete record of them as in a world archive" (*SS* 5: 230 / *RS*, 298). The "objective fact" gives itself forth as what is natural, uncontrived, pure, and unformed by its linguistic presentation. The text registers and delivers up the fact to the reading public; its registration seems, at first, to add nothing.

The *art of prose*, in contrast, disrupts the boundary between language and its theme. The fact is a metaphor, a poetic technique, a textual substitute that has subsumed and presented the referent in compliance with a literary form dictated by a literary (here, journalistic) tradition. Pointing out that the fact is a stylistic device, Heine confesses that he aims to transgress this prescribed convention:

> I therefore had to take care to clothe everything that I wanted to insinuate, the event as well as my opinion of it, everything I thought and felt, in the form of a fact; and I did this sometimes by placing my private views in the mouths of others or by proceeding parabolically. My letters thus contain many little stories and arabesques whose symbolic [*Symbolik*] is not always comprehensible and which the crude gaper could take as petty anecdotes or even as *commerage*. In the endeavor to let the form of the fact prevail, the tone [*Tonart*] was also an important means that enabled me to report on the most dangerous things. The most proven tone, however, was indifference. (*SS* 5: 230–31 / *RS*, 298)

Heine's digressions—the arabesques, anecdotes, and imaginary reported conversations and dialogues—he claims, are the means by which he insinuates his singularity, "everything I thought and felt," into "objective" report. They open the space in which he develops his stylistic individuality—and evades the censor. The foregrounding of facts produces an illusion of reference; this illusion is further supported by the stylistic techniques of anecdote and the distribution of speech into mouthpieces. These stylistic techniques are generally explained as devices for sidestepping censorship. Yet Heine is saying something more about the difficulties of expression by means of received conventions and public forms of language.

Heine's digressions cannot be delimited either as "subjective outpourings" or as colorful yet referentially bound reports. The "symbolic" of digression diverges from referential space, interrupting the forward movement, the direct line, from language to referent. These stylistic devices deviate from the literal and veer into the figurative. Once this break takes place, inaugurating figurative space within Heine's historical narrative, part of the function of figurative elaborations will be precisely this: to occupy and retain space. As individuality becomes identifiable with style, it adheres to the irreducible space it takes up. The symbolic of digression presents the possible incomprehensibility of mere extension; the displacement of language onto foreign personages or mouthpieces takes the place of the irreducible "foreignness" of writing. For Heine not only attributes his own speech to others, but he also does not hesitate to place foreign opinions in his own mouth. The foreignness of his own speech, evident in Heine's blatantly plagiaristic practices, structures his journalistic writing itself, as he remarks, in the "strangeness" differentiating the *I* in style over time.

When stylistic digression is made to stand as the center and point of departure of Heine's narrative, the text announces its origin in idiosyncratic aberration. This focus on communication by style opens the space for individual expression; but at the same time, it undermines the illusion of reference. If the "merely reproductive" aspect of the journalistic text is sacrificed, the referent would clearly show itself to be a product of its representation. To countermand this tendency, Heine explicitly subordinates his stylistic arabesques to the veracity of representation. He must do this precisely because digression cannot be a center; it cannot persist independently of that from which it digresses. Heine himself allies his performance of digressive arabesques with entertainment, mere ornamentation added on to the stability of facts: "To render the doleful accounts more cheerful, I wove into them sketches from the realm of art and learning, from the ballrooms of both good and bad society" (*SS* 5: 239 / *Works* 8: 26). On the one hand, Heine *must* present it in this way to preserve a notion of truth or fidelity; but on the other hand, the picture would not be complete without the aberrance added on to it by its representation: "And if I, among such arabesques, drew too many mischievous virtuoso's grimaces, it was not done to deeply grieve some long-vanished honest man of the pianoforte or Jew's-harp, but to give a picture of the time in its minutest nuances (*SS* 5: 239 / *Works* 8: 26). The adjoining of the time and its image turns on the *virtuoso's grimace*. Is the grimace a trait of the "object itself"—a fact merely copied by the reporter? Or is it the displaced thoughts and feelings of the journalistic hand, *drawn* and produced with the ingenuity of an expressive inscription? Who or what is the virtuoso, and why does the figure of the virtuoso come consistently to stand in this pivotal position between reference and digression? The virtuoso's relationship to the technical level of the instrument is like the narrator's strange relationship to the referential function of the linguistic instrument in Heine's prose: his manipulations similarly exploit the instrument in causing it to disappear.

The relationship between the *I* of Heine's individual entries and the editorial *I* cannot be read in terms of a unified subject or brought into line with the stable chronology of a life. This divided *I* has much in common with the virtuoso, an unstable and performing figure that can give only the temporary unification of aggregation, a unity not proceeding from an ideal structure but with a technical origin in spatial position on the stage and on the page. The virtuoso belongs to the guild of the rhapsode, a problematic figure standing at the beginning—and not the origin—of literature, the scribe whose tongue or pen makes possible the emergence of the author and the ideal origin of speech. His public appearance, interrupting and punctuating an errant and disappearing existence, is not a distortion or repetition but is his very emergence, just as Heine's *I* first comes forth on the stage of his dated articles. Heine's historical pictures of time are not "immediate" reflections but have always been subjected to the mediation—interpretation, formation or deformation, translation, edition, revision, calculation—of a technical medium's drawing hand. It originates not in an ideal structure or a unified conception but in the technical juxtaposition (*Zusammenstellen*) of organized and manipulated articulation, in the co-positioning on the page that subsumes disparate and self-contradictory entries under the homogeneity of the proper name. The following is frequently cited as a claim for the historical veracity of *Lutetia*:

> An honest daguerreotype must truly repeat a fly as accurately as the proudest horse, and my reports are a daguerreotyped book of history in which every day depicted itself [*sich selber abkonterfeite*], and, by juxtaposing [*durch die Zusammenstellung*] such pictures collectively, the ordering spirit of the artist has delivered a work in which that which is represented authenticates itself. (*SS* 5: 239 / *Works* 8: 25–26)

Here Heine describes the production of individual entries as the same action of collection and juxtapositioning, *Zusammenstellung*, operated by the later editor.

But instead of an *I*, we find a technical medium standing in the place of subject, a mechanical depersonalization of the authorial figure. This self-documentation of what is textually presented locates authenticity in the autonomy of the written text. The position of subject is handed over to a technical instrument: the daguerreotype, juxtaposed with the empty generality of "the ordering spirit of the artist." In the same way, Heine pictures incommensurability—here the horse and the fly—and cracks the unity of the framed picture.

These gestures share one side of virtuosity: the side that exposes the instrument as the source and place of generation, in material history, of meaning. Virtuosity proceeds out of and cannot be detached from the manipulation of its instruments, the materiality it splits and exploits. Yet it shows another side, emerging where the instrument is effaced and forgotten even as it persists and is drawn into focus. The "sense" we get of the era—the historical veracity—is the "other," or successful, side of virtuosity—where the technicality of printed matter is transcended and moves toward communication.

In "Die Wunde Heine" ("Heine the Wound") Adorno describes the action of this oscillation in Heine's use of language precisely in terms of virtuosity:

> If all expression is the trace of suffering, then Heine was able to recast his own inadequacy, the muteness of his language [*die Sprachlosigkeit seiner Sprache*], as an expression of rupture. So great was the virtuosity of this man, who imitated language as if playing it back on a keyboard [*der die Sprache gleichwie auf einer Klaviatur nachspielte*], that he raised even the inadequacy of his language to the medium of one to whom it was granted to say what he suffered. (*Noten*, 98 / *Notes* 1: 83)

How does it stand with Heine's "virtuosity"? For Adorno, the success of expression as break involves a dialectic reversal: "Failure reverses itself into success" (98/83), without, however, making the Hegelian restitution of what has failed. That is, the "success" does not absorb, elevate, retain, and replace the failure. This success remains *spread out*, *aus-gedrückt*, printed and expressed and cannot be recollected into a conceptual interior. The explicit comparison, *gleichwie*, "as if," delays the absorption of exteriority in an interiorty of sense by pointing to, and thus preserving, the irreducible materiality of the instrument. The simile *gleichwie* both connects and holds apart music and writing. The linguistic simile itself functions like the keyboard, like a mechanical tool given to the individual that can be used to obscure itself. The figure of the musical instrument can underscore the disparity between the musical and the linguistic instrument. Yet the figurative function of music and its instruments can also serve to conceal the break it instates between referential and figurative language. The musical figure serves to cover up the irreparable difference between the historicity of the text of history and that which is presumed to be outside of it—whether it be a transcendent subject or what is called an objectively existing space. Music is the mode by which the outside enters the interior of history and marks their division: the point at which the exterior of an instrument is appropriated, *verinnerlicht*, interiorized, where passive and active cannot be clearly distinguished: where repetition and originality coincide.

# 2. The Musical Alibi in Theories of Performativity

The more language is experienced as a standardized formal apparatus given by society, the more "originality" and innovation are relegated to the marks of particular use—to tone, style, and the particularity of specific combinations. It is not coincidental that Adorno's description of Heine's language allies the musical with the performative. It has become rather commonplace to assume that identities are constructed and produced through acts of language and other media. But it is not so clear what "performance" or "performativity" is. The concept of performance has been generally enlisted to stress process and production of subjectivities rather than appended predicates of a prior substance. This notion of performance has a recent history in structuralist linguistics and semiology as well as in speech-act theory. These theories are essentially formalist and provide some vocabulary for recognizing nonsubjectivist features of linguistic acts and gestures. It is important to recall this aspect, for otherwise performance is posited as a purely individualistic and spontaneous event free of social codes and constraints. At the same time, a formal approach to the problem of "actualization" or, more generally, "mise-en-scène," can never really explain itself and thus opens up an excess that it is meant to contain.

For Saussure, "performance" bridges the gap between *langue* and *parole* (usually translated as "language" and "speech"), between the general system of a language and any particular use of it. He isolates *langue* to delimit what can be an object of knowledge from the historical data out of which it is abstracted. The systematic nature of *langue* is what renders language knowable: "Language [*langue*] . . . is a self-contained whole and a principle of classifications. As soon as we give language first place among linguistic facts [*les faits de langage*], we introduce a natural order into a mass that lends itself to no other classification" (25/9). The distinction between the system and its individual manifestations places them in a hierarchy favoring the totality of a system, transparent to knowledge, over the individual: "In separating language from speaking we are at the same time separating: (1) what is social from what is individual; and (2) what is essential from what is accessory and more or less accidental" (30/14). *Parole* represents a mass of insignificant variations complying with normative rules; the stability of the rules is significant, says Saussure, but the variation is not: "Among all the individuals that are linked together by speech, some sort of average will be set up; all will reproduce—not exactly of course, but approximately—the same signs united with the same concepts" (29/13). *Langue*, "a collection of necessary conventions that have been adopted by a social body to permit individuals to exercise that faculty [of language]" (25/9), can be accurately represented in dictionaries and grammars (32/15); it is the condition of possibility and the origin of individual usage: "Language [*langue*] is not a function of the speaker; it is a product that is passively assimilated by the individual" (30/14).

What is at stake in this discussion is not simply certain epistemological problems of linguistics but rather a more general problem of the relation of what is conceived to be an essential structure to its individual (accessory and accidental) manifestations. Saussure clearly organizes *langue* and *parole* in a hierarchy. To describe the fundamental identity of *langue* within, and despite, its inessential manifestations, Saussure uses the following comparison: "Language [*langue*] is comparable to a symphony in that what the symphony actually is stands completely apart from how it is performed; the mistakes that musicians make in playing the symphony do not compromise this fact" (36/18). A musical comparison is called in to explain the very possibility of language practice. In accordance with his epistemology, Saussure's simile here relegates musical performance, indissolubly attached to the material conditions of physical instruments and individual realizations, to a flawed arena of history.[1] However, it is not certain that this "reality" is actually musical; indeed, it is not clear that, for musicians, the "symphony itself" could be said to exist autonomously. Whether the problematic passage from structure to individual instance is presented as an epistemological thorn or a moment of celebration, musical terms appear consistently to "explain" this passage. Nelson Goodman, whose work *Languages of Art* is widely cited in both musicology and Anglo-American aesthetics, has used an expanded sense of the term *score* to establish identity within variation in evaluating the problem of the reproduction of artworks. The privileging of the compositional score, as an idealized system of pure notation, over any particular realization has not been limited to the sphere of logicians.[2] Indeed, Avital Ronell has disrupted this idealization in *Finitude's Score*.

It is easy to attack the privileging of structure over performance as a logical and metaphysical rejection of "the body" and its attendant materiality. However, simple critiques of this kind assume a naive and direct access to "the body" that denies its discursive construction.[3] In several essays, Émile Benveniste has approached the problem of actualization with somewhat more subtlety in his elaboration of the formal apparatus of enunciation. This kind of analysis is useful, in that it demarcates the difference between discursively generated positions and the position of empirical naturalized bodies with which they are so easily confused. An instance of discourse or its "present" has nothing to do with the "presence" of an empirical agent. The moment of inscription, as Derrida has argued, generated in a context is at the same time a rupturing of that context: "By the same token, a written sign carries with it a force of breaking [ *force de rupture*] with its context, that is, the set of presences which organize the moment of its inscription. This force of breaking is not an accidental predicate, but the very structure of the written" (*Marges*, 377 / *Margins*, 317).

The framework of enunciation allows an examination of the relation of "subjectivity" and language through the analysis of formal relations articulated in a text without presupposing a prior subject. Benveniste defines it as follows: "The 'subjectivity' we are discussing here is the capacity of the speaker to posit himself as 'subject.' . . . 'Ego' is the one who *says* 'ego.' That is where we see the foundation of 'subjectivity,' which is determined by the linguistic status of 'person'" (1: 259–60 / 224). The *locuteur* and the *ego*, according to Benveniste, are formal relations originating in a linguistic structure; the *locuteur* is a position marked out in discourse by personal pronouns. Personal pronouns and temporal and spatial deictics set up an orientational frame within discourse. Benveniste writes:

> *I* refers to the act of individual discourse in which it is pronounced, and by this it designates the speaker. It is a term that cannot be identified except in what we have called elsewhere an instance of discourse and that has only a momentary reference. The reality to which it refers is the reality of the discourse. It is in the instance of discourse in which *I* designates the speaker that the speaker proclaims himself as the "subject." (1: 261–62 / 226)

The orientational points within discourse are self-referential and can be understood formally without extradiscursive referentiality, as in fiction, citation, or grammatical examples. They remain functional even when they are not explicitly present; the absence of personal discursive markers suggests "objective discourse."[4] Every kind of text, whether scientific or confessional, requires its discursivity; its ability to communicate depends on the instantiation of discourse embedded in the historical nature of language—what Derrida would call "spacing," the material aspect of articulation.

Benveniste's stress on the formal status of enunciation indicates that the capacity to pose oneself as a subject resides not in an individual "subject" but is given by the general pronomial structure of a language and thus is a component of *langue*. *Langue*, a sociohistorical system, is conceived as the condition of possibility of particular utterances; the system must precede and be given to the individual.[5] The formal apparatus of enunciation provides a framework, then, for examining the relation of general given forms (conventions, rules, and so on) to individual deployment, understood as the activation of these forms. Benveniste writes: "Enunciation is the putting into operation of language [*la langue*] by an individual act of utilization" (2: 80). There is therefore no direct access to these generalities, which cannot be known apart from their being used. For Benveniste, *langue* does not, strictly speaking, "exist" apart from its realization, although it is structurally independent: "Before enunciation, language [*la langue*] is nothing but the possibility of language. After enunciation, language is effectuated in an instance of discourse" (2: 81). Since these individual acts of realization occur within the irreversible time of *parole*, every enunciation, in principle, would be new and unique; the self-reference of personal pronouns is activated anew in each use. Individual existence would be marked out by the insertion into the totality of existing utterances: "Man disposes of no other means of living the 'now' and making it actual than through its realization by the insertion of discourse into the world" (2: 83). The "present" of each unique instantiation would thus interrupt and disrupt the totality of prior discourse.

An individual subject would first emerge in its insertion into discourse or its inscription—that is, its individuality would consist in the difference between this enunciation and all others, in this particular deployment of *langue*. The stability of an *I* could only emerge through a synthesis of the various uses of *I* over time and space. This synthesis depends on the extension of articulation in time and space; it is a synthesis of reading through which repeated marks are gathered up and attributed to an anthropomorphic figure: namely, the *locuteur*, whether it be the author or a fictional character.[6] Because this synthetic unity remains dependent on the dispersion out of which it is gathered, it is historical rather than transcendental.[7] Because of the persistent difference and dispersion of the instances of enunciation, the position of the author or speaker (*sujet d'énonciation*) cannot completely coincide with any particular instance of *I*. In Derrida's words, the iterability that makes the use of the word *I* possible also makes its consistency and identity impossible, without rendering discourse illegible (see "Signature Event Context"). In "Position Exposed," Werner Hamacher gives a brilliant exposition of the paradoxes of linguistic performativity and demonstrates the impossibilities of the idealist claim to identity through positing. The only subjectivity that can come to be through propositional assertion, Hamacher argues, is "in the experience of the irreducibility of positing to itself *as* positing . . . in the experience of positing as inconsistency and expositing" (*Premises*, 236). This fundamental inconsistency emerges in the operation of articulation itself. Hamacher continues: "This leap in the proposition—the hiatus in the transcendental—transposes and translates an absolute and absolutely free, prepredicative positing into a conditioned positivity, the being-posited of a self-predicative assertion that first results from this positing" (237).

In a number of texts, Louis Marin has dealt with the problem of the dislocation of the locutionary subject, especially in autobiography. He describes the process of "gathering" and unifying discursive instances as a synthetic effect that does not sublate the extension of articulation. He writes: "Autobiographical writing operates *like* [*comme*]—and this is the process of simulation—a synthesis of the subject and the present, *like* a transcendental constitution of person and of the present" (*La Voix excommuniée*, 26). In "Un certain regard du sujet," too, he approaches the problem of the simulacrum and linguistic machinations of such a synthesis. Interestingly, he uses the musical terms *syncope* and *reprise* to describe the syntheses of reading that create ligaments between graphically dispersed marks on a page but prevent their absorption into a conceptual unity independent of its material extension.

The constitutive difference and actual noncoincidence of the speaker and the locutionary subject do not, however, effect the structure of enunciation; they do not effect the discursive self-referentiality of pronouns and deictic markers, which functions independently of any actual speaker. Nor, however, can the enunciated subject (*sujet d'énoncé*) be conflated with the enunciating subject (*sujet d'énonciation*)—a position that can only open up with respect to the act of discursive production. Benveniste explains: "One must be careful in describing the specific condition of enunciation: it is the act itself of producing an utterance [*énoncé*] and not the text of the utterance [*énoncé*] which is our object" (2: 80). The act of enunciation is marked out by and can be formally studied from within, but is not identical with, the discourse it produces.[8] There can be no direct access to this "act itself," but it can be formally analyzed in terms of combination, selection, illocutionary conventions, and so forth. Paul de Man has perhaps worked more than anyone on this paradox at the limit of legibility. In

"Semiology and Rhetoric," the opening essay in *Allegories of Reading*, he especially stresses the discontinuity (a disruption that is not structured as a binary opposition) between grammar and rhetoric, where grammar comprises the iterable rules that make language production possible, and rhetoric, those deployments that submit to structural analysis but cannot be reduced to cases of grammatical compliance. The discontinuity between grammar and trope points to a constitutive uncertainty about the ability of grammar to guarantee meaning. In *The Rhetoric of Romanticism*, de Man is increasingly interested in the random and ungrounded emergence of rhetorical "acts," marked by the incision of tropes.[9]

The production of discourse from the point of view of enunciation is not to be conflated with historical empirical acts—the particular situation and conditions of the production of language. These chance circumstances are not reconstructible, and there can be no access to the indeterminate conditions, extending through a range of differences, that cannot be registered precisely because enunciative registration is a *rupture* from a context it produces in differentiating itself from it. Speculations striving to reconstruct historical specificities of context are impossible *in principle*, and can be only comforting fictionalizations and projections on the part of the reader. Structural relations of enunciation, on the other hand, inhere in or adhere to the *énoncé* and need not be fantastically imported from an extratextual world; they can thus be helpful in understanding acts of language, expression, and the emergence of "subjectivity" in language without presupposing a psychological entity to whose intention the text must be brought into conformity.

While enunciation gives a formal model for the articulation of subjectivity and individuality in language, this space for "particularity" and genuine expression is rendered ambiguous by the repeatability of language. The gap within the relation between structure and use of the word *I* disrupts the indexical reference of *I* to a present speaker. As the *I* is written, the speaker is already potentially absent (see *Marges*). In the most extreme case of the performative utterance, the individual act of utterance is constitutive of its meaning and always unique.[10] Yet illocutionary force is immediately a function of convention and linguistic form, not of subjective utterance or action.[11] The performative aspect, or act of enunciation, depends on an idealized moment of individual appropriation through which *langue* is converted into *parole*. "As an individual realization, enunciation can be defined with respect to language [*la langue*] as a process of *appropriation*. The speaker appropriates the formal apparatus of language [*la langue*] and enunciates his position as speaker [*locuteur*] by means of specific indices" (2: 82). However, since the indices are formal structures and not private inventions, they precede, and subsist independently of, their genuine appropriation. A particular utterance must presuppose a set of already produced examples and instances, a synchrony of already manufactured free-floating signifying elements, that is, texts. Concepts like Hans Robert Jauss's "horizon of expectation" mediate between the historical conditions of production—that is, the relationship between the possibility of a textual production in terms of all those already existing texts—and the structural relationship of *langue* and *parole*.[12] The empirical givenness of the synchrony of texts allows for horizontal transfers that need not involve any realization of linguistic structures. Language, or pieces of discourse, can be mechanically reproduced, performative sentences stated without performing anything, and enunciations quoted, copied, or variously produced without any act of appropriation and conversion of *langue* into *parole*. There is no way to know for sure when a "genuine" act of conversion has taken place and how to distinguish it from the "empty" repetition or mechanical reproduction of a convention. In other words, the genuine act of language appropriation, which occupies an ideal position in the frame of enunciation, cannot "appear" but is always in disappearance. The individuality and uniqueness of the instantiations of discourse are subject to erosion from the moment they are put forth; performance cannot be preserved. "Being an individual and historical act, a performative utterance cannot be repeated. Each reproduction is a new act performed by someone. . . . Otherwise, the reproduction of the performative utterance by someone else necessarily transforms it into a constative utterance" (1: 273 / 236).

Interestingly, Benveniste locates novelty, innovation, and genuine appropriation of language in an "individual and historical" act that cannot be the object of knowledge. They are located in a certain kind of *reproduction*, the kind stressing the difference of repetition. In the same way, although *langue* is granted a theoretical priority as the condition of possibility of *parole*, through enunciation, it is seen to be dependent on its realization through individual acts that cannot be thoroughly prescribed by or reduced to formal linguistic structures. The maintenance of formal parameters precisely allows self-differentiation to be articulated; it prevents the singular and individual event from collapsing into a model of spontaneous subjective autonomy, or what would have been called "immediate expressivity."

At the same time, enunciative novelty approaches sheer arithmetical addition as the expressiveness of the *énoncé* erodes. This is the situation in which Heine is writing, the situation of acceleration of printed matter and the attendant commodification of language. The larger the distribution made possible by printing, the more language is used as a product to sell rather than as a means of communication or "expression." In Heine's time, writers were exposed to the fact that machines could produce language, viewed as constative products, as well as—in fact, faster than—people could. As Wagner's testimony about his own writing for the *AZ* so clearly shows, journalism hyperbolically displays the unreliability of the *I* posing as authority, author, or historical witness. The increase in printed matter provides overwhelming evidence of the standardization of what J. L. Austin would call "parasitic" deviants of speech acts or what John Searle would describe as nonstandard derivatives of the illocutionary model of a first-person statement. Journalistic report institutionalizes a dual system of conditions of production: the narratively explicit context of what is reported or reviewed, on the one hand, and the "suppressed" sphere of temporal and material constraints based on layout and editing and the economic need connected with the particular situatedness of a particular writer at a particular time, on the other. This "particularity" operates as a manufacturer and not as an "author" or a source of expression or information.

One might say that the domination of *langue*, as a normative average of language, over *parole* is a way of presenting the classical concept of alienation. If *langue* represents a linguistic community, it is also the common ground—both the condition of possibility and the geographical territory—subtending the individual utterance. As a "natural" (national) language, the realm of the *lieu commun* and of standardization, is experienced as something foreign, a "nonalienated" relation to language is sought elsewhere. Since Rousseau, this "nonalienated" language has been especially associated with music, considered the language of a sensible subject. The comparison of music to the sense of discourse "in general" is already strongly stated by Rousseau, who identifies the expressive aspect of music precisely in composition. He writes: "There must be a sense, there must be a coherence, in music as in language." He compares the absence of expressive sense in music with the bare and indecipherable materiality of writing: "If in fact this music has no perceptible measure, it is nothing but a confused collection of words, taken at random and written down in no particular order, in which the reader cannot find any sense" (15: 172). The inscription of expression is the composer's task alone; correspondingly, Rousseau places no original value on performance, which he perceives as mere mechanical reproduction: "Regarding the actual production of sounds by voices or by instruments which we call *execution*—this is the purely mechanical and operational part of music" (14: 66). Rousseau's privileging of the composer, which goes hand in hand with his theory of musical expression, has more to do with his interest in the position of "author" than with any musical practice. Similarly, his project for a new musical notation is based on logocentric assumptions about the exteriority of the sign to its sense.

Because music has no words, it is not structured by the orientational point of the word *I*. The constitutive iterability of the first-person pronoun, its availability for general use, obstructs its ability to "express"; because it is detachable from its user, it can never be unique. The necessity of the dispersion of articulation separates different instances of *I*; the necessary dislocation of enunciation makes impossible the coincidence of *énonciation* and *énoncé*, introducing a necessary difference within the *I*. If we interpret *langue* as a representative of a geopolitical territory, it is apparent that the division of enunciation *must* separate the particular utterance from its *langue* as a ground or homeland—and that this division is the condition of any utterance at all. It is through this division, understood as an interruption and break in existing *énoncés*, that the utterance of a particular identity could take place and allow the emergence of a subject at all. The stylization of this division as opposition, break, and conflict can be read in the consistent nineteenth-century thematics of wanderers and of *Heimweh*: the longing for a solid and enclosed ground to house the isolated *I*, abandoned in its dispersion.

Music, however, is considered a place of nondivision between *langue* and *parole*. While music is conceived to be the most trenchant expression of the particularity of sentiment, it is also thought of as the most universal and immediately comprehensible language. There seems to be a direct passage between individual speaker and national language in music. In the tradition of the ethical interpretation of music, music "immediately reproduces" the character of its producer.[13] It also functions as the language of national character, presenting an image of *langue* speaking directly out of particular instances of music. The many debates about the relative merits of Italian, French, and German music reflect this relation. Rousseau, of course, claims that music is directly imitative of natural languages.[14] This tendency in the history of interpretation of music attributes to it a peculiar relation between structure (composition) and articulation; the particular utterance is differentiated from, but not opposed to or in strife with, the generality of *langue*. This relation, an immanent coincidence of *langue* and *parole*, is inconceivable in Saussure's linguistic terms. It would indicate the instant in which the present instantiation of discourse—inscription of difference as a break from history—has rejoined the history it interrupted. It presents an *ideal* relation in which novelty and originality, defined in opposition to the past, would still be integrated in a communal tradition.

The idealization of the relation between *langue* and *parole* in music points not only to a utopian vision of music but also to the difficulty in linguistic theory of explaining the passage from structure to instance. In *Langage, musique, poésie*, the musical semiotician Nicolas Ruwet criticizes certain views about music precisely because they defy the Saussurian hierarchy of *langue* and *parole*. He criticizes Henri Pousseur and Pierre Boulez because they "confuse the two planes, or much more, they reduce language to the single term of speech [ *pa-*

*role*]" (28). The debate revolves explicitly around the principle of identity. Ruwet continues: "Given that music unfolds in time, a reprise can never be considered as a pure and simple repetition. In music, A is never equal to A. But we would say that, on the plane of language [*langue*], of the system, A is equal to A, while on the plane of speech [*parole*], they are not" (29). This is not a neutral judgment, but establishes a hierarchy; identity on the plane of *langue* grounds the possibility of differences on the level of *parole*. But it is not clear that such a principle of identity obtains in music, especially since there is no such thing as a single note, all tones being composites of resonances that influence composition and the possibility of recognizing similarities.

At the same time, the possibility of immanent coincidence of rule and instance that de Man puts so severely into question repeatedly emerges to solve the dilemma of instantiation. Searle, in reply to Derrida, claims that the performance of a speech act itself puts into action the intention already formally encoded: "In serious literal speech the sentences are precisely the realizations of the intentions: there need be no *gulf* at all between the illocutionary intention and its expression. The sentences are, so to speak, fungible intentions. Often, especially in writing, one forms one's intentions (or meanings) in the process of forming the sentences: there need not be two separate processes" (*Glyph* 1: 202). In another vein, the musicologist Rose Rosengard Subotnik attributes this same immanent coincidence to Western music in the classical period: "The choice and treatment of premises in a classical work could always be referred . . . to more general classical principles . . . the one hundred-odd symphonies of Haydn . . . could be related to some normative conception of genre not literally embodied by any one of them." Such norms, she continues, were not "imposed as restraints upon classical music. On the contrary, far from preexisting and even predetermining composition in the manner of ancient generic models, classical models, such as Haydn's symphonic norm, were very largely created by the classicists themselves" (*Developing Variations*, 179). For Subotnik, in a sense the classical composition really does present the Golden Age relation of balance between individual freedom and general comprehensibility: "Embodying its own meaning yet retaining in that meaning a basis for generalization (that is, a second structure), classical music became a paradigm for later composers hoping to avoid public lack of understanding or misunderstanding" (180).

This ideal point overlaps precisely with the passage from *langue* to *parole*. Following a long tradition, Benveniste, too, tries to solve the explanatory problem of this transition through music. In "Sémiologie de la langue," Benveniste argues that music is not directly comparable to language as a system because it has no semiotics—no sign unity comparable to that of language (2: 55). Because it has no words, its sense can be located only in "the selection and arrangement" of a particular work (2: 58). The performative innovation of the individual act of language was located in the particular repetition of a general structure—a repetition embedded in a nonreconstructible historical situation. This edge of enunciation cannot itself be enunciated, for it becomes immediately subject to reification. Benveniste turns to music to characterize the individual production of language: "But it remains permissible, by means of metaphors, to assimilate the execution of a musical composition to the production of a linguistic utterance; one could speak of a musical 'discourse' which can be analyzed into 'phrases' separated by 'rests,' etc." (2: 60). I note here the peculiar ambiguity of Benveniste's formulation, "the execution of a musical composition." This formulation seems to attribute *signifiance*—a general but indefinable sense—to the performance of the piece; but the structures metaphorically linking music to discourse are not first produced in the performance, but rather are already inscribed in the composition. The elision between composition and execution or performance characteristic of music is set up as a paradigm of *signifiance* eluding the conventions imposed by the repeatability of semantic content and socially prescribed conventions of language.

This paradigm is also that of the individual expression, the creation of language, by a particular individual. For Benveniste, music, along with the other arts, belongs among "those systems in which *signifiance* is imprinted on the work by the author . . . the *signifiance* of art never refers to or relies on a convention identically received between partners" (2: 59), but is invented anew for each work. Art thus provides the remedy for linguistics, providing a legal space for individual deviation. This deviation is not dangerous, for it remains securely attached to a subject as its source: the unique expressive work is its signature or stamp, its "expression." The "musical" point of view voiced in Benveniste's essay allows discursive production ("execution") to be constitutive of meaning in a way that Saussure cannot allow. Yet this view remains within a recuperable system of intention and expression originating in a unified author. The composer remains the master of musical execution, just as for Saussure the individual is "master" of the execution of *parole* (30).

The formal quality of enunciation allows it to be coarticulated with nonsubjective systems, codes, and cultural patterns and constraints in general. That is, it insists that individual subjectivity is not self-originating or immediately self-identical. Saussure and Benveniste, while advocating such a framework, at the same time deprecate the contingency of material finitude that the category of instantiation necessarily implies. Rather than affirming the productivity of articulation in language, the positive version of its uncalculability and ultimate unintelligibility is displaced onto the musical, enlisted as an "other" to mend the flaw within the explanatory relation between *langue* and *parole*. This displacement is not subversive but in fact serves to protect language from a threat from within by expulsing it. This, it seems to me, is the problem with the semiological alliance of music with the concept of *signifiance*, meaning the productivity or generativity of articulated utterance "in general."

The alliance of music with *signifiance* organizes the relationship between composition and performance in analogy to that between *langue* and *parole*; the constraints thus placed on *parole* are compensated by a projection onto music of pure *parole*—one might say, pure performance with no content. Julia Kristeva, for example, uses "music" as the generalized metaphor for the direct infusion of semiotic drives into a work. "Music" stands as the representative of an aspect abstracted from the structure of language. The problem is clear in the following passage:

> There are nonverbal signifying systems that are constructed exclusively on the basis of the semiotic (music, for example). But, as we shall see, this exclusivity is relative, precisely because of the necessary dialectic between the two modalities of the signifying process, which is constitutive of the subject. Because the subject is always *both* semiotic *and* symbolic, no signifying system he produces can be either "exclusively" semiotic or "exclusively" symbolic, and is instead necessarily marked by an indebtedness to both. (*Révolution*, 22 / *Revolution*, 24)

This "exclusively semiotic" music, therefore, must be something other than simply music: it occupies an ideal position exceeding the literal art of music. "Music" is actually a metaphor used to describe what "properly" belongs to poetic production, described as: "The semiotic's breach of the symbolic in the practice that is called poetic. . . . Language . . . tends to be drawn out of its symbolic function (sign-syntax) and is opened out within a semiotic articulation; with a material support such as the voice, this semiotic network gives a 'music' in letters" (*Rev.*, 62 / 62–63). In *Le Langage, cet inconnu*, Kristeva agrees with Benveniste that music is not a system of signs. Instead, "Music leads us to the limit of the system of the sign" (306). The linguistic structure of the sign, giving the triangle of referent-signifier-signified, thus cannot be said to structure music, and this is why music communicates no determinate sense. Kristeva points out the importance of this difference:

> If the fundamental function of language is the *communicative* function and if it transmits a sense, music deviates from this principle of communication. It transmits a "message" between a subject and an addressee, but it is difficult to say that it transmits a precise sense. . . . Here is a system of differences that is not a system that *means* [*veut dire*]. (305–6)

While music seems to want to say *in general*, somewhere this generality ceases to be language and becomes something fundamentally other, presenting a transmission that is not communication, a language that does not follow the model of language. Its "deviance," allied with the direct transmission of presymbolic drives into signification (that is, the very principle of *La Révolution du langage poétique*), similarly duplicates a site where the individual can escape coded constraints and freely "express" itself. "Music" retains the privileged semiotic position that not only precedes the symbolic but also allows its translation *into* the symbolic. It is precisely the recognition of "laws" and "codes" of desire in *écriture*, according to Kristeva (citing Roland Barthes), that allows the "musical," that is, the poetic, to persist in signification. Music is thus the very means by which bodily subjectivity becomes legible; "a harmony organizes noises" (*Polylogue*, 52). The attention to this "harmonic" organization is supposed to preserve the heterogeneity of the subject of enunciation and check its absorption into a model of a transcendental *cogito*. In short, an aspect of linguistic *signifiance* is abstracted, given the name of music, and used to explain both the origin of the poetic as instinctually singular and its instantaneous transposition into socially mediated codes and forms.

Benveniste points to music as a limit to the empire of the sign, as a system that can be characterized as a "language" only by metaphor; he points explicitly to the central position occupied by language as the privileged medium of interpretation that is both semiotic and semantic. He explains:

> There is a SEMIOTIC MODELING [*modélage*] that language exerts, of which the principle cannot conceivably be located anywhere but in language [*la langue*]. The nature of language, its representative function . . . its role in the life of relatedness, make it the grand semiotic matrix, the modeling structure of which the other structures reproduce features and the mode of action. (2: 63)

Benveniste suggests, then, a mimetic projection of language onto other media; and it may not be possible to avoid this "modeling" or to speak about music in any other way. Nevertheless, it is possible, and indeed necessary, to examine the points at which linguistic conditions determine the interpretation of nonverbal media and to distinguish what metaphors of music conflate. Paul de Man, for example, assimilates harmony and melody to the linguistic axes of the paradigmatic and the syntagmatic in "The Rhetoric of Blindness: Jacques Derrida's Reading of Rousseau" (in *Blindness and Insight*). In "Sémiologie de la langue," Benveniste shows that this analogy does not hold with respect to music. De Man is not really concerned with music in his essay; rather, musical terms are frankly dummy figures for language: "It would not be fruitful to dispute these statements on the basis of a different phenomenology of music; the avowed thesis of the *Essai* equates music with language and makes it clear that, throughout the text, Rousseau never ceased to speak about the nature of language" (131). Yet this does not stop de Man from making extremely strong statements subordinating music to a linguistic model and transferring to it a set of values heavily colored by the pathos of the "lack of identity": "Music becomes a mere structure because it is hollow at the core . . . the musical sign can have no assurance of existence. It can never be identical with itself or with prospective repetitions of itself. . . . This movement . . . is determined by the nature of the sign as *signifiant*, by the nature of music as language" (128–29). In particular, music is made to act out the frustration of meaning: "Music is condemned to exist always as a moment, as a persistently frustrated intent toward meaning" (129). But there is no evidence that music is driven by this kind of "intent toward meaning" or that it is necessary to think of it as condemned and frustrated—though it may frustrate the intent toward meaning of the linguistically oriented interpreter.[15] Benveniste's and others' references to music in fact regress to the notion of a preexisting subject freed of formal and structural constraint; they say much more about language, and the deadlock of formal analysis in attempting to deal with the possibility of actual language production, than about music.

Despite attempts to the contrary, Kristeva ultimately reinstalls an expressive model of music idealizing the relation of bodily continuity with the musical instrument, parallel to the relation of the poetic subject to the maternal body. "Music" provides the place of nondistinction between form and instantiation. Barthes, too, shows the same tendency, though with more awareness of the rhetorical limitations of his reasoning. With reference to Benveniste's terminology, Barthes defines "the grain of the voice" as "the very precise space (genre) of *the encounter between a language and a voice*" (*L'Obvie*, 237 / *Image*, 181), pointing to this point of contact between individual utterance and *langue*. He describes this corporeally bound individuality as follows: "This voice is not personal: it expresses nothing of the cantor, of his soul; it is not original . . . and at the same time it is individual: it has us hear a body which has no civil identity, no 'personality,' but which is nevertheless a separate body" (238/182). Emphasizing that this individuality is not "subjectivity," Barthes wants to distance himself from an expressive theory based on the preexistence of a rational cogito. However, as for Kristeva, since the analysis is based on a linguistic model, it is hard to know how the suspension of signification attributed to music finally differs from a model of "expression." While Barthes affirms that the same relations would persist in the case of instrumental music, the fact that he tends to focus on vocal music is indicative of his linguistic orientation, interpreting music as *signifiance* or wanting to say in general. He states explicitly: "My evaluation of music goes by way of the voice," a recurrent object of meditation "which has often carried me beyond music toward text and language—the French language" (247). However, Barthes is straightforward about the use of music to figure an aspect of language. He concludes: "And perhaps this, in fact, is the value of music: to be a good metaphor" (252).

Music thus stands as a mythical realm for these linguistically oriented writers. The metaphoric convergence of musical and linguistic performance, starting primarily with Rousseau, continues to play the same role in sketches of general semiology. These sketches organize contemporaneous media structurally to solve logical problems. What this really indicates is a structural synchronization of what, during the eighteenth century, was primarily articulated in terms of a historical model. Music is the semiologists' Golden Age.

The articulation of the concepts of *langue* and *parole* by Saussure, and of enunciation by Benveniste, as well as analyses of performatives by Austin and Searle, set formal limits to individual production in order to render it knowable. But this delimitation, of course, produces simultaneously a region of excess that exposes its own explanatory limitations. *Enunciation* can theorize theorization's limit, pointing to the primacy of discursive extension and the ultimate emptiness or nonsubstantiality of its subject position. The work of Philippe Lacoue-Labarthe and Jean-Luc Nancy in particular has focused on this movement of reversal. In "Typographie," Lacoue-Labarthe describes enunciation, allied with *lexis*, as a constant "depropriation" because the possible absence of the subject of enunciation is inscribed in the very possibility of an utterance (263/132). This "depropriation" is inscribed in the practice of language in general and is not simply an addition that could be avoided: "The cleavage(s) of enunciation is a law of language" (264). The subject of enunciation cannot be thought of as "properly transcendental," as a stable entity separate from an *énoncé*; but nor can it be reduced to the empirical subject of enunciation. In *L'Absolu littéraire*, the problem of presentation—*Darstellung* or *mise-en-oeuvre*—is analyzed rigorously as a moment of writing. The focus on articulation places the process of presentation—enunciation as "actualization"—as the space of generativity in general. The same "cleavage" comes to the fore in Nancy's reading of Kant in *Discours de la syncope*. The rhythmic/musical term *syncope* delineates a self-division of discursivity that forever sunders the region of presentation from the transcendental ego Kant would have as its seat or origin. The schism of syncopation is most critical in Kant's transcendental schematism—that is, precisely the section of the *Critique of Pure Reason* that tries to explain the possibility of the application of general concepts to particular objects or instances. Schematism is tautologically defined as the activity of the imagination of subsumption or application that makes application possible; the schema is the figure of the activity of application that provides the rules for its own application (A: 134). This infamous moment recedes in its very emergence, as Kant writes: "This schematism of our understanding, in its application to appearances and their mere form, is an art hidden in the depths of the human soul, whose true machinations (*Handgriffe*) nature is hardly likely ever to allow us to discover or to lay unconcealed before our eyes" (A: 141 / B: 181).

The work of this invisible hand and its manipulations continues to structure negotiations between general structures—rules of language, social norms, and cultural constraints—and individual possibilities and instances. The question is, and remains, how are such generalities "assumed" by individual instances and how exactly are they "appropriated," "enacted," reproduced, and criticized through individual deployments? Pierre Bourdieu, for one, draws an explicit analogy between Saussure's conceptualization of *langue* and *parole* in linguistics and a parallel relation for anthropology between *culture* and *conduite* (culture and conduct) (*Le Sens pratique*, 51). To simplify, Bourdieu is interested in two things: how to approach practices as primary and thus avoid their classification in terms of the realization or transgression of an "intellectualist" rule, and thus mere material addenda, and how to explain the generative position of behaviors and practices not as spontaneous individual acts, free of all constraint, but with respect to general social structures, "structured structures predisposed to function like structuring structures" (88). To interpret social action as either compliance or infractions of rules is to reduce them to "executions of scores or applications of blueprints" (87). Instead, Bourdieu proposes a model of social regulation and regularity, "without in any respect being the product of obedience to rules," that is "collectively orchestrated without being the product of the organizing action of a conductor" (88–89). He continues to use the phrase "orchestration without conductor" (*orchestration sans chef d'orchestre*) to describe the spontaneous self-regulation of social practice and the relation of the social "habitus" to the possibility of individual behaviors and actions.

While rejecting Saussure's "intellectualist" favoring of *langue* over *parole*, Bourdieu nevertheless shares the same hierarchizing assumption that denigrates "the execution of a score." He also assumes that we know what "the execution of a score" means and that this aspect of musical practice can be unproblematically translated into a conceptual sphere. At the same time, the concept or metaphor of an orchestra is central in the articulation of his model, again erasing any historical and material specificity of the character of "orchestra" within a social and ideologically overdetermined history of musical practice. In *Bodies That Matter*, Judith Butler, too, is concerned with specifying "performativity" and the way in which general constraints contact individual deployments in ways that both reinforce regulatory structures and allow critical reworkings. Her self-critical reworking strives to limit the claim for spontaneous individual agency and also allow for differentiation within the deployment of norms. She locates agency "as a reiterative or rearticulatory practice" that is produced by the regulatory system it can criticize. Importantly, she argues that the "imaginary morphology" that makes such reworking possible "is not a presocial or presymbolic operation, but is itself *orchestrated* through regulatory schemas" (13–14, my emphasis). Butler uses various forms of the word *orchestration* consistently to indicate the difficult logic of deployment, instantiation, interpellation, or "assumption" (8, 28).

Musical terms operate consistently to describe a nonidealist model in which practices and instantiations generate the rule of their production that they presuppose. Music provides a privileged vocabulary drawing on the history of interpretation of music that understands it as disruptive of a logocentric organization of meaning—a disruption that privileges precisely the discursive extension of enunciation. The critical potential of musical analogy lies in the nonoppositional and nonhierarchical relationship between composition and performance. Yet these terms tend to be immediately co-opted by a linguistic orientation and are called in to mend a linguistic problem encountered in binary terms. The double valence of the virtuoso duplicates a standard opposition between poetry and prose; the oscillating protrusion and disappearance of musical terms is symptomatic of performativity's disruption of context and the concomitant production of a dual context.

It is crucial not to repeat the gesture that posits music as a self-evident, natural, and naive "other," dwelling somewhere outside of language. However, music itself is not historyless; its terms and tensions appear in discourse about music as well as in socially mediated musical practices. Western theorizations of music (to which I limit the sphere of reference here) and musical practices have worked together to forge an ideology of music that can play its part in a logocentric system. One need only think of Plato's division of musical modes in Book 3 of the *Republic*. Just as with genres of literature, musical modes are evaluated, some included and some forbidden. Moreover, instruments that provide an unmanageable range of variety are prohibited: "We shall not need in our songs and airs instruments of many strings or whose compass includes all the harmonies . . . we shall not maintain makers on triangles and harps and all other many-stringed and polyharmonic instruments" (3: 399c–d). Musical instruments bear the ability to inculcate "affinity" to proper ethics as well as the potential excess that exceeds good character and legibility. The reduction of musical instruments and forms serves to subordinate music to language and the body to the soul; the "foot and air" of correct musical composition should conform to correct speech "and not the speech to the foot and the tune" (400a). In this typical reduction, the sense of "harmony," originally a carpentry term meaning "well fitting," is sublimated to mean the subordinated correspondence of the body to the soul. This "harmony" becomes the general principle of which music and musicians are inferior imitations. "Then he who best blends gymnastics with music and applies them most suitably to the soul is the man whom we should most rightly pronounce to be the most perfect and harmonious musician, far rather than the one who brings the strings into unison with one another" (412a).

The general principle of correct "blending" as true harmony rids Plato's text of the untoward vibrations of instruments that might disturb the composition of the body and the soul, or of the Republic. At the same time, specific problems of musical practice vanish as they are replaced by their "true" conceptual counterparts, transparent and knowable principles available to the reasoning philosopher. The music positioned as "first" in experience (the inculcation of norms and affinities through songs of the nurse) is conceptually rendered last, ancillary, and nonessential. But the remnant of musical instruments and experience cannot be erased or absorbed by Socrates' theorizing. In attempting to describe and decide which rhythms may be permitted along with which musical modes, Socrates and his interlocutor are forced to take recourse to *the absent musical expert*:

> That there are some three forms from which the feet are combined, just as there are four in the notes of the voice whence come all harmonies, is a thing that I have observed and could tell. But which are imitations of which sort of life, I am unable to say.
>
> Well, said I [Socrates], on this point we will take counsel with Damon, too, as to which are the feet appropriate to illiberality, and insolence or madness or other evils, and what rhythms we must leave for their opposites. And I believe I have heard him obscurely speaking of a foot . . . which he arranged, I know not how, to be equal up and down in the interchange of long and short, and unless I am mistaken he used the term iambic. . . . And in some of these, I believe, he censured and commended the tempo of the foot no less than the rhythm itself, or else some combination of the two, I can't say. But, as I said, let this matter be postponed for Damon's consideration. For to determine the truth of these would require no little discourse. (400b)

I quote this passage because of the striking shift of tone; Socrates becomes uncertain, recalls vaguely by hearsay, and cannot provide the specific details of the instantiations of the rule he is articulating. For a moment, Socrates is no longer the omniscient harmonist of the soul, but a simple locutionary subject whose knowledge falls short at the border of someone else's professional expertise. This temporary lapse around music recontextualizes, finitizes, and positions

Socrates as the maker of a finite discourse that requires supplementation from the expert in another science. The musical "truth" is always elsewhere, for it is no "truth" at all in Plato's sense. The discourse required to define it is not simply of excessive length and difficulty but is fundamentally no discourse at all— or none that could be cited or recited in the *Republic*. The apparition of the figure "Damon" installs a musical alterity in the *Republic* that limits its own explanatory capacity; the lateral reference to Damon is "like," but not identical to, the expulsed materiality of certain musical modes and instruments. Damon emblematizes the point at which musical practice controls the knowledge of its own principles of rule and application and cannot simply be translated into the *Republic*. Even the omniscience of a Hegel, as I shall discuss later, reaches an impasse when it comes to the technical details of musical knowledge. Even he cannot penetrate the secret knowledge of the musician.

Kant's *Critique of Judgement* enacts the same dual expulsion of the musical. On the one hand, in conformity with the theory that aesthetic judgment responds only to formal and not to affective qualities, Kant separates rigorously the play of musical structures, based on mathematical relations, from the bodily affects of musical sounds, closely associated, in fact, with the inappropriate convulsions of laughter (272–75/177–81). He is careful to explain that it is the language-like interplay, worked out through mathematical proportions, of general communication that causes aesthetic pleasure. "To this mathematical form alone, although not represented by determinate concepts, attaches the satisfaction that unites the mere reflection upon such a number of concomitant or consecutive sensations with this their play, as a condition of its beauty valid for everyone. It is this alone which permits taste to claim in advance a rightful authority over everyone's judgment" (268/173). This expulsion of the bodily is perhaps rather to be expected. But music is disturbingly inseparable from its motions, the motions that transmit and affect the body of the auditor. In fact, it is difficult to keep its vibrations out; melodies recur involuntarily in the memory, and then "we find them to be more of a burden than a pleasure" (269/174). It seems virtually impossible for the philosopher to get rid of music; and this point leads us not to a clear-minded thinking subject exposing general rules but to the shadowing image of a man sitting at his desk trying to work:

> Moreover, music has a certain lack of urbanity; primarily because of the constitution of its instruments, it tends to spread its influence further than one might want—on the neighbors—and so to speak obtrudes and does violence to the freedom of others outside of the musical society; which the arts that speak to the eyes do not do, since one need only turn one's eyes away if one does not wish to admit their impressions. (269–70/174)

In this passage, the locutionary position of the theoretical text itself temporarily descends to its neighborly dialogic position in a lateral relation to a specified group, the "musical society." No amount of theoretical purification can block out the intrusion of the neighbors' music—an uncontrollable intrusiveness grounded in the very characteristics of the musical instrument. Music invades the philosophical text in a way that exceeds the control exerted upon it through focus on compositional form and denigration of bodily affection.

What is at stake here is not simply the "otherness" of music but the "otherness" of "otherness" itself. I have argued that, on the one hand, "music" becomes the name for abstracted properties of language based on a formalist model and that the "difference" and "absencing" thus carried out is itself *linguistic* in character. In this sense, music becomes a dummy figure for reflecting language, a figure for language's failure or inability to explain itself linguistically. On the other hand, I do not posit a "music" wholly external and immune to language and linguistic conditions; the problem is rather one of distinguishing between the referential and nonreferential force of the word *music* and terms associated with it. The semiological references to music I have discussed above preserve a naive reliance on the referential effect of "music." The result is twofold. On the one hand, "music" is appropriated to cover a theoretical flaw or gap, thus producing a "musical" exterior as something utterly "other" in contradistinction to the metaphoric music of its own vocabulary. The second problem is that the theoretical text, which after all is attempting to explain, that is, to *know* something, assumes the position of subject while circumscribing "music" as an object. This inevitably happens when the focus is on the absence of pronomial voice in music as an "other"; its ability to speak will then always be prescribed, defined, and described by language as "the master matrix" of expressive and communicative possibility.

The organization of language and music as a relation between subject and object installs an ambiguity in its definition of difference that in fact makes the distinction between subject and object impossible. This pivotal border becomes apparent in Adorno's *Einleitung in die Musiksoziologie* (*Introduction to the Sociology of Music*). The juxtapositioning of "the good listener" and "the emotional listener" shows the epistemological ambiguity involved here quite clearly. The good listener, Adorno writes, though not an expert, can still hear correctly:

He listens beyond the musically singular; spontaneously completes contexts, judges with grounds, not just according to categories of prestige or arbitrariness of taste. But he is not conscious, or not fully conscious, of the technical and structural implications. He understands music something like the way one understands one's own language, even when one knows little or nothing about its grammar and syntax—unconsciously master of the immanent musical logic. (*Gesammelte Schriften* 14: 183)

The emotional listener, in contrast, also constructs a metadiscourse, but one that is utterly unrelated to "the music itself." Such listeners react to music with their own representations and associations that are somehow stimulated by, but do not originate in, the music:

> Sometimes they like to use music as a container into which they pour their "free-floating" anxiety-provoking emotions. . . . In truth, even adequate listening is not thinkable without affective cathexis. But in this case, the thing itself [*die Sache selbst*] is cathected and the psychic energy is absorbed into the concentration on it; while for the emotional listener, the music is only a means to an end in his own libidinal economy. He does not externalize himself [*entäußert sich nicht*] in terms of the thing itself; rather, he alters its function into that of a medium of sheer projection. (14: 187)

This distinction may seem self-explanatory, but the question is how to tell the difference between adequate response and projection. The one "understands" music *like a language*; the other also reads the text but reads only himself into it. The only way to distinguish, then, would be to allow some formal linguistic parameters to connect the response to the music or text; the link, in fact, seems to be in the word *like*, in the process of *simile* that connects and differentiates simultaneously. Simile allows sameness and difference to come forth together, persisting and extending through articulation rather than condensing into the substitution of metaphor. Is this ability of simile strictly linguistic?

Perhaps the *rhetoric of simile* is precisely what exceeds the linguistic tendency to move toward conceptual meaning and cannot be contained in a strictly linguistic origin. This is indeed what Adorno suggests in "Fragment über Musik und Sprache" (Fragment on music and language), where he begins quite precisely: "Music is language-like [*sprachähnlich*]" (*Gesammelte Schriften* 16: 251). This does not simply mean that music is "like" language; it means, instead, that what music gives is the very concept of simile, the sameness that will always be different: in other words, a *metaphor* of *metaphor* that will always differentiate identity; it is a *metaphorical* similitude: "But music is not language. . . . Whoever takes it literally as language will be led astray by it" (16: 251).

The "correct" link of response to music, to return to Adorno's grammatical simile, emerges precisely in the differing model of repetition in music, that is, in the difference between musical performance and linguistic performance. Adorno describes this difference as follows:

Here one must take recourse to interpretation. Music and language require this equally but completely differently. To interpret language means: to understand language. To interpret music: to make music. Musical interpretation is the completion and actualization which, as synthesis, holds fast to language-likeness [*Sprachähnlichkeit*] and at the same time annihilates any particular likeness to language [*Sprachähnlichkeit*]. That is why the idea of interpretation belongs to music itself and is not simply accidental to it. To play music correctly is, above all, to speak its language correctly. This demands imitation of itself, not decipherment. Only in mimetic praxis, which of course might be internalized in the silent imagination, in the manner of silent reading, does music reveal itself; never to observation that interprets it independently of its realization. (16: 253)

This mimetic practice—the performance of a score—is similar to, but only similar to, the repetition of linguistic performance. What is added is not an addendum but a completion that is also actualization. The greatest similarity between music and language, then, would be in the point of its utter dissimilarity, in the duplicitous extension of simile. "If one wanted to compare an act in signifying language to the musical act, it would be more the manual copying of text than its significant grasping" (16: 253).

The most "productive" aspect of musical performance is compared to the most purely mechanical reproduction of language. The confrontation of music and language here brings to the fore the utter inadequacy of linguistic comparison to describe constitutive performance—musical or otherwise. One logical "way out" has been to restrict this limitation to the sphere of music, as the place where structure and instantiation, origin and repetition, supplement each other. This confinement and quarantine of music allows the conceptual power of theoretical language to persist, to ignore its own inability to describe its own performance, its own conditions of possibility. The alternative is to read in "music" a fundamental critique of meaning itself and a limit to the possibility of explanation. Nancy writes:

> The musical score (text?) . . . is inseparable from what we call, in a remarkable way, its interpretation: the sense of this word oscillating between a hermeneutic of sense and a technique of "rendering" [*du rendu*]. The interpretation or *execution*, the putting into action, music entelechy, cannot simply be "meaningful." What it is concerned with is not, or at least not only, sense in this sense. And in turn, the execution cannot itself be signified without remnant; one cannot *say* what it has *made* "the text" *say*. The execution can only be executed: it can only *be* executed. (*Le Sens du monde*, 136)

# 3.   Instruments of Virtuosity

With typical irony, Heine prefigures both Adorno and Nancy in pointing to music's adherence to its execution. "The very best musical criticism—the only kind, perhaps, which proves anything—I heard last year," Heine reports, describing a vehement debate about Rossini and Meyerbeer. "As soon as the one gave the highest merit to the Italian," Heine continues,

> the other opposed him, but not with dry words—rather, he trilled out some of the especially beautiful melodies from "Robert le Diable." The first one knew no sharper repartee than to send back eagerly some scraps of "The Barber of Seville." . . . Instead of a noisy exchange of speeches that say nothing, they gave us the most delightful table-music, and in the end I had to admit that one should dispute about music either not at all, or in this realistic way.
> (SS 3: 333–34 / *Works* 4: 244)

This anecdote promises little in the way of what language might have to say about music. The narrator, a fellow at table, both partakes and does not partake of the polemical repast. The anecdotal narrative frames and delivers the musical communication from which it excludes itself. This narrative technique exhibits Heine's ambivalent attitude toward music. While he sometimes seems to subscribe to the Romantic adulation of music, at other moments he is unenthusiastic. Heine's rejection of music shows an obvious anxiety collecting especially around the musical instrument. His ambivalence toward music can be traced along the fault line between the "mere" instrument and the musical instrument. The prominence of technique and the centrality of the material instrument in music problematize the commonplace Romantic emphasis on music as a language of subjective expression that transcends its means of production. Music lasts only as long as its instruments resound. The finite bodies of both performer and audience remain in physical contact with the vibrating instrument. As much as the metaphoric "spirit world" of music may temporarily obscure its material origins, the timbre of the resounding body can always reassert itself. The irreducible specificity of these bodies becomes clear when technique and the particularities of performance overshadow the musical message. The "mere" instrument is brought into focus by the "mere" player, who begins to dominate the picture with details of the concrete materiality of a body in direct contiguity with the thinglike qualities of an instrument. This aspect of musical performance highlights the hand instead of the script.

Heine's musical reportage is limited in scope and strongly colored by his amateur relation to music. Ludwig Börne, in a letter published in *Heine in Paris*, a colorful exhibition catalogue, testifies to Heine's lack of technical expertise, described in amusing detail:

> Heine sat next to me at Hiller's concert. He is so ignorant about music that he took the four movements of the grand symphony for separate pieces, and applied to them the numbers from the program in the order in which they appeared. So he thought the second movement of the symphony was the alto solo announced; that the 3rd was a cello solo, and the 4th the overture to Faust! Since he was so bored, he was very happy that everything went so quickly, and was dumbstruck when he found out from me that only No. 1 was over. (quoted in Kruse and Werner, eds., 67–69)

Michael Mann has thoroughly documented Heine's treatments of music and the conditions surrounding their production. As Mann shows, Heine's writing about music begins, in his letters *Über die französische Bühne* (On the French stage), by following commonplaces, almost to the point of plagiarism. German papers criticized Heine's approval of Meyerbeer, claiming that Heine's taste in music was "too French." Since much of his earlier remarks were copied or imitated from Parisian periodicals, it is not surprising that his views would seem "French" to German musicians and music critics.[1]

On the other hand, precisely because of his amateur status, Heine addresses problems of music and its reception from the point of view of a more generalized aesthetics. In the ninth letter in *Über die französische Bühne*, Heine asks directly: "But what is music?" (*SS* 3: 332 / *Works* 4: 242). In response, he positions music as a figure of mediation between the particularity of matter and the universality of spirit, but as a mediation that cannot be absorbed within the stability of conceptual knowledge. Heine writes of music: "It stands between thought and appearance; as a dim mediation, it stands between spirit and material. It is related to both, yet different from both. It is spirit, but spirit that needs the measure of time; it is material, but material that can do without space" (*SS* 3: 332–33 / *Works* 4: 242). Music cannot be absorbed into the simultaneity of a concept; thus, Heine says, musical criticism is an "experiential science" and should be based on the subjective impressions that are directly contiguous with the musical experience they render. For Heine, music's formal structure, which could be named by technical terms, does not properly belong to the sphere of musical criticism; instead, the effects of music on a subject are its essential measure: "Certainly there are laws here," writes Heine, "determinate mathematical laws. But these laws are not music; rather, they are its condition, just as the art of drawing and the doctrine of colors, or even palette and brush, are not painting, but only necessary means. The essence of music is revelation" (*SS* 3: 333 / *Works* 4: 243). Thus, the essence of music, for Heine, lies not in its formal conditions but rather in an intended sense that exceeds the necessary, but external, means of its realization. Heine's move away from technical analysis toward colorful translation is typical of much Romantic writing about music (see Rousseau, Hoffmann, and Liszt, for example). This move presupposes a division between the subjective or "spiritual" ends and the material means of communication and privileges an impression or sense over the technical means of its delivery. But this separation is not specifically musical; but rather, it originates in the Western conception of the linguistic sign that has interpreted it as a composite of a material and a "spiritual" component. The division of language into an interior and an exterior is an ideological structure prescribing the reflex that seeks a place in which this split might be mended. This linguistic split makes possible the displacement onto music of an ideal adequation between idea and appearance, or between the inside of the subject and the outside of its means of expression. The ideal of adequate expression—the relation of "revelation," as Heine calls it—cannot be achieved in language as long as the materiality of writing and the dispersion of syntax are considered to be external instruments of a unified interior. Music is called in to enact the non-differentiation of means and end, or outside and inside. Yet music holds apart the material and spirit it is said to bind, for it remains within mortality and thus preserves the materiality it dissolves. In the same way, Heine's exclusion of technique from expression in music reproduces the bare instrumentality—the palette and brush, the paper and pen—it strives to erase.

In the ninth letter, Heine praises Meyerbeer's music in terms of an aesthetic of expression in which the external work mirrors the internal sentiments of the composer. In this turn away from technical details, Heine digresses from the referential dimension of his own language, which could indicate "objective" formal conditions of the work, and diverts attention instead to a metaphorics of communication (transmission and revelation). "In *The Huguenots*," Heine writes, "Meyerbeer finally reveals himself without reserve. Here, he has drawn with bold outlines the entirety of his thought and has dared to speak out in unrestrained tones everything that moved his heart" (*SS* 3: 340 / *Works* 4: 254). The expressive gesture is clearly assimilated to writing and speaking.

Heine identifies with the composer's sovereign position in considering the communicative and expressive intent of Meyerbeer's work to be the *essential* aspect of his art, to which material and formal elements—including the arabesque—are subordinate or merely instrumental. The expressive communication Heine privileges raises Meyerbeer out of the sphere of everyday language and places him onto a poetic communicative terrain: "Not until this work did Meyerbeer win his right to immortal citizenship in the eternal city of spirits [*ewige Geisterstadt*], in the heavenly Jerusalem of art" (*SS* 3: 340 / *Works* 4: 254). As material details of individual works and arts are left behind, the *ewige Geisterstadt*, city of spirits or spiritual city, projects a poetic model as the common homeland of *all* arts, a land in which *all* kinds of artists communicate through a universal metaphoric language. Heine's assimilation of the musical to the poetic is even more explicit in his discussions of Chopin. While Heine repeatedly expresses his admiration for Chopin, he does not describe either his performances or his compositions directly. Again, this absence of formal analysis can be related both to Heine's ignorance and to the aesthetics of expression that understands subjective impressions as the proper decoding of a musical message. In *Über die französische Bühne*, Heine stresses Chopin's character as composer, raising him to an elite position dissociated from the horizontal, technical plane of the keyboard: "Chopin . . . is not only brilliantly distinguished as a virtuoso by his technical perfection, but also made the highest achievements as a composer" (*SS* 3:352 / *Works* 4: 277). Chopin's virtues in fact emerge as the technical specificities of his music disappear. In *Lutetia*, Heine says directly that Chopin is "much more a composer than a virtuoso. In Chopin's case, I completely forget the mastery of piano-playing, and sink into the sweet abysses [*Abgründe*] of his music, into the painful sweetness of his equally deep and tender creations. Chopin is the great genius tone-poet" (*SS* 5: 442). The dissolution of Chopin from the bonds of the instrument releases him, too, from the particularity of both individual nationality and the individual art. As he is elevated to the status of a "universal artist," that is, a *poet*, historical dispersion also disappears in a dream of common origin in the true fatherland:

> Yes, we must attribute genius to Chopin in the full sense of the word: he is not merely a virtuoso, he is also a poet, he can bring to our intuition the poetry that lives in his soul, he is a tone-poet, and nothing equals the pleasure he creates for us when he sits at the piano and improvises. Then he is neither Pole, nor Frenchman, nor German—then he betrays a much higher origin and we recognize that he hails from the land of Mozart, Raffael, Goethe: his true fatherland is the dream-realm of poetry. (*SS* 3: 353 / *Works* 4: 278–79)

The more Chopin is a composer, the more he is a poet. Chopin's performance detaches him from the literal ground of geographical origin and attaches him to a metaphoric ground beyond both spatial and temporal division. The language spoken in this land is *poetic* yet synaesthetic; all the arts communicate through the figures of Mozart, Raphael, and Goethe. As the physical aspects of Chopin's performance recede or are withdrawn, music is experienced not as the ground of Heine's description but as its *Abgrund*, its lack of a ground. Historical reference—that is, the fact that this is supposed to be a narrative description of a historical performance—is uprooted as it swerves into the very process of metaphorization. Forgetting technical mastery, Heine focuses instead on the communicative aspect of music and thus on Chopin as a poet and composer. "Mere virtuosity" is left behind with the geographical divisions of literal nations.

This swerving, as we have seen, is habitually identified as the greatly praised and innovative "subjectivity of style" of Heine's journalism. Michael Mann also identifies this as Heine's deviation from the "sources" on music from which he consistently "sought advice"; for Mann, these deviations represent Heine's original contribution to music criticism. At the same time, Heine, with Hoffmann and others before him, has defined this swerve away from technical exteriority to metaphoric generalization precisely as *music itself*, whose essence, we recall, is *Offenbarung*, revelation. Music is understood here as the figure of signification itself, held in suspense and never arriving at a definite sense. It is the action of signifying in general, generated within a material means of communication.

It is impossible to know in what way this definition pertains to music and in what sense it merely subsumes music under displaced poetic ideals to the benefit of the professional poet. Indeed, in identifying Chopin's performance as a metaphor of—that is, a substitute for—a poetic message, Heine inscribes himself in the scenario as the recipient: "When he sits at the piano and improvises, it is as if a fellow countryman were visiting from the beloved homeland and telling me the most peculiar things that have happened there during my absence" (*SS* 3: 353 / *Works* 4: 279–89). "Chopin" thus allows the poetic message to return to itself; Heine's metaphoric reading of Chopin's performance itself sets up the communicative community of artists in which Heine, too, is now included. This musical performance provides the background for Heine's poetic voice to begin to speak:

> Sometimes I would like to interrupt him with questions: and how is the beautiful nymph, who used to know so well how to tie up her silver veil so coquettishly about her green locks? Does the white-bearded sea god still pursue her, with his stale old love? Are the roses at home still as proud as flames? Do the trees still sing so beautifully in the moonlight? (*SS* 3: 353 / *Works* 4: 280)

Heine uses Chopin here as a figure to reflect his own reflection about "poetic" communication, a figure allowing him to voice a series of images clearly reminiscent of his own poetic idiom. The literal event described—Chopin's performance—fades out as Heine translates it into a metaphor of a poetic message. This metaphoric report brings near the absent "homeland," now a figurative one that is both the place of origin and an integrated community brought into being through the communicative bond between Heine and Chopin. The virtuoso's journalistic report from home is transformed, through Heine's rhetorical questions, into poetic dialogue.

As a model of the ideal poet, Chopin serves as a vehicle for Heine's own lyricism, as the occasion for a lyrical intrusion into a prosaic historical text. Heine's tenuous subjunctives—"it is as if a fellow countryman were visiting . . . and telling me . . . I would like to ask"—remain bound to, but divert attention from, the narrative extension that produces this "poetic illusion" of a metaphoric fusion of individuals in a phantasmatic dialogue and homeland. Deviating from a referential narrative into this brief "fantasy" or arabesque, Heine makes no attempt to explicitly relate Chopin's actual performance to the effect it produces. For the effect depends precisely on the disappearance of the relation out of which it came—on the forgetting of technical mastery. The narrative technique of this transport—from a literal narrative to its metaphoric translation—itself puts into operation the temporary obfuscation of the relation between formal-technical means and the "meaning" to which it gives rise. This disappearance of technique, which Heine attributes to Chopin, is induced by the text itself, and it allows Heine, too, to make contact with the synaesthetic and atemporal homeland. The displacement of the origin of poetic communication onto the musician, Chopin, makes possible the lyrical arabesque Heine performs here. Through the animation of the mouthpiece "Chopin," the "musical" aspect of writing can come forth. Heine's text and Chopin's performance converge in the common properties of their effects. The singularity of style emerges through the suspension of reference or content, just as the rhetorical questions Heine would like to ask Chopin are not a search for answers, but an occasion to speak. The musical report itself delivered by Chopin makes both present and absent the content of the poetic message; in the same way, Heine's report defers its referent: Chopin's performance, its very center and origin.[2]

This reading offers some commentary on Nancy's remarks quoted at the end of Chapter 2. Nancy's text stresses the musical indissociability of sense and its production; its interpretation, then, oscillates between "a hermeneutic of sense and a technique of 'rendering'" (*une herméneutique du sens et une technique du "rendu"*) (*Le Sens du monde*, 136). In one sense, Heine's text partakes of the music he describes; the relation between Heine and Chopin is one of identification. But at the same time, this "musical" aspect of writing must be understood as an analogy or metaphor marked by the *difference* between the performance of written enunciation and musical performance—the difference that adds the durability of paper and script. The musical-poetic subjunctive, which unites what is prosaically divided, has no enduring autonomy; it can be only a temporary digression from the circumstances of prosaic division out of which it emerges. While the extension of the metaphoric dialogue strives to open a space for a stylistic intrusion of lyric expressivity within a historical narrative, that expressivity has already been turned over to the autonomy of writing.

While the musical-poetic dialogue is meant to bring near what is separated, the writtenness of Heine's text recalls and in fact depends on separation—in particular, on his separation from Germany. Heine's absence from his homeland is precisely what makes his text possible, both economically and thematically. Were it not for this geographical division, the space separating the origin and the addressee of the journalistic message, there would be no need and nothing to report. Heine's situation merely exaggerates the necessary difference between event and witness that makes journalistic report necessary and possible in the first place. Within the literal realm of journalistic division, there can be no simultaneity of communication, no assurance that the message will arrive at its address. Chopin's address elevated him above the mortal sphere of temporal division into the eternal city; his report from the homeland thus preserves the content it defers. His murmuring message brings near the absent "homeland" in the medium of *Heimweh* (homesickness): "Ach!" Heine exclaims, "I have already lived abroad for a long time, and with my fabulous homesickness [*fabelhafte Heimweh*], I feel almost like the flying Dutchman" (*SS* 3: 353 / *Works* 4: 280). The stylization of *Heimweh* makes possible the idea that there is a land or ground to which one could belong, although it may be circumstantially absent.

We cannot tell, for certain, whether Heine's exile is in France or in the dispersion of prose; for the written letter can only travel across geographical boundaries and further disperse the poet who is supposed to be expressed there. Heine concludes the letter containing the discussion of Chopin and indeed the whole collection of letters: "I hope, dear friend, that these letters find you happy and cheerful, in the rosy light of life, and that things don't happen to me as they did the flying Dutchman, whose letters are usually addressed to persons who have long since died in the homeland during his absence" (*SS* 3: 354 / *Works* 4: 280–81). Writing implies the absence of the addressee; in particular, journalistic writing implies an indefinite and unformed addressee (the public), whether it be near or far. Whether or not these people are dead, most certainly the *I* inscribed there will have passed away, into this inscription, before the eyes of the reading addressee, even if it be Heine himself. The anxiety in this passage draws attention to the narrative conditions of Heine's text—conditions denied by the idealized communication presented in the musical scene.

The instantaneous transformation of music into text—its interpretation as communication—grasps the poetic side of virtuosity, the side that can be assimilated to poetry and composition and can be rendered in a portrait. But it cannot hold its other side—the side that remains attached to the piano and the sonorous bodies of its production. In the poetic translation, or metaphorization, of music, something is lost. Music cannot be translated; it stands as a limit of language's ability to master and contain the power of translation, the ability to carry across, common to both language and music. This point can be compared to the kernel of untranslatability that, for Walter Benjamin, characterizes not the original, but the translation—the "translatedness" that cannot offer itself to further translation.[3] Music preserves and reproduces the ends it is said to synthesize, just as Heine's interpretations and metaphors re-create their excluded doubles—their pens and palettes, pianos and presses.

Heine's presentation of music is two-faced. His privileging of the composer stresses the idealizing poetic function of sympathetic communication on a metaphoric ground. This ground is projected as the "eternal city of spirits," the common homeland of all arts, a land in which all kinds of artists communicate through a universal metaphoric language. Yet this image of poetic eternity, totality, and simultaneity remains structured and bound by, and thus derivative of, the political terminology it strives to transcend; the autonomy of the poetic *Reich* is illusory. Music can go no higher than the worldly universality of nationality: "Yes, Italy will always be the homeland of music!" (*SS* 1: 570), Heine says elsewhere. The interruption of the sociopolitical world already occurs within its vocabulary. Chopin embodies an *elevation*, opening a vertical space that yet falls back within the horizontal differences against which it is defined. Heine describes him: "This is a man of the highest rank. . . . His fame is of an aristocratic kind" (*SS* 3: 352–53 / *Works* 4: 278). He is the "highest," of the first

rank, an aristocrat. The superlative and the word *first* are supported by the average and the horizontal series of numbers, just as aristocracy can only emerge
in distinction from other classes. The realm of artists establishes a communicative elite, dissociated from yet contained within the common ground of the
technique of the piano.

In contrast, the figure of the virtuoso is firmly articulated on historical
ground. In Heine's descriptions of Franz Liszt in the *Musikalische Saison von 1844*
(The musical season of 1844), appended to *Lutetia*, stylistic elements, not statements, impart the difference between the composer and the virtuoso. Unlike
Chopin and Meyerbeer, Liszt is not primarily a composer but rather above all a
virtuoso, a technical performer. Heine presents him with gusto: "He is here!"
Heine exclaims, "our Liszt, who, despite all perversions, inversions and sharp
edges still remains our cherished Liszt and at this very moment has once again
aroused the *beaumonde* of Paris. Yes, he is here, the great agitator" (*SS* 5: 531 /
*Works* 4: 414). Liszt is presented "at this very moment" in physical contact with
the worldy space of Paris to which he imparts vibrations. Heine continues to
string together contradictory epithets, culminating in the giant-dwarf: "He is
here, the modern Homer, whom Germany, Hungary and France, the three
greatest nations, claim as their native child. . . . He is here, the Atilla, the
scourge of God . . . he is here, the mad, beautiful, ugly, enigmatic, terrible, and
often very childish child of his time, the gigantic dwarf" (*SS* 5: 531 / *Works* 4:
414–15). Liszt's transnationalism does not elevate but only mixes together the
many lands he has traversed—lands bearing historical and geographical and not
mythopoetic names. While Meyerbeer and Chopin open a path to the poetic
homeland, Liszt remains bound to the prosaic ground of literal territories. Indeed, he is connected with Atilla the Hun and the violence "from the East" that
he represents. This violence, attached to the "scourge" as well, underscores the
engagement of the body and its political interests. It suggests, too, the performative violence that came to be associated first with Paganini, known for breaking violin strings, and later with Liszt, who at times performed with two pianos
on stage, since he too sometimes played so thunderously that piano strings
broke.[4] The "modern Homer" presents the rhapsodic face of the first poet: the
traveling technician, the prosaic remnant of the metaphor of the poet, elevated
and positioned to stand at the origin of literature.

In quest of an explanation of the audience's stupendous reaction to Liszt,
Heine reads Liszt not as a poetic substitution but as the concatenation of prose.
He suggests:

> Yet perhaps the solution to the question does not lie in such deep and strange
> mysteries, *but rather on a very prosaic superficial surface*. It seems to me that the

whole spell-binding witchery can be explained by the fact that no one in this world knows how to organize his successes so well, or much more, their mise-en-scène, than our Franz Liszt. (*SS* 5: 533, my emphasis / *Works* 4: 419)

Liszt is prosaic, working within the historical horizon of divided languages and nations—what Lukács has called the "prose of capitalism." Liszt's universal appeal does not raise him into the realm of immortal spirits; his art remains historical, bound in quotidian technical communication. Here, prose indicates the organizational planning of mise-en-scène. It is a kind of manipulation that is not driven by an ideal intent to communicate; rather, it works a medium to produce effects on finite subjects of worldly communication. Within the prosaic order, there is no "natural" relation between the performance and its effect on the public.

To support his prosaic reading, Heine cites Liszt's hiring of claqueurs to applaud his performance and shower the stage with flowers in order to instigate further applause and his manipulation of the press. The cheering of members of both the public and the press is bought and paid for; what affects the public and arouses the jubilatory Lisztian furor is not Liszt "himself," his music, or its execution—that is, not the work's realization of an idea. Rather, it is the staged dissimulation of this very effect. The public is infected by what appears to be other people affected by the performance; but what they catch is the mechanical imitation of cheers detached from what they should be responding to.

In other words, the original Lisztian presence is essentially a superlative newspaper review written by Liszt himself. This is why Liszt is *verkehrt*, inverted; there is no original presence behind his appearance, for his presence as Liszt consists precisely of his staged appearance. Liszt's art is not *composition*, expression in revelation, but performance: the organization and realization within time of the technical means of producing effects. "In this art he is a genius, a Philadelphia, a Bosco,—yes, *even a Meyerbeer*" (*SS* 5: 533, my emphasis / *Works* 4: 419–20). (Incidentally, the English translator adds "the celebrated Houdin" to Heine's list here.) The performing Liszt is the Meyerbeer of the anti-Meyerbeerian art, the author of the authentic expression in the medium of inauthenticity; he inscribes veritable expression into the dissimulating traits of the virtuoso performance. If Liszt's art is "prosaic," grounded in the manipulation of extrinsic techniques, by the same token Liszt is a figure of the *art* of prose par excellence, which of course is also Heine's art—or at least one of them. As technique, prose stands in opposition to art yet has the power, too, to transform itself into art.

In his focus on the composer, Heine reads the musical work as an expression of a subject, according to a model of poetic expression; music appears to be a metaphor for poetry. Correspondingly, the performative aspect of virtuosity, exemplified by Liszt, falls off into the model of prose. "Mere virtuosity" uses prosaic techniques and exposes the bare instrument in its necessary persistence. In mere virtuosity, the effect is caused by mechanical instruments and techniques, not by the intended expression of a transcendent subject. Read in this way, music would simply reproduce and reflect the linguistic functions of poetry and prose—nothing is said about it specifically. Its essence would be language; its material specificity would fall away, like writing, from its linguistic sense.

In adopting this deprecating stance toward prose, Heine joins in a "melocentric" tradition that privileges the expressive nature of figurative language, which music is said to embody, over the technical and rational means of its production, aligned with writing, harmony, and exteriority.[5] Yet to say that Heine simply shares this view would be to ignore the irony of his writing and to take him at his word at an isolated moment. It would be like reading the recurrence of Romantic topoi in Heine's poetry as a simple continuation of Romantic traditions of poetry. But Heine is above all concerned with the mechanical repetition of what were once expressive topoi; his relation to Romanticism is skewed and critical. What is new in Heine's poetry, what exceeds and criticizes Romanticism, brings this reversal to the forefront.[6] But it is a reversal that cannot be pinned down to any one place or unified in a concept; it consists, instead, in the processes first opened up in his texts.

The division of music into poetry and prose, represented by Meyerbeer and Liszt respectively, reduces the relation between composition and performance to the hierarchically controlled relation between conception and execution. There would be no problem if we simply let it go at that; Meyerbeer would be the composer who remains the same, Liszt the dissimulating performer who constantly changes. But just as we have seen Liszt invert into Meyerbeer, Heine, too, reverses his opinions. With the passage of time, he changes his mind and tends to contradict himself.[7]

Liszt is not always a charlatan; sometimes he, too, transcends the instrument and reveals the musical art. Sometimes he becomes Chopin-like. And just as there are two sides to Liszt, who is sometimes Meyerbeer, Meyerbeer also is not always himself. The combination of contradictory traits in Meyerbeer does not always come to rest in peaceful harmony. Meyerbeer in fact exercises the master's control over the execution of parts. Heine explains that it is the "domination of harmony . . . that characterizes Meyerbeer's music as a socially modern music. [The melodies] must not protrude sharply, I'd like to say egotistically, but must serve the whole; they are disciplined" (*SS* 3: 344 / *Works* 4: 261). Just as the individual voices are disciplined to serve the harmonic whole, the composer strives to dominate and control the realization of the work in time and space. Heine points to Meyerbeer's tendency to control performers, his obsessive efforts to correct the errors inevitably incurred in the transference of conception to paper, and his "mania for perfection in correcting the proofs" (*SS* 3: 342 / *Works* 4: 258), even when the works are already virtually in print.

In *Lutetia*, Heine accuses Meyerbeer of manipulating the press to enhance his own fame. Here, Heine depicts Meyerbeer's self-extension not as poetic expression but as a self-interested inflation aimed toward the immortality of personal renown. This reversal takes place in Heine's text by means of a figurative use of musical terms:

> But what will become of his fame when he himself, the celebrated Master, is suddenly torn from the scene of his triumph by death? Only the great Giacomo himself, who is not only the general music director of all Royal Prussian musical productions, but also the director of the Meyerbeerish fame, only He can conduct the monstrous orchestra of this fame. (*SS* 5: 363)

Seen as a finite rhetorical subject threatened by death, Meyerbeer, like Liszt, is limited to the mortal immortality of historical extension in language: fame takes the place of the immortal city of spirits. Heine's recontextualization of Meyerbeer into the mundane spheres of government and employment reveals that he, too, is practiced in the prosaic art of manipulation working within time. To indicate this manipulation, Heine shifts from a literal to a figurative sense of musical terms. The reversal of the "good virtuoso" (a poet) into the "bad virtuoso" (a prose manipulator) is enacted by Heine's shift from the literal to the figurative. Through this shift, he relates the effect on the audience not to the genuine expression engraved in the musical work but to the devices of its presentation. The manipulation of these devices instrumentalizes and exploits the language and actions of others, enlisting them in the service of the production of an effect. Heine writes: "Indeed, no other composer has understood instrumentation as well as Meyerbeer—that is, the art of using all possible people as instruments . . . and through their cooperation [*Zusammenwirken*] to conjure up a consensus in public recognition that verges on the fabulous [*ans Fabelhafte*]" (*SS* 5: 364). The poetic effect of music, which erases its technique, is deflated by Heine's *underlining* of instruments, by the blatancy of his own use of figurative language. The source of the effect is not the transcendent passion of a subject but the communicative device itself; the autonomous *Zusammenwirken*, or cooperation, of instruments has been calculated to produce an effect on the public. The communication pointed to here is not musical or expressive but rather journalistic, reminiscent of the historical *Zusammenstellen*, juxtapositioning, of horse and fly discussed in Heine's prefaces. Heine's reversal of literal musical terms into figures exposes the instrumental use of language itself. As our attention turns to the critique of rhetorical instrumentation Heine describes, the specificity of musical instruments falls away; the instruments have merely been used to say something else. This figurative use of musical instruments—a *prosaic* or instrumental use—points not to music but rather to its own linguistic function.

The autonomy of the resounding device brings forth a general agreement of the public; the instruments of persuasion work through the mechanics of cause and effect within boundaries of a single immanent plane in which particular differences are eradicated. The manipulation of journalism imposes this pseudo-universality, bringing about a mechanically produced uniformity of effect. Heine describes the correlation among the uniformity of applause, reviews, and effect:

> The masterworks of our noble Meyerbeer find the most undivided applause even at the very first performance, and the very next day, all the journals deliver the earned articles of praise. This happens thanks to the harmonious cooperation of instruments; in melody, Meyerbeer stands behind the other two masters, but he soars above them in instrumentation. Heaven knows that he often uses the lowliest instruments; but perhaps it is through these that he brings about the huge effects on the great crowds that admire him, worship, honor and even respect him. (*SS* 5: 364)

Instrumentation functions as a metaphor for the journalistic reversal between cause and effect according to which the public report produces the effect it claims to describe. The unanimity of public opinion is no necessary sign of the internal qualities of the musical work performed. In the critique of the composer as manipulator, the border of the fabulous verges not on revelation of the beyond, but on the false and inauthentic. Calculation is patent in the unanimity of harmony and undivided applause.

We must remember, for a moment, that these texts are themselves journalistic texts, written in the same instrumental language, possibly already dissimulated and manipulated toward some self-interested end. Heine himself has an interest in separating the literal from the figurative. He seeks to break the persuasive effect of rhetorical devices. For how else could he himself speak? Through the breaking of his own language, Heine constitutes a critical space, a slight opening in the immanence of mechanical repetition. Yet this opening occurs within the public's space and time; Heine, too, writes journalistic pieces for a public. Heine does not presuppose an authority of his own language that would override the journalistic conditions he describes, and he does not take up a position that would stand outside the medium of his critique. The inconsistency of Heine's remarks on various musicians and his tendency to contradict himself do not simply reflect Heine's character or changes of opinion; they are unavoidable and unresolvable. It is the very persistence of contradictions that allows the "material" side of writing to flourish, marked as they are by the inevitable imperfection of expression in time through a medium. Heine's critique of language comes forth in his use of it, and not in isolated statements. This is why he must often change his mind and why the virtuosity of his own style makes it impossible for him to thoroughly reject Liszt.

The singularity of Heine's voice emerges, momentarily, in the breaks of his language. In his breaking of musical terms in his critique of Meyerbeer, Heine manages to make a slight difference through which he can establish himself. Disengaging himself from the homogeneous mass of the duped public, Heine holds himself apart from the unified effect to which the public falls victim. This tendency to hold himself apart as an indifferent observer is the reason for much contemporary criticism of his political position. In the context of his discussion of Meyerbeer, Heine describes his detached position in political terms:

> But my sensations always departed a bit from the sensations of others; I knew how they felt, but I felt quite differently . . . and even if I rode about heartily on my battle horse and thrashed away with my sword at the enemy, the fever, the lust, or the fear of the kill never really grabbed me. But I sometimes had an uncanny feeling about my inner calm; for I noticed that my thoughts dwelled elsewhere even when I thrashed about in the thickest press of party wars. (*SS* 3: 334–35 / *Works* 4: 245–46)

Through this distance, Heine evades the "fear of the kill," striving to retreat into a still interior; yet this retreat gives rise to the anxiety of duplicity, the uncanniness (*Unheimlichkeit*) of the separation of exterior and interior. This self-division can be described in terms of Heine's use of the word *I*. Heine's double anxiety expresses dread of the absorption of the *I* in a tumultuous and violent exterior—mortality and instability—on the one hand; and on the other, his anxiety results from the distance from this sphere established by breaking the identification of the speaking voice with the word *I*, that is, precisely by alienating himself from his own language.

The experience of listening to Meyerbeer's music exemplifies the absorption of a particular *I*, a finite body sitting in the audience, within the programmed effect planned by another. This absorption signals the suffocation or extinguishing of the individual. Pointing out his own anxiety, Heine admits that he prefers to avoid this experience: "I for one confess that my heart never beat so stormily as during the fourth act of the *Huguenots*, and that I very gladly avoid this act and its excitements" (*SS* 3: 343 / *Works* 4: 260). Heine further characterizes the division between the absorbed *I* and the distanced observer by jux-taposing the naive public and the expert: "While the great multitude is carried away by the content, the calmer observer admires the enormous advances of the art, the new forms that appear here" (*SS* 3: 343 / *Works* 4: 259). Amateur that he is, having excluded these "forms" from the sphere of music criticism, Heine is in something of a bind. Yet we find the same dissociation between the ab-sorbed experience and contemplative distance in Heine's use of the word *I*, sug-gesting that the full identification with this word is something like the extinc-tion of an *I* in the musical performance, the manipulated absorption of the public into the rhetoric of the virtuoso.

In his contradictory presentation of Liszt, Heine stylizes and instrumental-izes the device of speech itself, dissociating the word *I* from the sense of its ut-terance that survives it. The performative manner of Heine's description sug-gests that he is directly transcribing the experience of the astonishing effect he describes; his exclamations draw attention to the linguistic act of an agitated *I*.[8] But the performative and deictic character of this description, voiced as the ut-terance of an *I*, is revealed to be a calculated device, and not an immediate ex-clamation proceeding directly from a genuine experience. Heine presents "our Liszt," "the child of his time . . . whose madness confounds our very sense, and to whom we offer, in any case, the loyal service of bringing to public notice here the great *furore* that he arouses" (*SS* 5: 532 / *Works* 4: 412). Heine's text seems to be a subjective reaction to Liszt, but it shows itself to be a mere recording of the Lisztian furor it imitates and narrates. The public journalist uses the *I* as a tool for stating generalities. Now "we" speak no longer of Heine's private opinion but rather of a public and communal fact:

> We confirm unambiguously the fact of this monstrous success; how we
> interpret this fact according to our private opinion, and whether we give or
> withhold our private applause from the celebrated virtuoso must be of the
> utmost indifference to him; for our voice is only that of a single person and
> our authority in the art of music is not of special importance. (*SS* 5: 532 /
> *Works* 4: 416)

Heine's report is made persuasive by the device of a performative enthusi-asm that affects the genuine conviction of an *I*. By explicitly drawing a distinc-tion between his private opinion and the general opinion he reports, Heine dis-tances himself from the masses, withdraws from identification with the word *I*, and removes himself from the mechanical influence of the musical transmission. In this shift, the sympathetic furor aroused by the agitating Liszt is itself bro-ken. For the possibility of Heine's generalized statements about Liszt in no way depends on his actual performance; his description is not an immediate transcription of an actual sentiment but merely the repetition of the speech of others. Thus, "Heine" emerges in his deviation from that represented speech—a deviation marked out by the breaks implied in his manipulation of expressive devices. Liszt, then, stands between the narrating Heine and the resounding body of the musical performance.

It is not surprising, then, that Heine might have trouble maintaining his "own" position, an inevitable difficulty, since articulation is presented as a constant process of depropriation. In *Lutetia*, increasing anxiety shows up; it can be traced in the narrative attempts to master and control it in the figure of the virtuoso. This anxiety already appeared in Heine's aversion to the fourth act of *The Huguenots*. Indeed, the more strongly events reverberate, the greater the anxiety about the autonomy of subjectivity. Music's ability to affect "spirit" without mediation is thus both the reason for its success and for the anxiety it provokes. Heine's anxiety extends to Liszt as well:

> For I must admit to you that, however much I love Liszt, his music does not have a pleasant effect on my state of mind, all the more so because I see ghosts which others only hear; and that, as you know, with every sound the hand strikes on the piano, the corresponding figure [*Klangfigur*] rises up in my mind—in short, the music becomes visible to my inner eye. My very understanding still trembles in my head when I remember the concert where I last heard Liszt play. (*SS* 3: 351–52 / *Works* 4: 273)

The *Klangfigur*, or Chladni figure, is often invoked in nineteenth-century writing in discussions of theories of correspondence. Specifically, the term refers to experiments in which sand was placed on metal or glass plates that were then made to resound with a bow, and the vibrations caused consistent shapes to form in the sand.[9] As an epistemological model, the *Klangfigur* guarantees an accurate recording or translation of music into textual images. But at the same time, this quasi-mimeticism presents a threat, suggesting that thinking is nothing but mechanical reproduction, that the origin of thought lies elsewhere than in itself. The narrator's very technique causes the author anxiety. Understanding itself is destabilized by its explicit connection to a bodily origin. This is Heine's anxiety of hyperimmanence, in which the signified takes on a plastic contour, retaining an explicit connection to the materiality of the signifier.

Heine's conception of transcendence remains historically and aesthetically bound, as in the metaphor of the spiritual *Heimat* uniting all the arts. Because there is no theological or transcendent ground to pick up the slack—the excesses and absences within the finite—"transcendence" can only be temporary, momentary, or punctual events in passage that do not lead to any higher unity. This transcendence isolates but does not liberate, dissociates but remains attached.

The utopian ideal of a poetic homeland attempts to gather up these points of isolated subjective transcendence and give them a dwelling place. The differentiation of the individual from the crowd can only be performed in passing. Individuality (singularity) emerges in the temporary interruption of history (something like the artificial time of musical performance) within history.

The virtuoso is the ideal model of this paradoxical event in which individuality is distinguished from its surroundings but does not dissipate into isolated insanity. The elevation above but still within history is the excess of the technical that remains bound to it. The virtuoso embodies *excellence*. While Liszt may sometimes appear to be a manipulative charlatan, he is also the author of the uncanny *Klangfigur* in the mind of the early Heine; he, too, is a Meyerbeer of expression. In the "successful" version of instrumental virtuosity, the instrument disappears in the face of what it reveals. Indeed, "revelation" proceeds by the same "musical" movement by which excellence steps forth and the hero stands out as the representative of the mass. Here, Liszt and Chopin are paired as the "true" pianists:

> Next to him [Liszt], all pianists disappear—with the single exception of Chopin, the Raffael of the pianoforte. In truth, with the exception of him alone, all other piano players whom we heard in countless concerts this year are just that: piano players; they excel in the accuracy with which they handle the stringed wood. But with Liszt one no longer thinks of difficulty overcome; the piano disappears and Music is revealed. (*SS* 5: 358)

It is precisely Liszt who mediates between matter and spirit in the process of dissolution, in passage, on the way from the piano to music. Music embodies, suspends, and presents this process of dissolution, of departure from a ground not yet arrived, on its way to the poetic *Heimat*. It enacts the loss of content, the dissolution from a referent, which takes place through the focus on style. Style imitates music: it remains attached to its instrument, but, as it disappears in the face of what it reveals, it cannot reveal music; that is, it does not disappear but rather persists and displays itself in its failure to refer or signify, in its failure to reveal *something*. Like Chopin's music, the persistent extension of style reveals itself as a nonground, an *Abgrund*, emitting indeterminate tones.

Music exposes stylistic transmission itself without arriving at a sense. The thematization of music presents an abstraction, a specialized focus abstracted from language, following from a certain interpretation of language. Music, and its metaphoric version as stylistic extension in language, thus solicits the mortality of its own manner of communication; for the effect it produces, or what it reveals, cannot be separated from the process of the performance but can only emerge within it. The string breaks, the music stops, what is revealed disappears.

Music has nowhere to go; its inscription has no further destination. Borrowing a Hegelian schema of the history of the arts, Heine characterizes music as the last word within the lexis of history, not the first word of eternity:

> With the development of the life of consciousness, people lose all plastic gifts; in the end even the sense of color is extinguished, which is always bound to a determinate drawing or image. Increasing spirituality, abstract thought, strives towards sounds and tones to express a mumbling effusiveness which is perhaps nothing but the dissolution of the entire material world. Music is perhaps the last word of art, just as death is the last word of life. (*SS* 5: 357)

Music is the terminal station for the exchange of senses, pointing also to the future dissolution of all senses that would be pure spirit, or death, as the beyond of the body. Musical dissolution announces the death of the letter and the body, rupturing the texture of life but providing no place beyond it. Heine finds this morbid edge of music particularly disturbing in Liszt. He explains Liszt's taste for Beethoven as follows: "This composer would answer best to the taste of a Liszt. For Beethoven drives the spiritual art to that resounding agony of the world of appearance, to that annihilation of nature that fills me with a horror that I cannot conceal" (*SS* 5: 358). Heine is in a double bind. For this "resounding agony" itself breaks the contiguity of mechanical determination as well as the horizontal fusion of the masses that extinguishes all differences. Both these models present a spiritless immanence that Heine seeks to differentiate largely through altering repetitions in his journalistic performances. Heine must oscillate between two deaths: on the one hand the death of mechanical repetition, and that of material dissolution on the other.

Liszt embodies the dangerous moment of hyperimmanence, in which the signifier and the signified, presence and absence, are both present—when the effect itself has taken on a plastic form. This danger is itself inscribed in the model of adequation on which Heine relies: the liaison of "spirit," or a sense, with a "determinate drawing or image" (*bestimmte Zeichnung*), which itself describes the technique of rendering visible the musical effect, of translating it into a figure or image. Hyperimmanence collapses technique and its metaphoric effect, or signifier and signified, within the body. Heine criticizes this lack of differentiation, this hyperpresence of the effect in its cause, in the following description of the early Liszt. The ability of piano technique to produce effects is expressed through the assimilation of Liszt's body to the piano, the signifying instrument: "For example, when he played a storm, we saw the lightening bolts twitching through his own face, his members shivered and shook as if from the storm wind, and his long pig-tail dripped with the very rain he was representing" (*SS* 5: 358). What is unacceptable here is the identification of the performing subject with the materiality of the metaphors he is supposed to signify—the absorption of the presenting subject within the presentation. With this absorption—if there is no "extra" or excess subject, no invisible interior beyond or behind physical presence—there is no fundamental distinction between the performer and the instrument; subjectivity itself becomes a signifying machine. The metaphors are coexistent with the materiality of Liszt's body, just as musical tones remain contiguous with the instrument that produces them. The body thus duplicates the instrument's ability to appear and disappear, to function as a relay between materiality and spirit as that materiality that can give way to spirit.

Spirit has no protection against the musical instrument. It cannot succeed in transfiguring its action into an image; it cannot completely theorize it. Heine describes the all-pervasive intrusiveness of the musical instrument thus: "that pianoforte which one cannot block out anywhere, which one hears resounding in every house, in every society, day and night" (*SS* 5: 434–35). Narrator and virtuoso alike emerge in distinction from the mass, just as poetry differentiates itself from the geographical ground of prose. The autonomous action of instruments, indicated by the position of grammatical subject, threatens to absorb this difference: "These piercing clotted tones without any natural sense, these heartless whizzing noises, this arch-prosaic plodding and plucking, this pianoforte kills all our thinking and feeling and we become stupid, dumb, idiotic" (*SS* 5: 435). The automation and instrumentalization of subjects occurs through the replacement of the grammatical position of subject with bourgeois instruments; their expressionless and repetitive production of sound kills. Classed as "arch-prosaic," this reproduction of expressive form devoid of expression sounds rather like the dumb eloquence of the printing press. The "arch-prosaic" presents the mere extension of transmission; it designates the bare exterior of the written text. The autonomy of writing established in its fundamental and foundational separation from expression suggests an omnipresence of proliferating texts, pieces of writing not yet read—and, like the fatal forte of the piano, perhaps illegible.

The passage goes on to describe the more advanced Liszt: "Now, even when he plays the most tempestuous thunderstorm, he himself rises above it like the traveller who stands on the tip of one of the Alps while it storms in the valley below: the clouds gather far below him, the lightning twists about like snakes at his feet, and he raises his head, smiling, up into the pure aether" (*SS* 5: 358). In the sublime scenario Heine sets up here, the subject is elevated out of its errance and placed in a stable position of sovereignty. With this differentiation—the aetherization of the subject—the stable position takes control of its expressive elements. The lifting up of the head separates intention and effect, placing them in a hierarchical relation.

Heine's changing portrayal of Liszt ends up following a movement of aetherization comparable to the poeticization of Chopin. Heine attempts to rise above and gain control of this mechanical repetition in much the same way that we saw Liszt rise above the piano in the portrait of the dynamic sublime. He does so this time not by drawing a figure but by reading one. He thus draws the virtuosi into a representational frame, appropriating them into a general interpretive schema:

> The way this piano-playing has taken the upper hand, and especially the triumphal trains [*Triumphzüge*] of the piano virtuosi, are characteristic of our time and give veritable witness to the victory of machine over spirit. Technical ability, the precision of an automaton, the identification with the stringed wood, the resounding instrumentalization of human beings, is now praised and celebrated as the highest thing of all. (*SS* 5: 435)

In the same way, Heine's manipulations of physiognomic figures instrumentalizes humans to say something else. This is evident in his tendency to assimilate music to poetry, as it was fictionally worked out in his attribution of poetic speech to Chopin (prosopopoeia)—just as he "instrumentalizes" musical instruments to criticize the press.

The procession of virtuosi—their *Triumphzüge*—draws a line through the streets of Paris, rendering it legible: it stands as the *bestimmte Zeichnung*, the definite image, to which Heine's generalization can be attached. In the virtuosi's movement or trait (*Zug*, from *ziehen*, to draw or pull), they emerge as a general character. The stable character stands as a genuine and authentic witness of the vague background out of which it emerges. As a readable character, the virtuoso stands between space and the writer, between the unmarked generality of the time and its fixation in the text. In announcing his victory, the virtuoso allows the writer to say what he could never *say* himself: that the writer cannot "speak," that he can merely report or repeat the readable traits of another; that in using language, he has also identified with the "stringed wood" of the word *I* and has become an instrument of the press. The *I* cannot master the hand or ever take the upper hand but can only hand it over to another.

What the *I* loses, the historiographer gains. The victory of the virtuoso allows the interpretive scenario, re-placing the virtuoso in a sociohistorical context, so that the text appears to be neutral or merely reproductive. If the narrator can only reproduce the words of others—the original text of the world—at least he could gain the historical veracity of an accurate representation. But how to know that the traits and trains (*Triumphzüge*) of the piano virtuosi are really theirs and not those drawn by the hand of the narrator? The framing of the physiognomic figure renders it available to interpretation; Heine's manipulation of these human figures itself instrumentalizes humans to (make them) say something else. His use of prosopopoeia and manipulation of plastic figures itself enacts the "taking of the upper hand" (*Überhandnehmen*) he deplores. His narrative techniques themselves act out the identification with stringed wood, the "instrumentalization of human beings" (*Instrumentwerdung des Menschen*). This persistence of repetition, which threatens to efface difference, accounts for the anxiety Heine experiences at the hands of the musical instrument; when the instrument becomes a subject, the subject can also become an instrument.

If Heine himself acts as a kind of virtuoso, then we do not know if the message he emits originates in the world he wants to describe or in his own narrative instruments. We do not know if Heine is a rhapsode or a philologist, if he distorts, reports, or transmits. The virtuoso works on the margin between the piece of paper and the layout of the page. The piano virtuosi, Heine writes,

> come to Paris every winter. Paris serves them as a kind of announcement pillar on which their fame can be read in colossal letters. I say, their fame can be read here, for it is the Parisian press that makes them known to the gullible world, and those virtuosi understand with the greatest virtuosity the exploitation of the journals and the journalists. (*SS* 5: 435)

The text here enacts a break between the space of Paris and the spacing of the text. While the first phrase suggests that a message is about to emerge directly from historical space, the gigantic letters are deflated in what follows. Figurative letters are replaced by literal letters; there is no continuous passage from the one to the other. As the *I* explicitly reasserts itself—"I say"—its pronouncement instates breakage; the nonlinked passage through this instatement has turned the page from the spatiohistorical world of Paris to the text about it. Repetition links this nonlinkage; discontinuity appears through repetition, through contiguity, for "read" is no longer "read"; what appears to be the same is broken apart. This difference is communicated by the spatial distance highlighted within and by reading—by the extended syntax of Heine's text, which connects, yet holds apart, two instances of reading (*lesen*).

The second occurrence of *lesen* refers the figurative letters of the virtuoso's fame not to an actual effect of a performance, a historical event, but to the report of this fame by the press. The shift from the figurative report emerging out of physical space (like the "report" of a revolver) to the literal report in the press breaks the interpretive authority of the figurative character, the physiognomic sign embedded in a spatial tableau or historical context. Heine himself thus sets a limit to the reliability of the physiognomic character; the prior world it reveals is not a "world" but other texts. The proliferation of journalistic texts, of printed articles, forms the background, or the arch-prosaic ground of mechanical repetition, for Heine's production of physiognomic portraits. These figures emerge not from "direct observation" but from acts of reading and editing.

The greatest virtuosity opens onto the corruption of the press; the fame of the virtuoso is grounded not in his actual ability but in the calculated and bought manipulation of the report of it, designed to produce and extend the fame it records. This intervention of printed matter between the performance and its effect makes impossible the final distinction between technical precision and artistic (poetic) expression, for it displaces the origin of the effect from the spotlight of the performer onto the context of manipulated techniques: to the keyboard, the stage, the claqueur, the journalistic report, the advertisement. Moreover, fame is not simply added on to but is constitutive of the virtuoso; without it, he would not be a virtuoso any more than there could be a spotlight without a stage and the price of a ticket. Heine makes the connection between this constitutive fame and the relation of the virtuosi to the press: "Actually, they are all famous, especially in the advertisements that they manage to get printed, either by themselves or through a brother, or even a Madame Mother. It is unbelievable how humbly they beg in the newspaper offices for even the slightest expenditure of praise" (*SS* 5: 435–36). Recalling that Heine's text is also journalistic, we wonder whether his report does not potentially falsify his own voice. If the virtuoso exploits the journalist, then he does so no more than the journalist exploits the virtuoso, who provides a theme in public demand and a content to report and who steps forth as a character in an interpretive pattern. The virtuoso and the journalist mutually exploit each other.

Virtuosity presents a pattern that can be lifted up out of the mechanical determinism in which it originates, that can step forth as a singular individual and yet remain attached and not deviate and disintegrate into abstraction. Yet the price is paid in its lack of durability, for it disappears at the moment it comes into being, finding its lasting existence always elsewhere: in reports marking its absence. Virtuosity presents a poetic side, which effaces its techniques to give way to a poetic terrain suspending time, producing prose as its opposite. Yet it also performs within its historical extension, just as music remains in time, and it cannot be fully replaced by its poetic counterpart. The metaphor of music remains within the circuit of "natural" communication—of the language of the heart—which the persistent autonomy of the instrument will continue to disrupt. The instrumentalization of instruments—their figurative meaning in Heine's text—repeats what it would interrupt. Virtuosity presents a side of language that cannot be subsumed under "prose" understood in dialectical opposition to "poetry." It points to that specificity of musical performance that cannot be absorbed by language, and thus to a deficiency in language, which can capture neither music nor its own "musicality." The assimilation of musical per-

formance to the poetic homeland inevitably reproduces the foreign exterior—
the amalgamation of literal nations and languages, the mechanical repetition of
barbarian language, gathered up and unified in the figure of "Liszt." In the same
way, historical figures become significant physiognomic characters as Heine se-
lects and edits the haphazard frame of journalistic reading. Heine's reading and
translation of historical figures attempts to control what is always potentially illegible—the illegibility and unmanageability of the technical instrument itself,
which exceeds expressive control.

In the ideal figure of adequation, the heart and the music beat time together.
Virtuosity is temporarily saved as it is brought into line with this heartbeat—
when the physical contact with the materiality of the instrument is replaced by
this figurative physical contact. The instrument is rescued, divided now between piano and violin:

> For violinists, virtuosity is not altogether the result of mechanical finger-ability
> and mere technique, as it is for the pianists. The violin is an instrument that has
> almost human moods and stands, so to speak, in a sympathetic rapport with
> the mood of the player: the smallest discontent, the slightest mood tremor, a
> breath of feeling, all find immediate resonance here. That is probably because
> the violin is pressed so close to the breast and even perceives our heartbeat.
> (*SS* 5: 437)

In this kind of expressive transmission, following the poetic model, the exterior
renders visible an interior; yet this doubling of the interior in its exterior in-
duces the hyperimmanence it should delay. Consistency itself works against the
expression it should present:

> But this is only the case for artists who really have in their breast a heart that
> beats, who have a soul at all. The more sober and heartless the violinplayer, the
> more uniform his execution will be, and he can count on the obedience of his
> fiddle at any hour, in any place. But this prized assurance is only the result of a
> spiritual narrowness. (*SS* 5: 437)

The "genius" of expression breaks and is, in principle, broken: "I have never
heard anyone play better, but also at other times worse, than Paganini, and I can
say the same of Ernst. This latter, Ernst, perhaps the greatest violinist of our
time, resembles Paganini in his flaws [*Gebrechen*] as in his genius" (*SS* 5: 437).

Consistency marks the domination of composition over performance, the
calculated manipulation of figures that manipulates them toward a determinate
end. While we have seen this tendency in Heine's texts, it is regularly countered
by a notable inconsistency. This inconsistency is marked by differences of reading, which holds together but does not conflate disparate segments of extended

text. The moment at which Liszt becomes the Meyerbeer of the anti-Meyer-beerian art compresses composition and execution—the giant-dwarf—but does not reduce them to a unity. Virtuosity, which characterizes this working through extension, produces inconsistency and disruption within the mechanical repetition of the word *I*. Heine cannot condone or condemn virtuosity once and for all, for many of his own techniques would fall subject to the same critique.

The physiognomic reading Heine proposes thus still presupposes the mechanical reproduction from which it differentiates itself. Heine associates this kind of repetition not only with the technique of the musical instrument but also with that of the printing press: "Haumann, the son of the Brussels bootleg printer [*Nachdrucker*], practices his father's métier on the violin: what he fiddles are pure reprints of the most excellent violinists who ornament the texts here and there with superfluous original notes and increase it with brilliant typos" (*SS* 5: 360). The "bad" virtuoso practices empty mechanical techniques and mars the work he plagiarizes as he performs. His deviations (his "originality") are errors that refer only to the particular performer and do not lead to the idea of the work, just as the instrumental manipulation of journalism and public opinion circulate, by means of money and applause, back into the fame of a particular individual. The arabesque of the nongeneralizable *I* is a deviant from the idea of originality—the idea of origination in the idea. The worldly charlatan, the virtuoso, is a typographical error. In virtuosity, the idea digresses.

# 4. Virtuosity, Rhapsody, and Romantic Philology

In *Der Fall Wagner*, Nietzsche notes: *"The emergence of the actor in music*: a capital event. . . . In formula: 'Wagner and Liszt'"* (*Kritische Studienausgabe* 6: 37 / *The Case of Wagner*, 178–79). Nietzsche has nothing more to say about Liszt here; he enlists him to draw out the spectacular and virtuoso qualities he is criticizing in Wagner. The formula "Wagner and Liszt" is in fact a predicate modifying Wagner. It has become commonplace to link Liszt to Wagner in this way, to imply that Liszt is a mere continuation of what Wagner began, a sideshow to Wagner's center, a cultural trill. Much of Liszt's contributions to musical production and publication—to its distribution or dissemination beyond the sphere of his own hands—remain largely forgotten. After retiring from his career as performer at the age of 35, Liszt was enormously active in his position as *Kapellmeister* at Weimar in a variety of ways that spread music beyond the sphere of his own two hands. He produced huge numbers of transcriptions and arrangements of orchestral pieces for keyboard or smaller ensembles and also worked to find funding for many artists, including Wagner.

A vague but consistent dismissal of Liszt as musical marginalia participates in the specific kind of distinction between composition and performance that Heine has, in part, put forth. Wagner himself articulates this distinction even more strongly. However, the standards organizing and evaluating composition and performance are not specifically musical but are generated by a linguistic context. Philological characterizations of the Greek rhapsodes, the nameless singers of antiquity, in the tradition of "the Homer question," pave the way for the appearance of the virtuoso and the *querelle* between composition and performance.[1]

Virtuosity's oscillations maintain the two poles that would disappear in a phantasmatic unity of composition and performance. As argued in Chapter 2, this imagined unity, modeled after the linguistic relationship of *langue* and *parole*, projects a nonalienated utopia. This utopia in turn projects an ideal relation in which novelty and originality, defined in opposition to the past, would still be integrated in a communal tradition. Idealized interpretations of the Homeric epic, in which the expression of an individual is also that of a social generality, combine the linguistic structure of enunciation with a narrative of literary history. The attribution of "organic totality," the balanced integration of part and whole or the particular and the general, to the era of classical Greece and the Homeric epic, its representative genre, has been a critical commonplace since the seventeenth century.[2] While the name "Homer" functions as a unifying principle in this utopian structure, the rhapsodes carry the blame for the diversions, digressions, and excessive ornamentation that "blemish" epic unity. The corrupting character of rhapsodic transmission originates in its technical status, suggested by the questionable though often invoked etymology construing the term from *raptein* ("to sew or stitch") + *(h)odos* ("songs"). The rhapsodes' relation to manual technique, horizontal aggregation, and juxtaposition parallels the musical performers' attachment to their instruments, while the "unitarian" interpretation of Homer reinforces the authorial principle of the composition.

Giambattista Vico first challenged Homeric unity with the thesis that the Homeric epics were popular collective works and that the name "Homer" gathered together common traits of all the Greek peoples (*The New Science*, 324). The name *Homer* is itself a kind of "rhapsody," according to the spurious etymology Vico reports: "[the common noun] homeros is said to come from *homou*, together, and *eirein*, to link" (318). Interestingly, the fusion of performative repetition with poetic composition coincides with the confusion of the common and proper name; in this way, individual and collective population are indistinguishable. In the eighteenth century, the nostalgia for epic enclosure is understood as a symptom of the modern lack of intimacy between man and nature (or "subject" and "object") in Johann Winckelmann and Friedrich Schiller, for example.[3] The emergence of the modern author's prestige coincides with a falling off of the epic and a rise of the "subjective genres": the modern lyric and music. For Hegel, music stands at the center of the Romantic arts, which have "subjectivity" as their principle, a subjectivity that is empty and abstract: "What alone is proper for the musical expression is the object-free inner life, abstract subjectivity as such. This is our entirely empty I, the self without any further content" (*Ästhetik* 2: 261 / *Aesthetics* 2: 891). Idealizations of the Greek world and its epic form are attempts to fill this emptiness.

On the other hand, it is precisely this lack of content that permits the configuration of unity between traditional generality and a particular performance. Just as many linguists use musical metaphors to describe the relation between *langue* and *parole*. Milman Parry, for example, characterizes the relation between Homer and his community in similar terms. In the following passage, Parry describes the beauty of Homeric language in analogy to music:

> The first impression which this use of ornamental words makes upon the reader is one of utter loveliness. They flow unceasingly through the changing moods of the poetry, inobtrusively blending with it, and yet, by their indifference to the story, giving a permanent, unchanging sense of strength and beauty. They are like a rhythmic motive in the accompaniment of a musical composition, strong and lovely, regularly recurring while the theme may change to a tone of passion or quiet. (426–27)

Parry's famous innovation is his insistence that the Homeric poems were composed performatively; he argues that metrical shape determines diction. For Parry, poetic composition, "winged" diction in particular, depends largely on "convenience" rather than on content, on materiality rather than on meaning: "This need for filling in space in the metrical pattern seems to have entered invariably into the use of ornamental adjectives" (427). Parry sees the adaptation of meaning to metrical shape as the collective work of a whole "race." This collective origin offsets the negative qualities of technical reproduction. "Such is the need of filling-in," Parry writes:

> The words which they chose for the filling were those which generations of poets and audiences had selected as producing the highest artistic effect, as being most beautiful and appropriate to the subject. The fact that every epic poet used them is nothing to disparage: in their case the race was the artist, and the artist satisfied an artistic need and made of that need an opportunity for extraordinary beauty. (428)[4]

In the nineteenth century, the need to fill up space has not disappeared, but has shifted to the columns of newspapers and the auditoriums of performance halls. The same issues governing several centuries of "the Homer question" also structure debates about the relation between composition and performance in music. Despite his professional status as a musician, Wagner allies himself with

the authorial position. As we have seen, the evaluative organization of composition and performance parallels an unstated interpretation of language that
similarly elevates and privileges "meaning" and deprecates rhetorical extension
and historical contingency even as they are exploited. These two positions are
allied with composer and virtuoso; the hierarchical relation between them subordinates musical production to a linguistically oriented authorial model. But
just as in writing, in the end the hierarchy will not remain in place. Like the
rhapsode in literary history, the virtuoso has an aberrant existence that can
never quite be controlled by the compositional figure it supplements.

In his early essay "Der Virtuos und der Künstler" (The virtuoso and the
artist) (1840), Wagner makes clear that the compositional thought is the prior
origin of the performance; he conceives of execution primarily as adequate repetition. This relation ought to duplicate an original internal repetition issuing
in the written composition. Wagner writes:

> The most important thing for you must be . . . that the musical piece should
> correspond exactly with your inner perception of it when you wrote it down;
> that is, the composer's intention should be reproduced with conscientious
> fidelity so that the spiritual thoughts are transmitted to the organs of percep-
> tion without disfigurement or distortion. (*GS* 1: 169 / *WPW*, 53)

Yet Wagner's very definition of music calls for the spatiotemporal extension of
the work into its resounding performance. Music, the art of sounds, must be
performed in order to be itself. Wagner states this imperative succinctly to his
fellow composers: "The tones you have written down must resound aloud; you
want to hear it, and you want others to hear it" (*GS* 1: 169 / *WPW*, 53). Because
the compositional thought is the prior origin of the performance, execution is
considered a relation of identical repetition, almost like that of the printing
press to a manuscript.

Ideally, only the composer himself could perform the work, since the written composition itself is foremost a spatiotemporal extension of the "spiritual
thought"; but when anything but solo music is composed, this is of course impossible. The composer therefore essentially needs the performer, to whom he
must entrust his own work. For Wagner, this mutual dependence and the system of division of labor implicitly inscribed in the structure of "expression"
originate in history, understood as a dividing fall into finitude. This division
also parallels that between the arts and particular languages and thus the need
and solution of the *Gesamtkunstwerk*. Wagner tells composers:

> You need the virtuoso; and if he is a proper one [*der rechte*], he needs you com-
> posers too. . . . To be sure, something has come to pass that opened up a divi-

sion between virtuoso and artist. Surely it was easier, at one time, to be one's own virtuoso. But you composers became ambitious and made it so difficult for yourselves, that now you must relegate this labor of execution to one who devotes his whole life to this: to be the other half of your work. *Truly, you must be grateful to him*. (*GS* 1: 172, my emphasis / *WPW*, 55)

The composer is thus only half himself and owes a debt to his other half, the usurper of his identity, the delegate of himself: "You composers only want your piece of music to be executed as you have thought it out to yourselves; the virtuoso should neither add nor take away anything; he should be *you yourselves*" (*GS* 1: 172, my emphasis / *WPW*, 57).[5]

The composer, according to Wagner, strives to produce the exact reproduction of the "spiritual idea" in which the composition originates. The "proper virtuoso" also ought to do precisely this and work as an extension of the composer's pen. But just as the technicality of writing entails a certain generic constraint, distortion, and typographical error, the virtuoso tends to digress from the composer's intention. This digression overlaps with the particularity and autonomy of the virtuoso, forming the circuit among digression, ornamentation, and improvisation, historical variability, the spatiotemporal contingency of the performance—and the fame, glory, and money paid to the virtuoso. These last fall within the government of the particular interests of the performer, deriving in no way from the compositional idea and serving instead to institutionalize the identity of the performer. The proper (*rechte*) virtuoso is required to give up the authorial model of proper expression. The composer will remain himself in his extension, but the extended performance must strive to become an other, to become the extension of an intention originating elsewhere. Wagner describes the ideal virtuoso in these terms:

So the greatest merit of the performing artist, the virtuoso, must consist in the pure reproduction of the thought of the composer. This can only be assured through a real appropriation of and assimilation to the composer's intention; this can only be insured through a complete renunciation of his own power of invention. (*GS* 1: 169–70 / *WPW*, 53)

Ideally, the virtuoso would be a musical instrument, that is, the kind of instrument that is thoroughly effaced in the presence of the ends it serves. The virtuoso is called in as the necessary mediation between the idea and the material signifier:

His position as mediator of the artistic intention, indeed, even as the true representative of the creative master, especially obligates him to preserve the seriousness and the purity of art in general. He is the point of passage

[*Durchgangspunkt*] for the artistic idea, which in a sense can only attain to a real existence through him. (*GS* I: 170 / *WPW*, 54)

The proper characteristic of the virtuoso is to have no proper characteristics; the proper quality of extension in time is to efface itself toward the meaning that has prescribed it. But even Wagner cannot really require that the virtuoso not exist at all, for then the composition would never resound. The virtuoso must therefore possess his own and proper *creative force*. His specific character is pliability, mutability, extendability, in service to the principle of allopreservation. The best virtuoso, Wagner says, will be one

> who is gifted with enough creative force of his own to be able to measure the value of preserving the purity of the artistic intentions of others in accordance with his own values. At the same time, he must be endowed with a special loving pliability [*liebevolle Schmiegsamkeit*]. Artists would stand in line to get virtuosi like these, who make no demands for their own invention, and in a sense only belong to Art insofar as they are able to interiorize and appropriate, make their own, alien art works. This performer would have to have enough modesty to keep his own characteristics and properties . . . out of play so that in the execution, neither his good nor his bad points would attract any attention: for, finally, only the art work, in a pure reproduction, ought to appear before us, while the particularity of the executor should not draw any attention to itself, that is, should not divert from the art work in any way. (*GS* I: 170 / *WPW*, 53–54)

But as this property is granted the virtuoso, propriety itself is distorted as it is written and handed over to the personal characteristics of the performer. This kind of improper identity overflows the structure of the centered self. The conceptual hierarchization of composition over performance protects the stability or fixity of the structure of the originary *I* that nevertheless is threatened simultaneously by the contemplation of the virtuoso's pliability (*Schmiegsamkeit*). The productivity and creativity of the virtuoso endanger not only the propriety of the *I* as source but also the value of originality and the status of the produced work as the private property of its producer.

In the same way, as Lacoue-Labarthe has shown, Wagner found it necessary to supplement his musical works with critical texts published in various journals.[6] The public's inability to understand immediately the Wagnerian musical opus on its own terms is a sign of the division between the arts and a mark of finitude. The division of labor between music and writing, then, parallels that between composition and performance and is only provisional. With the artwork of the future, Wagner writes, these divisions will be overcome.

> But when this is achieved in the real work of art, when the thing we have willed
> stands before us to determine our feeling—then, too, our criticism is at an end;
> then we are redeemed from critics into artists and art-enjoying people. And
> then, honoured friend, you can close your Journal for Music: it dies, because
> the work of art lives! (*GS* 5: 64 / *WPW*, 73)

But until that time, Wagner gladly takes up space in contemporary journalism.
The author-composer must rely on favors from the instruments of his extension for his distribution. The Wagnerian theory of the artwork of the future is
an ideological recovery of the loss the composer suffers in the hands of the virtuoso; it mends the break and fall into history that is both the historical origin
of the division of composer and virtuoso—and the necessity of performance
itself.

Thus, Wagner is compelled to compose the flaw in the model of self-identity
with the very same stroke with which he hopes to protect it. The delineation of
the proper self of the virtuoso, insofar as he represents the deficiency of the
composer, structurally alters the model of the subject as the origin of which
historical extension is the copy. In "The Virtuoso and the Artist," Wagner
clearly does not include Liszt among the "proper virtuosi," accusing him of the
mere display of his own technical ability. Later Wagner changes his mind and
redefines his criticism of Liszt. In his correspondence with Liszt, Wagner urges
him to compose, for he considers the performative activity to be essentially in-
complete:

> In single, aphoristic things we never attain repose; only in a great whole is
> great power self-contained, strong, and therefore, in spite of all excitement,
> reposeful. Unrest in what we do is a proof that our activity is not perfectly
> self-contained, that not our whole power, but only a detached particle of that
> power, is in action. This unrest I have found in your compositions. . . . I com-
> pare it to the claw by which I recognise the lion; but now I call out to you,
> Show us the complete lion: in other words, write or finish soon an opera.
> (*Correspondence*, 47)

Wagner clearly strives to integrate performance into a hermeneutic totality
dominated by composition. But the very figure that articulates his position continues to reproduce and depend on the autonomy of rhetorical division and extension—on the "claws."

The claws endanger Wagner's ideal of authentic expression; for the virtuoso,
like the actor, always speaks the words of another. There is something disagreeable about this "speaking the words of another" viewed with respect to the desire for originality within a logic of production. Wagner writes to Liszt: "I must

confess that it would be absolutely impossible for me simply to write music to another man's poems, not because I consider this beneath me, but because I know, and know by experience, that my music would be bad and meaningless" (*Corr.*, 56). The fixation and rigid identification with the typeface of an *I*, which establishes the authorial position, is a mode of identification with one's language or words as one's "own" language. Indeed, while in exile in Paris, Wagner had a great deal of difficulty writing for a French public, and he lamented the political and economic necessity to move outside the sphere of his native language. He writes to Liszt: "The reason why for a long time I could not warm to the idea of writing an opera for Paris was a certain artistic dislike of the French language which is peculiar to me. You will not understand this, being at home in all Europe, while I came into the world in a specifically Teutonic manner" (*Corr.*, 56). While Wagner disdains this speaking of another's language, this is of course Liszt's vocation. In contrast, Liszt does not overtly defy the structure of own and other, for example, but critiques it by offending against proper use. The duality of the structural relation between composer and virtuoso becomes evident in the reversal of dependence in the relationship between Wagner and Liszt, who helped to support Wagner financially, was responsible for the performance of many of Wagner's works, and of course eventually became his father-in-law.[7] Longing to hear himself, to obtain completion in the resonance of his work, Wagner writes to Liszt:

> Dear friend, I have just been looking through the score of my *Lohengrin*. I very seldom read my own works. An immense desire has sprung up in me to have this work performed. I address this wish to your heart:
>     Perform my *Lohengrin*! *You are the only one* to whom I could address this prayer; to none but you could I entrust the creation of this opera. (*Corr.*, 62–63)

Political circumstances prohibited Wagner's attendance at the premiere of *Lohengrin*, which Liszt did in fact produce in 1850. But Wagner suggests:

> One thing more: tell me, dear Liszt, how could we make it possible that I could attend the first performance in Weimar *incognito*? . . . I promise faithfully to preserve my *incognito* in the most stoical manner, to lie *perdu* in Weimar for a little time, and to go straight back, guaranteeing all the time the strictest secrecy from abroad also. (*Corr.*, 67)

It is interesting that Wagner should clothe his offer to efface himself in a clandestine visit to his homeland—in order to hear himself and fulfill the longing set astir in his self-reading—precisely in foreign words such as *incognito* and *perdu*, in the French he so dislikes. But Liszt replies: "Your return to Germany and visit to Weimar for the performance of *Lohengrin* is an *absolute impossibility*" (*Corr.*, 72). It is Liszt, employed as musical director to the court at Weimar, who is in good standing with the political powers and therefore has access to the necessary funds for the production of *Lohengrin*. While his employment here or there is surely accidental, it is possible that what has often been characterized as his opportunism, his *pliability of opinion*, is not at all accidental. The fact that Liszt finds himself financially established at Weimar, and thus socially installed with the means of producing Wagner's opera, has as much or as little to do with chance as his lack of a maternal language, what Wagner calls his cosmopolitanism. Because of his transnationalism, no single language is any more inherently offensive to Liszt than any other, since all are assumed (compare Chapter 5). The importance of the relation of dependence here, on the level of the physical subsistence of both Wagner and his works, should not be underestimated, since it belongs to the *essence* of music to come into existence in the world. Wagner describes it thus: "I know that I am safe with you as a child in its mother's bosom. What more is required beyond gratitude and love?" (*Corr.*, 78).

We must, perhaps, concede to Liszt when he writes: "The virtuoso definitively has the right of life and death over the works whose thoughts, feelings and excitement the composer has momentarily entrusted to him. . . . He can let them live a glorious life of fame [*Ruhm*], like that enjoyed by the heroes in the Elysian fields; or he can let them die an ignoble, ridiculous death!" (*Über die Musik der Zigeuner*, GS 6: 334 / *Gipsy*, 267). The composer—or rather the poet or author in general—must entrust his work to the hands of the virtuoso, delivering it *momentarily*, through and into the moment, into mortality. The sphere of life and death in which the work is realized—the *Darstellung*—lends the same renown as the epic narration of the lives of heroes. The delivery in time of the work of another (as its source and essence) through the voice of a particular but anonymous performer—an inessential servant who adds and subtracts nothing—is of course the very model of epic narration. The handing over of the work of others, homologous to the narrative delivery of tradition, is, like "tradition," regulated and controlled by notions of fidelity to the source; yet as Wagner points out, the purity of what is handed over depends for its very life on subjective judgment, grounded in nothing but the particularity of the performer. This silent and unmarked editing is the work of the virtuoso and the rhapsode: epic singer and aboriginal newspaper. There is no book of music—no Bible, no *Odyssey*, no notion of the fixed integrity of a text to control the musical tradition. The performer plays the role of printing press, typescript, and editor at once and relates directly to "the art" itself, standing side by side with, rather than beneath, the composer.

The dependence of tradition, and the newspaper, on their delivery, like Wagner's dependence on Liszt, is also, but not simply or exclusively, a chance circumstance of history. For Liszt, the performance is essential and of equal rank with composition, similarly enjoying the status of an autonomous art. For Wagner, the virtuoso's execution ought to repeat the original repetition within the composer between the "thought" (conception) and the composition. But for Liszt, this "first" repetition has no existence, since the composer's imagination is not music:

> Without the virtuosi, the composer's existence would be a perpetual Hell, since the latter can neither himself present what his creative genius has thought up, nor objectify what fills him, nor can he make present to himself that which makes his pulse beat, which ignites his imagination, occupies his thoughts and absorbs his whole being. If all this is not performed for him by human voice, an instrument or an orchestra, he would be in endless torment with no hope of deliverance. (*GS* 6: 336 / *Gipsy*, 268)

The persistent resistance of the instrument, lodged in its autonomy, resurfaces continually in the tensions between composer and performer. The intertwining relation of technology, time, and the written intention in fact intervenes in Liszt's production of *Lohengrin*. He writes to Wagner: "If you will do me a service, dear friend, send me, if possible by return of post, some metronomical indications for the introduction and several other important pieces. . . . I believe I am not mistaken as to your wishes and intentions, but should still prefer to have conviction *in figures* as to this matter" (*Corr.*, 80, my emphasis).

Wagner supplies the figures, but writes:

> You ask me for a few metronomical indications of the tempo. I consider this quite unnecessary, because I rely in all things on your artistic sympathy so thoroughly as to know that you need only be in a good humour with my work to find out the right thing everywhere; for the right thing consists in this only: that the effect corresponds with the intention. (*Corr.*, 83)

Wagner, unable to attend the premiere, must depend on the reports of eyewitnesses to judge this "effect." After receiving reports about the performance, he writes to Liszt:

> So much is certain: that the performance has caused fatigue by the length of its duration. I confess I was horrorstruck when I heard that the opera had lasted until close upon eleven at night. When I had finished the opera, I timed it exactly, and according to my calculation the first act would last not much over an hour, the second an hour and a quarter, the third again a little more than an hour, so that, counting the entr'actes, I calculated the duration of the opera

from six o'clock to a quarter to ten at the latest. I should have been doubtful whether you had taken the tempi according to my calculation if musical friends, well acquainted with the opera, had not assured me particularly that you had taken the tempi throughout as they knew them from me, and now and then rather a little quicker than slower. I must therefore assume that *the dragging took place where you, as conductor, lost your immediate power, viz., in the recitatives. (Corr.,* 89, my emphasis)

The point here is not to decide what actually happened to create this misunderstanding, but one cannot help wondering how, exactly, Wagner timed his opera. For if Liszt, in possession of the metronomic figures, understood Wagner's "intention" better than he did himself, it must be because whatever Wagner timed did not conform to the actual conditions of performance. But it is plain that Wagner explains the discrepancy by the faulty and deficient character of the particularity of the performance—the time and materiality of instruments—and precisely where the conductor, the stand-in for the composer, could not sufficiently manipulate the particular voices of the singers—where deviance exceeds the control of the authorial-compositional idea. The division and distance of space, between Weimar and Zürich, in the passage of the musical intention from composer to performance, is itself the possibility of distortion that compels the "letter" as a means of communication from afar; and the letter bears with it the necessary detour of the (metronomic) "figure" as that which ought to secure what this distance endangers. We see here only that the "figure," as an objective and mechanical safety measure, is incapable of ensuring the transmission of sympathetic vibrations, for its necessity is born of the spatial interruption of these very vibrations.

While the limitations and deficiencies of presentation imposed by any particular performance may issue from chance and empirical circumstance, the dependence of composition on performance in general is necessary, for it bears directly on the theoretical determination of what music is. This determination proffers consistently a reversed image of writing. Within a traditional concept of writing, the meaning is an interiority gathered together (*legein*) from an inessential extension of the physical text; the *logos* goes out in order to come back in. But in music, the composition is there only to go out; its exile is its fulfillment and homeland. For Liszt, the performer relates directly to "the art" itself, standing side by side with rather than beneath the composer. Liszt alters the paternal relation between composer and performer to one of fraternity; insofar as the performance is essential, music can never proceed from the single hand of one creator: "For the virtuoso, because he gives music its tangible and perceptible essence, himself *creates Music* [*schafft die Musik*], and by that act he establishes the claim of his art to be ranked with those called autonomous" (*GS* 6: 336 / *Gipsy*, 270). In this alteration of the authorial model, the fraternal replaces the paternal as the site of productivity.

What Wagner has called "loving pliability" (*liebevolle Schmiegsamkeit*) is the common ground of both the failures and the successes of performance. The pliability needed for the art of constant self-transformation is one of Liszt's standard attributes; both Wagner and Heine comment consistently on it. This characteristic, actually a sort of lack of character, has much to do with Liszt's tenuous position within the musical canon. The tradition portrays him as an admixture of the sublime and the ridiculous, and he was criticized for his devotion to popularity and effect, for his personal vanity and ambition, and for his subordination of "artistic ideals" to economic gain and self-interest. Similarly, the troubling "bizarrerie" of his music might be said to consist of the apparently indiscriminate juxtaposition of highly "emotional" or "expressive" passages with utterly commonplace borrowings from the burlesque stage; one cannot help thinking that Liszt often does not seem to know the difference. For Béla Bartók, Liszt's peculiar inconsistencies account for his largely negative reception. "What does repel," Bartók writes, "is rather Liszt's many-sidedness, his eclecticism, his over-susceptibility to all musical sensations, from the most commonplace to the most rare. Everything he had ever experienced in music, whether trivial or sublime, left a lasting imprint upon his work" (451). Liszt's combination of disparate cultural elements does not conform to modern standards of unity and originality; it does, however, reconnect him to a sociohistorical background that renders him a kind of living epic or sounding board: "Liszt," writes Bartók, "did not start from any one point, nor fuse together in his own works several related things; he submitted himself to the influence of the most diverse, contradictory and almost irreconcilable elements" (502). Like the rhapsode, the virtuoso stands between his world and its representation and becomes the very site through which tradition, like the musical composition, passes.

The Romantic interest in popular culture aims to establish a bond between the isolated and empty "subjectivity" of the modern author and a national or "Volk" tradition, like the contemporaneous idealization of the epic world or "Golden Age." These issues are brilliantly coarticulated in Nietzsche's essay "Homer und die Klassische Philologie" (Homer and classical philology), in which he examines the "Homer question" as the center of a "cultural-historical determination of value" that is enormously important (*Werke* 3: 161 / *Collected Works* 3: 151). Quoting Goethe, Nietzsche points out the modern need and desire to think of Homer as a single author:

Scharfsinnig habt ihr, wie Ihr seid,
von aller Verehrung uns befreit, und wir bekannten überfrei,
daß Ilias nur ein Flickwerk sei.
Mög unser Abfall niemand kränken; denn Jugend weiß uns zu
   entzünden,
daß wir ihn lieber als Ganzes denken,
als Ganzes freudig ihn empfinden.

    *(3: 160)*

With subtle wit you took away
  Our former adoration;
The Iliad, you may us say,
  Was mere conglomeration.
Think it not crime in any way:
  Youth's fervent adoration
Leads us to know the verity,
  And feel the poet's unity.

    *(CW 3: 149)*

Nietzsche shows how the unity of "Homer" is constructed precisely through the separation of a cohesive unified work from its diversities, falsifications, and errors. These flaws, split off from the authorial center, are the *Flickwerk* ("conglomeration": literally, patchwork) attributed to the deliverers of the tradition, both rhapsodes and philologists:

> at the same time, one had come up with a history of the Homeric poems and their tradition according to which these diversities were not blamed on Homer, but rather on his editors and singers. One imagined that Homer's poems had been passed down orally for quite a long time and thus exposed to the deformations of improving and sometimes forgetful singers. (3: 163 / 3: 153)

Friedrich August Wolf's *Prolegomena* argued that the Homeric epics were the aggregate work of bard, rhapsodes, and philologists alike. Johann Gottfried Herder, along with Vico, understood Homer as the collective work of a folk tradition, thus accounting for its "diversities." The division between rhapsode and poet works in the service of an opposition between a general cultural collectivity and the individual, an opposition mirroring the division separating the internal "unity" of a work from its delivery through tradition, understood as an external appendage. The characterization of the rhapsode thus proceeds out of the opposition between collective and individual, or in Nietzsche's words, out of the "superstition that opposes popular poetry to individual poetry. . . . But in reality, this opposition does not exist at all" (3: 167 / 3: 160).

Nietzsche's presentation of the Homer question works against the opposition of author and rhapsode, an opposition valuing the author as a creative source and deprecating the rhapsode as a "merely reproductive" delivery system. This is not surprising, since the philologists—and Nietzsche is himself of course among them—belong to the class of rhapsodes. At the beginning of the essay, Nietzsche describes classical philology in obvious analogy to the art of the rhapsode, pointing out especially its lack of conceptual unity: "At the present day, no clear and consistent opinion seems to be held regarding classical philology. . . . The cause of this lies in its many-sided character, in the lack of a conceptual unity, in the inorganic aggregation of heterogeneous scientific activities which are connected with each other only through the name 'philology'" (3: 157 / 3: 147). Philology works in the sphere of finitude, expending its "blood and sweat" to unearth the "immortal masterpieces of the Hellenic spirit." Philology gains prestige precisely through its ability to deliver tradition and thus provide access to it. Where the disclosure of the immortal is seen to depend on these mortal means, the repetition that reveals it is raised to an essential position. In Nietzsche's positive evaluation of delivery, the terminology shifts significantly: "Of course philology is not the creator of that world, it is not the composer [*Tondichter*] of this immortal music; but is it not also a merit, and indeed a great merit, to be a virtuoso and be the first to let resound once more that music which for so long lay in the corner, undeciphered and unvalued?" (3: 173 / 3: 169). The virtuoso replaces a figure of the past with one of the present day through which the past resounds. The insertion of musical terminology allows for an exchange of values; what was previously the source of corruption now becomes the opening of possibility.

Philological discussions of Homeric epic abound with questions about the compositional role of the rhapsode: To what extent does improvisation coincide with authorship? Or was there a Homer, or any poet at all, who was distinct from and prior to the performances? No matter what the answers, the questions themselves display a conflict, a problem with considering the rhapsode an "author" as well as a need to distinguish between rhapsode and author. Wolf, for example, distinguishes between bard and rhapsode, even though the same person might perform the duties of both at different moments. This distinction must be made to guarantee the reliability of the concept of author, which simultaneously sets limits on what exceeds philological research. In "What Is an Author?" Michel Foucault analyzes the way in which the principle of an author controls meaning: "The author does not precede the works, he is a certain functional principle by which, in our culture, one limits, excludes, and chooses; in short, by which one impedes the free circulation, the free manipulation, the free composition, decomposition, and recomposition of fiction. . . . The author is therefore the ideological figure by which one marks the manner in which we fear the proliferation of meaning" (159). The rhapsode, a coproduct of the authorial principle, stands in the place of this feared proliferation, which, in Foucault's words, the rhapsode "makes manifest, but does not divulge" (*Archaeology of Knowledge*, 225–26). The rhapsode maintains contact with this disorder yet protects the present from it. The rhapsodic dimension refers to a singular existence in historical time and space and thus presents a limit to what can be known or reconstituted of that space. The "unity of a world" transmitted by the rhapsodic tradition cannot be ideally circumscribed and known or understood. It consists of the lack of differentiation between individuals and community by virtue of which there is no barrier between the totality of utterances and an individual utterance.

The figure of the Greek rhapsode, known to tradition only by representations on vases and mentions in written texts, presents a vague and uncontrolled background out of which poetry, or text in general, is said to emerge.[8] The term *rhapsode* refers to historical individuals identified as a professional economic group. The figure of the rhapsode amalgamates the indeterminate wanderings of concrete individual bodies with the representation that survives them in the delimited function of performance within a definite stage or platform. According to tradition, most clearly articulated in Plato's *Ion*, the rhapsode, as a concrete individual, is driven by the meanness of material self-interest: the desire to win money and fame through the excellence of his performance. Rhapsodic performance is always polemical, establishing excellence through comparison and competition. The fixation on exteriority and materiality, articulated in the rhapsode's concern with clothes, personal appearance, praise, and prizes, cannot be dissociated from the polemics of rhapsodic performance. Part of the rhapsode's role is to play out this exteriority and display its attachment to the poetry it presents.

The art of attachment is vital to the rhapsode. Plato's *Ion* presents the famous image of the Muse as lodestone, transmitting magnetically through poet, rhapsode, and spectator.[9] The rhapsode's physical performance, when successful, sets up this communicative chain, animating the dead letters of the poetry he recites as he comes into metonymic contact with the Muse. When this chain is set up, the specific character of the rhapsode is obscured, as are the characteristics of clothes, appearance, staging, acting, and so forth. The poetic word is spread by means of the temporary effacement of the rhapsode. Despite the rhapsode's fixation on exteriority, self-effacement or disappearance is nevertheless also constitutive of the rhapsode's profession—his identity is thus marked as a deface-ment or destabilization of identity.[10]

The instability of the rhapsode's identity structure is reflected in his wander-ing lifestyle—a fundamentally improper existence. In Plato's version, Ion claims that he cannot normally occupy the position of general, for example, since he is a foreigner from the occupied territory of Ephesus. Ion's "improper" citizen-ship is translated, too, into an impropriety of language; he contradicts himself, claims to know what he cannot know, and flatly rejects the rules of Socratic di-alogue. The problem is that his mode of production, literally the stitching to-gether of songs, does not properly produce anything, but only reforms, com-bines, gathers, and presents.[11] Just as the rhapsodic performance can be subor-dinate to the particular material interests of the individual performer, the rhapsodically produced work originates not in an idea but in dispersed material that forms only an aggregate. This materiality remains in contiguity with the ir-retrievable expanse of the territory over which the rhapsode has wandered, a background that cannot be taken in by a theoretical gaze but only retroactively inferred. Foucault's anonymous "murmuring" allows the world to resound without being represented, without passing through the strictures of a "sub-ject." The double valence of the rhapsode permits the belief in historical verac-ity at the same time that it delimits the region of error to that of technology.[12]

The epic delivery of tradition installs a technical origin to what will come to be thought of as an "immediate" expression of a world that provides reliable historical information about that world. This illusion is produced by the seem-ing identity of the subjects of *énonciation* and *énoncé*, which appear to coincide in the bodily presence of performance. But the rhapsode's oral presentation is already a kind of writing.[13] Distinguishing between rhapsodic performance and later lyric and musical performance, Friedrich Schlegel points to the function of performance as mnemonic technique, dispelling any sense of pure immediacy: "The singers differed from the later lyric poets, who were all also musicians, in this respect: they presented everything narratively and merely from memory, while the lyric poets presented their feelings musically" (11: 36). What the rhap-sode conveys is fundamentally not his own. Schlegel invokes music and lyric as the genres that protect "proper" expression, binding a now differentiated inte-rior and exterior. For Schlegel, music falls on the expressive side of transmission in opposition to the technical transmission of the rhapsode.

The rhapsodes, just as they form an independent guild, present the auton-omy of a communicative instrument or technique dissociated from any trans-mitted content. Because of this autonomy, the rhapsode has been conceived not only as the means of transmission of tradition but also as the permanent source of corruption and distortion. The work delivered by the rhapsode is neither "originary" nor the "original" work of an author—not, in Schlegel's words, *"one* whole art-composition of a *single man,* but rather . . . the superb fragments and monuments [*Bruchstücke und Denkmäler*] of the poetry of an entire age" (11: 36). The Homeric epics in their present form, Schlegel continues, acquired their shape through philological work: "The collection and writing down [of the poems] out of the mouths of the rhapsodes makes it clear with the highest certainty that we do not possess them in their original shape [*Gestalt*]."

The gathering and collecting suggests that the unified form of the Homeric poems is not only not originary but in fact results from a twofold process of technical sifting, combination, and selection: that of the rhapsode and that of the editor or scribe. The general picture of the era is thus dependent on the specific and calculated labor of singular individuals. Like Heine's daguerreotype, it emerges as a technical, not a conceptual, construction. "Secondary" activities install order and first produce unified shapes. The creative transmission of a tradition thus both alters and produces what it transmits. Schlegel, with Nietzsche, allies these activities with philology:

> The art of the rhapsode consisted in the *arbitrary* connection of different poems through transitions and patched-in verses [*Flickverse*]. This art itself attests to the disorder in which these poems existed in the most ancient Greek times (compared to their present composition [*Zusammenstellung*]). . . . The Greeks called those who collected these rhapsodies "orderers" [*Anordner*], *diaskeuasten.*
> (11: 37)

The rhapsodes are the first philologists, the first editors. The insertion of the proper name—"Homer," for example—asserts the excellence and distinction of the fragments it gathers, allowing the technical and idiosyncratic origin—pointing always to a possibility of self-interested aberrance—to be forgotten and replaced by a framed portrait of a unified world, an authentic historical picture, or the unity of a work as the product of a subject. The name *Homer* stands as an emblem of this substitution.

The figure of the rhapsode provides a foothold for philological fictionalization, making possible a claim for historical grounding even in the very gesture of figuration that severs the character from its spacing. The unique quality of rhapsodic presentation is obstructed and terminated by writing—by the reproducibility of the performance of combination and selection, traceable in writing as the marks of enunciation. The figure of the rhapsode goes one step beyond the subject of enunciation; it is an aggregate and fictional figure, with its one side marked by elocutionary positions and the other extending to the empirical person, the literal body—the technical hand, the potentially dissimulating source of what has been produced. The rhapsode thus can have no proper place in literature, since it is a figure of the transition from the page of history to what is legible on it—a margin or space that cannot be stated in print, since the untranslatable difference from it is what allows it to come forth in the first place. In a nineteenth-century context, this function, both productive and reproductive, unique and yet representative, is taken over by musical performance and acted out by the virtuoso. At the instant that the rhapsode is delimited and represented—on the stage, the vase, or the page—something is lost, but the rhapsode loses nothing, for he only comes into being in this representation. In the same way, the nineteenth-century virtuoso is necessarily a social and public figure constituted by predicates, harboring no interiority apart from a public image shaped by the many reviews and accounts that produce it.

The intermingling of philology and music through the coupling of the rhapsode and the virtuoso recalls the difficulty of the term *interpretation*, which links reading and music. The performance of musical works creates an arena for interpretion in which the proper characteristics of the particular performer—his "own" and proper creative force—render forth the work. The musical performance hyperbolizes the creative aspect of reception, innovative precisely as distortion through the particular perspective of an *I*; for there is no pure performance of a musical work, and to identify accuracy with the essence of the work is to misunderstand music completely. It is not surprising that Liszt, within the Romantic tradition, should conceive of the productivity of performance along the lines of philological interpretation: "The virtuoso . . . is not the passive instrument that reproduces the feelings and thoughts of others, adding nothing of his own. He is not the more or less clever and experienced reader of works that have no margin for his glosses, or have no need for commentary on what is said between the lines" (*GS* 6: 332 / *Gipsy*, 265–66). Liszt's prodigious ability to sight-read is perhaps the most uncontested among the characteristics reported of him. It is said that he could play on the spot any score set before him. But this is not really "proper" reading.

The untranslatability of reading in this context reasserts the heterogeneity of language and music, despite the many parallels that have been drawn here. On the one hand, the relationships poet/rhapsode and composer/virtuoso are in fact different versions of the structure instituting the standard of authorial original and the subordination of execution and reproduction. At the same time, these terms have their own specificity; it is important to retain a sense of their difference and to not thoroughly reduce the relation composer/virtuoso to a literary model. The alterity of this relationship lodges not in some "other" mythical realm called "music" but rather can be located in the literary tradition itself insofar as the literary model—Homer—is already irreducible to the model of literature it puts forth. Paradoxically, Homer is both one of many and unique and foundational. The proper name of the poet, and the unity of the work, can only emerge through the elevation above, departure and difference from the rhapsodes. According to Aristotle's *Poetics*, poetry emerges out of the improvisations of "persons who have a special aptitude for these things, making improvements bit by bit." Poetry and poet alike appear distinguished by quality: "Homer was not only the master poet of the serious vein," Aristotle writes, "unique in the general excellence of his imitations . . . but also the first" (48). Homer indicates the point at which the *best* of many is differentiated from its background to become the *first* of a series of poets. The poet's proper name thus interrupts a process of amplification and accumulation, breaks off, and becomes different. Through this interruption, coincidental with the institution of writing, a text breaks forth from the world, a recording is made, and the individual is differentiated from an indeterminate historical mass.

Since authorial originality and the set of values, property, and propriety it institutes are grounded in the elevation of production over repetition, this origin must pass over the contradictory moment of productive repetition. At this scandalous limit, Homer retains contact with the authenticity of the rhapsodic world, an authenticity that he thus can transmit. Insofar as Homer is considered the "first" author, the contradictions sketched here constitute the area in which he cannot be fully subsumed under the concept of author that he initiates; Homer must exist before the concept modeled after him. Thus, there is a constitutive region within authorship that deviates from and exceeds the concept of a unified author. As a deviant, Homer is an author *sui generis*, a term articulated by both Liszt and Baudelaire. The term *sui generis* indicates a singular individual that is part of a genre but also stands alone in its class. It is thus an aberrant concept that covers only itself and, by definition, cannot serve the economy of abbreviation and generalization of conceptualization.

Like the rhapsode, the virtuoso is simultaneously the possibility and the impossibility of composition. Liszt holds the key both to its preservation and to its destruction, wielding the power of its success and failure, its existence and disappearance. The proper utterance of the composer, through which his word resounds abroad, is thus dependent on the virtuoso's ability to recite the work in a foreign language—to use language *improperly*—to efface himself and to speak the language of an other. Similarly, the rhapsodes repeat the words of others, concealing their own identity behind the language and name of a poet or muse. Their art is to present, not to produce. Thus, by definition, Liszt can never be a "proper author" either in music or in letters.

Literally, of course, Liszt was indeed an author who published frequently in the Parisian musical press, and he was an editor of the *Revue et gazette musicale*. His collected works were first published in a German version in six volumes edited by Lina Ramann.[14] Liszt has a complex and peculiar relationship to literature that cannot be easily summarized. He both modeled himself personally after literary figures and drew heavily on literary sources in his compositions. His symphonic poems—a form he was the first to introduce—after Dante and Faust, for example, are not simply musical representations or illustrations of literary works but rather are readings or interpretations of these works.[15] This subtle distinction in the conception of the symphonic poem is clearly related to Liszt's interpretation of repetition, reproduction, and presentation.

The issues of Liszt's writing, composition, and his appeal to epic generality come together around his *Hungarian Rhapsodies*, traditionally the most popular and well known of Liszt's compositions. Inspired by a trip to his native Hungary, Liszt composed this series of short pieces based on Hungarian folk music around 1840.[16] Since Liszt spent little of his life in Hungary, which he left when he was eight years old, his nationality is somewhat complicated, though he always considered himself Hungarian.[17] It is not coincidental that Liszt took an interest in and identified with the Gypsies, a marginal group he defined as both Hungarian and not Hungarian.[18]

Though a reader may be unable to call any one *Hungarian Rhapsody* to mind, it is likely that these pieces would be unmistakably familiar when heard. In the film *A Day at the Races*, for example, Harpo Marx begins to play "Rhapsody no. 2" until, frustrated at his inability to play further than the first few bars, he tears apart the piano, extricates the strings, and uses them as a harp. Harpo's frustration is not accidental, since the pieces, like much of Liszt's early works for piano, are known to be extremely difficult, as the title of the *Etudes transcendantes*, for example, suggests. Liszt of course installed this difficulty in order to display his own technical brilliance; the *Hungarian Rhapsodies* are often held in disrepute precisely because of their obvious "bravura."[19] Moreover, the pieces were thought to be inspired by an illiterate "low culture." For this reason, too, their legitimacy has been doubted. As recently as 1960, Albert Lord could still characterize the academic preference for literary tradition over oral culture as the discomfort of those who "cannot . . . tolerate the unwashed illiterate" (129). Liszt's biographer Alan Walker explains:

> From the start, Liszt was worried about the way the rhapsodies might be received by "cultivated" musicians, and later events were to justify this fear. It was not the first time in history that a great composer has descended to the "ethnic" level in search of material, but it had never before been attempted on such a bold scale, and never in connection with the Gypsies. Liszt therefore decided to "explain" the rhapsodies to the world by publishing an introduction to them. But it grew to such massive proportions that the first fifteen rhapsodies were

already in print before the "introduction" appeared, in 1859, almost twenty years after his first return from Hungary, in the form of the two-volume *Des Bohémiens et leur musique en Hongrie*. Though this book is a pioneer work, it is, alas, defective from both the ethnomusicological and the anthropological standpoint. (1: 338)

This book, of which Baudelaire owned an autographed copy, is a lengthy and potentially offensive work dealing with problems of national and ethnic identity, epic poetry, music, and many details about Hungarian and Gypsy music and musicians. Moreover, its history is complicated by a revision that was undertaken in 1881 by the Duchess von Sayn-Wittgenstein.[20] Since the work was meant to legitimate Liszt himself, the focus here will be on Liszt's idealization of and identification with the Gypsies and how these are meant to validate his own activities. For Liszt, the Gypsies present the model of the kind of impropriety in which Liszt himself partakes—an impropriety already suggested by the fact that his conceptual introduction in fact postdates his *Rhapsodies* by fifteen years.

In Liszt's view, the Gypsies are attached to no property or geographical territory; they report no history or origin. He attributes to them a dispersed national identity with no geographical ties. "This is indeed a strange people," writes Liszt,

> so strange as to resemble no other in anything whatever. It has neither fatherland, nor religion, nor history, nor any kind of code. It seems only to continue to exist because it absolutely refuses to cease to do so, or to be anything other than what it is. It allows no will, no persecution, no proselytizing any influence either to change, to modify itself, to disband or to be exterminated. (*GS* 6: 7 / *Gipsy*, 8)

Their character crystallizes as they simply remain the same through time and space. The unity of the Gypsies is thus defined by their ability to resist all change. They are defined as difference from and resistance to the structures of nationality. This difference is not safely projected onto a prehistorical and idyllic past but rather it persists in the present. The Gypsies thus represent the persistence of the ahistoric within the civilized world; they are defined against the culture whose standards and structures they reject. In particular, the Gypsies take no interest in territorialization or property. This people, says Liszt,

> spread over our continent, but without showing any desire for conquest; and without even demanding any right of permanent residence. It had evidently no desire to appropriate one single inch of land. . . . It carried with it no memory, it harbored no hope. It refused all possible benefits that might attach to colonisation . . . [it] lived on, satisfied with the rejection of every foreign element,

participated in no advantage of the civilization of Christianity with which it lived side by side. (*GS* 6: 6 / *Gipsy*, 8)

This side by side, a living relation of metonymic juxtaposition, is the threat of impropriety itself, which places together on a horizontal plane that which "ought" to be hierarchically (vertically) ordered. A pouch of historylessness within history, the unchanging identity of the Gypsies is constituted in their refusal of a teleology of history, their resistance to all development and technological projection. Liszt writes:

> To our eyes, this people lives a quasi animal life, having no knowledge and no concern about anything that goes on outside of itself. Centuries may come and go, nations march forward, the countries which shelter it, through war and peace, may change their masters and their views: but this people remains itself, unchanged. Impassable and indifferent, it lives in the day and profits from the confusion that decides the fates of other nations. (*GS* 6: 7 / *Gipsy*, 9)

The Gypsies hold themselves apart as an indifference to laws connecting past, present, and future. The Gypsies, "this people," writes Liszt, "that, as if it were sarcasm itself in the flesh, laughs at the ambitions and the tears, the struggles and the festivities, of others" (*GS* 6: 7 / *Gipsy*, 9), looks upon and exploits what it does not care about. The Gypsies' relation to property poses especially acute difficulties for the standards of value they challenge. Liszt does not idealize the Gypsies' relation to property as an idyllic utopia. While the Gypsies mock the principle of property, they do not scorn property itself, but rather steal it. They represent not only a state that comes before civilization but also one that must come after it, looking upon it, using it, and speaking to it in its own language.

Because of its lack of attachment to a territory, its lack of a stable circumscription of any kind, the Gypsy culture, says Liszt, lacks the conditions of poetic self-articulation: "It is not difficult to conceive that such a people, in the absence of all intellectual culture, with no piously preserved and elaborated history, for centuries without any attachment to native soil, fatherland or home, would also be unable to bring forth a poet" (*GS* 6: 9 / *Gipsy*, 11). Self-articulation in a national epic presupposes that the people articulated there are defined by the histories, codes, and so on that structure an epic recording. Liszt quotes a lengthy passage from Hegel (from which the following passage is excerpted)[21] describing the tenuous balance, characteristic of the epic genre, between the general and the particular, not yet developed to opposition: "The sense of right and morality must seem to originate and find support solely in manners and character. . . . It must not be that any understanding, in the form of prosaic reality, should establish itself in opposition to individual convictions and passion"

(*GS* 6: 15 / *Gipsy*, 16). This situation is fundamentally inconceivable for the one who produces it, who by definition has not yet grasped the difference between general and particular in the form of a "prosaic reality." One may say that this is the perspective through which Homer is still a rhapsode—a star, perhaps, but not yet the first author, a status first conferred by the invocative tradition of the Homeridae and then by the intervention of writing. This intervention—which at the same time lends semantic autonomy to the general values and structures implicit in the social code of a language—would, for Hegel, constitute the difference between the epic world and its literary representation. In the same passage, Hegel chronologizes this difference, explaining that the poetic representation of epic unity must necessarily postdate the immediacy of life that it represents. The beginning of the epic genre is the end and division of the epic existence it articulates, an existence that is therefore always located in the past. Given the conditions of nineteenth-century culture, therefore, there could be no epic production, no author unaware of himself and his language.

In the nineteenth century, the autonomy of the universal was firmly established in the positive form of writing. Borrowing Hegel's terms, Liszt allies the conceptual content of words with the positive aspect of "prosaic reality." The "poetic reality" that would contrast with this is, for Liszt, not poetry but rather *instrumental music*, the medium able to give forth the mere gesture of speaking without saying anything, to present performance with no constative interruption. The improvisational music of the Gypsies, Liszt claims, constitutes precisely such an epic, an epic which, unlike Hegel's, exists in the present. Music is the national epic of a languageless and nationless folk:

> We say "epic," although their poems and songs comprise no narration, refer to no event, and recall no memory. What they do instead is repeat the feelings that belong to all the individuals of this race, their inner type, and which include the expression of their entire sentient being. In this peculiar collective work, there is no fragment, however long or short, that expresses any personal, individual mood [*Stimmung*], any sentiment that is not also the sentiment of all, any expression so subjective that none from their midst could sympathize. Even the smallest scrap, the shortest strophe, any split shard of a poem . . . says only what all feel, sings and poetises only impressions proper to all.
> (*GS* 6: 8 / *Gipsy*, 10)

What Liszt suggests is really a very curious notion of epic that violates virtually every literary criterion of the genre (for example, criteria of episodic narrative and transmission of cultural norms). Epic thus presents a linguistic ideal that language is incapable of fulfilling. Instead, it is handed over to music to be *narrationless epic*. Narrationless epic cannot be a "proper" concept; for while it is possible to articulate its logic, no literary example can offer itself. It is thus an empty category, or a concept *sui generis*.

Narrationless epic installs a certain impropriety in its language. Freed of semantic generalities, such a work entails no identification either of or with an *I*. The absence of the word *I* permits a withholding from enunciation, whose subject insinuates itself and persists as something absent, something that does not present itself in an utterance. "This people," Liszt writes of the Gypsies,

> would only be able to relate its most intimate impressions in a language that does not make precise, does not betray its object, and would bring no light of day to lay bare the darkness in its heart and its own destiny; for its silence about itself, which it never violates and indeed can be called its only religion, precept and law, never allows this people to issue itself in a narration of which it itself would be the *sujet*. (*GS* 6: 9–10 / *Gipsy*, 11–12)

The Gypsies' identity, since they refuse to give it a content and represent it through the mediation of words, is defined as the preservation of a secret; this "identity" is constituted as the failure to disclose, as what is held back from the changes of linguistic representation. Ruled by the law refusing all law, this language violates the laws of property and propriety. The nonidentification of the speaker with his utterance due to the absence of the word *I* (or one fulfilling a comparable function) installs signatureless language that could always be dissimulation. It removes the standard of true utterance. Recalling that Liszt attributes this kind of language to the Gypsies, with whom he identifies, the possibility is opened up that this is also Liszt's own principle. If so, the reliability of what Liszt says itself decays; if he speaks not of the Gypsies but of himself—not as a linguistic *I* but as the "subject" of his own other medium (music) in which the subject is not a subject—he only destroys the possibility that what he says is true at all. In a sense, then, Liszt is not using language "properly"; rather, he posits an area of withheld subjectivity in anonymous dispersion, identifying himself as, and with, a subject that is absent and disjunct.

Liszt has set himself the task, then, of rendering accessible something that, in principle and like Liszt himself, eludes conceptual research. Nevertheless, Liszt has crossed the line from musical experience to textual representation in his work on the Gypsies, in which he attempts to render something accessible by bestowing the unity of an edition. In editing the *Hungarian Rhapsodies*, Liszt can only end in contradiction; for the intervention of the proper name and the solidity of writing stand forever at odds with the fluidity of the imagined epic or oral world.

It is evident how Liszt generally sides with the indispensability of what is performed in time by concrete individuals. But he remains plagued by the lack of a legitimate ground that this position necessarily entails. Remember that this text is supposed to be a legitimation, and perhaps a kind of advertisement, of Liszt's compositions and even of Liszt himself. Ultimately, his arguments and opinions are articulated in conformity to the standards of performance and assertion he puts forth: validity is claimed. The idea that value can simply be claimed and taken by linguistic performance is part and parcel of the violation of rules of linguistic propriety and property. Through this offense, Liszt continually asserts the equal rank of deliverer and producer, of plagiarist and author. The virtuosi give value to the style through which what needs to be performed can walk upon the earth: "It is the gipsy virtuosi who clothed gipsy melody with their blooming ornaments. . . . It is the gipsy virtuosi who let the rhythms resound which give the music profile and stature" (*GS* 6: 336 / *Gipsy*, 270). Indeed, these virtuosi possess the formative power of anthropomorphism without which no figure could speak, no author resound:

> They alone have interpreted this art as artists who understand its language, its secrets, its most hidden depths. . . . And only the gipsies have understood how to give them [popular motives] their full artistic value, their illumination and their renown, by their execution, their virtuosity and the feeling which they let flow into them. (*GS* 6: 336–37 / *Gipsy*, 270)

Virtuosity gives and takes the supplement of existence as the arena of value. If value originates in the transmission, rather than in the work, what is borrowed is equal to the original: property is gained by the taking. This is the most scandalous point in Liszt: that stealing, the theft that devalues the origin and the original, is permitted. The virtuoso, Liszt, is not the original producer but the one who has successfully appropriated or stolen what he holds: he is the hero who has slain the competitor.

Liszt's claim for the legitimacy of his *Hungarian Rhapsodies* is grounded in their popular and traditional origin. Unfortunately for Liszt, he unwittingly outlines how their presentation, meant as mere editing and repetition, has usurped the position of origin to which he attaches himself. And also unfortunately for Liszt, he can take up no position in this text other than the authorial one constituted in the organization of a unity. For the performing position to which he hands over the power cannot be sustained in print; what the virtuoso gains, the author has lost, even if the author is himself the virtuoso he describes. What is established, simply, is a division of Liszt by which the *I*, or the text representing the *I*, has lost access to Liszt himself.

The virtuosi, like the Gypsies, are defined in their dispersion in existence, an existence that cannot be directly transcribed but must be collected and, in this collection, differs from itself. Liszt describes the process of selection as follows:

> After having submitted a fair number of these pieces to the process of transcription, it began to dawn upon us that we should never finish. . . . The closer we came to our task, the more our work increased, and finally all limit vanished. A mountain of material was before us—it had to be compared, separated, eliminated—light had to be shed upon the matter! (*GS* 6: 388–89 / *Gipsy*, 333)

Liszt gives no reason other than this purely economic one, providing no other criterion of selection or arrangement. Indeed, it is out of this simple necessity that his epic theory emerges; what is striking is not so much the claim Liszt makes here, but the blatancy with which its justification is seen to be mere convenience. Liszt articulates the calculated and technical construction of a whole, passing through plastic fictionalization. He explicitly points not only to the mechanical and technical origin of unity but also to its ground in his own merely idiosyncratic beliefs. "The fragments," Liszt continues, "were edited, remodelled and joined with others. This was done with the intention of gathering the essential in them together into a body which, so cemented, would present a work that would more or less [*ungefähr*] correspond to what we have permitted ourselves to believe should be regarded as a Gipsy Epic" (*GS* 6: 389–90 / *Gipsy*, 334). This *ungefähr*, "more or less," is simply impossible and can only erode the notion of correspondence it puts forth; it opens the very margin of error it ought to close.

With this turn toward technical construction and editorial reproduction, Liszt in the meantime turns from the collector vacationing and listening to music in Hungary to the composer of the *Hungarian Rhapsodies*. Imperceptibly, his identification slides to the side of the philologists,

> who purified the songs of HOMER from the intercalations they suffered from the rhapsodes, who performed them and foisted upon them all kinds of errors, thus disfiguring and distorting the art work. . . . May we be forgiven for the ambitious comparison of our selective project with that of the Greek scholiasts, who undertook amongst innumerable versions, apocryphal and of doubtful value, to choose the most pure and worthy of their author . . . and bind them together into the one inimitable poem. (*GS* 6: 390 / *Gipsy*, 334–35)

Can this be the same Liszt writing this? No, it is not the same Liszt, for it is inevitably the Liszt of the pen and the text, not the Liszt withheld, dissimulated, in recession, and performing—in short, the virtuoso.

What Liszt has produced, he claims, is an "Epopeia *sui generis*," and that indeed it is, neither narrative nor genuine, idiosyncratically bound and given the name of a whole. In the willful figuration that gives an aggregate the name of a whole body, Liszt exposes not only his own impossible contrariness but also a series of contradictions structuring philological reconstitution and received ideas about genre. Yet this "Epopeia *sui generis*," in its violation of the concepts on which it depends, does not stand alone but partakes in a much broader contradiction characteristic of nineteenth-century aesthetics.

# 5.    Liszt's Bad Style

Liszt presents and represents a confusion of distinctions, a constant combining and recombining of contradictory traits that problematize the reliability of predication in general. Both overly popularized and notably neglected, Liszt is the very cliché of uniqueness, the commonplace of the bizarre. "Liszt" is an unexamined aggregate of images and associations, drawn perhaps from a portrait, a piece of music, a film, an unnoticed allusion. He is a legend subject to no particular rigor. The attempt to apply rigor to separate fact and fiction only increases the distance between the investigation and its theme, altering and containing it according to conventional philological standards. Philological practice would encourage a definite and precise examination of "sources" to clarify and elucidate this picture. Yet such an investigation is destined to fail, for the greater the accuracy of the research, the greater, finally, the deviance from what is meant by "Liszt." For Liszt *is* that unexamined impression, a vague character or image engraved with historical imprecision: he is a theme, a thought entertained by a member of the public, a word read by an indistinct and undistinguished reader. Liszt is an error that answers to no correction.

Just as Wagner prescribes that the virtuoso should overflow the boundary of a discrete ego, Liszt's predicates extend without limit or distinctions. There are no adequate criteria for determining the boundaries of "sources." Should one examine, and possibly privilege, his compositions, his visual images, or his texts? Should fictional works modeled after Liszt be included?[1] Do all have equal, or indeed any, authority? Liszt developed piano technique that has influenced keyboard pedagogy ever since; is not this, perhaps, the place to look for him? Can we be certain that, at any piano concert, we do not hear Liszt, who was the first to position a lone pianoforte lengthwise on the stage?[2] Does he not haunt the ordeals of piano lessons and the annual recitals of every bourgeois child? Or, as Bela Lugosi's hair becomes wild and disheveled amid exploding machines at the end of *The Black Cat*, can we be certain that we are not somehow seeing Liszt, whose B Minor Sonata makes up the score? Does Liszt ever end?

If Liszt is an impression, it is because the narrated impression is the very extension of the virtuoso himself, whether through bodily traits, musical tones, or verbal rumor. Hans Christian Andersen, for example, anticipating Liszt's performance, describes the concert-hall atmosphere: "Celebrity, with its mighty prestige, had opened the eyes and ears of the people. It seemed as if they recognised and felt already what was to follow" (quoted in Huneker, 230). This atmosphere is constitutive of the power of impression specifically connected with Liszt. Andersen continues: "Liszt's whole appearance and his mobility immediately indicate one of those personalities toward which one is attracted solely by their individuality. As he sat at the piano the first impression of his individuality and the trace of strong passions . . . made me imagine that he might be a demon" (quoted in Huneker, 231). Reports of Liszt focus on the uniqueness and specificity of his bodily presence and thus draw into focus the relative position of the narrating subject. The mere contact with Lisztian themes tends to emphasize the enunciative position of the subject who speaks of him, undermining claims to objective judgment or stable knowledge. The following passage from Nietzsche's early autobiographical text, "Über Stimmungen" (On moods), shows how Liszt draws out the writer's finitude. The passage begins by focusing on the writer's bodily position and his material paraphernalia: "Just picture how, on the first day of Easter, I sit at home wrapped up in my dressing-gown. . . . For a long time, I stare at the white paper lying before me with the quill in my hand" (*Werke* 3: 113). Liszt's music intervenes as Nietzsche describes how writing departs from its present, yet remaining within the horizon of the writer's finitude, stays linked to the experience it marks:

> On this day, I played Liszt's "Consolation" quite a bit, and I feel how the
> tones have infiltrated their way into me and resound in me in spiritualized
> form. And recently, I had a painful experience and had undergone a departure

or a non-departure [*Abschied oder Nichtabschied*], and now I notice how this feeling and those tones have fused and I believe that the music would not have pleased me so much if I had not had this experience. (*Werke* 3: 113)

Liszt somehow makes this experience possible for Nietzsche, an experience that parts but does not part, amalgamating the sensory tones and the feelings with which they coincide. What Nietzsche describes, it would seem, is affection itself: sense impression traveling beyond the limits of the senses, penetrating into the experiential realm of a writing *I*.

George Eliot, too, focuses on bodily presence in her description of breakfast at the Altenburg, Liszt's home in Weimar. Liszt again has something to do with the intermingling of writing and personal position. After describing the Princess von Sayn-Wittgenstein's clothing in great detail, Eliot writes:

> I sat next to Liszt, and my great delight was in watching him and in observing the sweetness of his expression. Genius, benevolence, and tenderness beam from his whole countenance, and his manners are in perfect harmony with it. Then came the thing I had longed for—his playing. I sat near him so that I could see both his hands and face. For the first time I heard the true tones of the piano. He played one of his own compositions. . . . There was nothing strange or excessive about his manner. His manipulation of the instrument was quiet and easy, and his face was simply grand—the lips compressed and the head thrown a little backward. . . . There was nothing petty or egotistic to mar the picture. (quoted in Huneker, 260–61)

The musical communication described here originates in the instrumentalist's manipulation; Eliot's judgment is grounded in a *manner* legible only on Liszt himself. This judgment emerges through the juxtaposition of individual bodies in a physical proximity outside of which communication would be impossible. Because of the essential dimension of the bodily position of the one speaking about Liszt, texts representing him tend to point to their own relatively, frequently foregrounding irreducible details and peculiarities. As Nietzsche says, "this so-called music of the future of a Liszt seeks somehow to show the most peculiar [*eigentümliche*] places possible" (3: 34).

Liszt's constant indication of the *eigentümliche*, the peculiar and idiosyncratic, parallels his favoring of performance and style. In *The Romantic Generation*, the musicologist and pianist Charles Rosen argues that Liszt's achievements as a composer lie precisely in his ability to generate compositional innovation through style and technique. Liszt's compositional method, based largely on "different ways of playing the same theme, changes of performance style" (48), shifts the emphasis of composition from formal features to the means of producing sound. Analyzing a passage from Liszt's tenth *Hungarian Rhapsody*, Rosen writes:

> This is, I imagine, the kind of writing that earned Liszt the contempt of his
> most distinguished colleagues, Schumann and Chopin. It is the zero degree of
> musical invention if we insist that invention must consist of melody, rhythm,
> harmony, and counterpoint. Nevertheless, played with a certain elegance, these
> pages are both dazzling and enchanting. The real invention concerns texture,
> density, tone, color, and intensity—the various noises that can be made with a
> piano—and it is startlingly original. The piano was taught to make new sounds.
> (492)

Rosen explains how, in Liszt's hands, technical innovations in areas like fingering, for example, expanded musical possibilities: "I do not wish to imply that
Liszt's innovation is a purely technical one of fingering: it means that Liszt was
the first composer in history to understand fully the musical significance . . . of
new techniques of execution" (496).

Liszt's identification with style and technique and his insistence on the productive quality of performance undermine the authority of identity.[3] Rosen argues that Liszt's compositional "paraphrases" of other composers are among his
best work. Just as Liszt's redefinition of technique makes the opposition of technique and meaning obsolete, the difference between paraphrase and composition is also destabilized. Many regret that Liszt was not more "original," Rosen
writes; but "at what point Liszt ceases to paraphrase and starts to compose is a
question that often makes very little sense. . . . Composition and paraphrase
were not identical for him, but they were so closely interwoven that separation
is impossible" (502–3). Production and reproduction, originality and repetition,
self and other, are not clearly or finally delimited by a stable difference.

Liszt presents a spectacle of alteration. His consistent inconsistency forms
the very consistency of the virtuoso—an inconsistency determined by the oscillation between egotistic protrusion and transmissive self-effacement. Liszt's
most disturbing trait is probably his ability to simulate the genuine with the
same ease as he produces the hyperbolically artificial, that is, to manipulate both
sides of the virtuoso's character. Liszt's simulation of identity is reported in the
following journalistic anecdote published in *Le Temps* (1874). When Chopin
gives a tear-inspiring performance in the dark, Liszt seems to agree with Heine's
opposition of the two. Liszt says to Chopin: "'Ah, my friend, you were right!
The works of a genius like yours are sacred; it's a profanation to touch them.
You are a true poet and I am nothing but a buffoon!' . . . Chopin believed he
had eclipsed Liszt on that evening." Chopin appears to have won the prize, but
Liszt will have his revenge on another occasion:

The group was reunited at the same hour, that is, around midnight. Liszt begged Chopin to play. After much fussing, Chopin consented. Then Liszt demanded that all the lamps be extinguished, all the candles, and that the curtains be lowered so that the darkness was complete. It was the caprice of an artist, one did what he wanted. But just at the moment when Chopin was going to sit down at the piano, Liszt whispered a few words into his ear and took his place. Chopin, who was very far from guessing what his comrade wanted to do, took a seat in a nearby arm-chair without a sound. Liszt proceeded to play exactly those compositions that Chopin had let us hear on that memorable evening of which we have already spoken, but he knew how to play them with such a marvelous imitation of the style and the manner of his rival that it was impossible not to mistake him; and indeed, everyone was mistaken. The same enchantment, the same emotion was renewed. When the ecstasy was at its height, Liszt eagerly struck a match and lit the candles of the piano. There was a cry of stupefaction in the assembly.

—What! it's you?

—As you see!

—But we thought it was Chopin!

—You see, said the virtuoso as he stood up, that Liszt can be Chopin when he wants; but could Chopin ever be Liszt?

It was a challenge; but Chopin did not wish, or did not dare, to accept it. Liszt was avenged. (quoted in Prod'homme, 23–24)

Liszt's impropriety is his most proper epithet. His ability to "become" Chopin and to imitate the inimitable only duplicates his own inconsistency. Like Heine and Wagner, Hector Berlioz describes this inconsistency in contrasting two of Liszt's performances of Beethoven's *Moonlight Sonata*. The first performance disfigures Beethoven's work, obstructed by the prominence of the pianist's ego:

One day thirty years ago, I was present when Liszt played this *Adagio* for a small gathering of friends. Following the custom he had adopted to win the applause of the fashionable public, he distorted the music: instead of playing those long sustained notes in the bass, instead of maintaining the severe uniformity of rhythm and tempo . . . he added trills and tremolos; he accelerated and slowed down the tempo, thus making passion intrude into the sad tranquillity. He made thunder growl in a cloudless sky, where the only source of darkness consists in the sun's vanishing. I suffered cruelly. (84/39)

The brokenness of the presentation, its interruptions and unevenness are correlated with the ornate additions that assert the performer's particular identity.

Berlioz describes the opposed movement in Liszt's later performance of the same piece, presented in total darkness:

> Then, after a pause to collect his thoughts, out of the darkness emerged the noble elegy that he had once so perversely distorted. It was now heard in its sublime simplicity; not a single note, not an accent, was added to the composer's notes and accents. It was the shade of Beethoven himself, his great voice that we heard, called forth by the virtuoso. Each of us felt the characteristic *frisson* in silence and, after the last chord died away, we were still silent—we were weeping. (85/40)

There are many Liszts: virtuoso, composer, conductor, Romantic hero, charlatan, dandy, artist. If nothing else, what is meant by "Liszt" here is a series of recognizable letters set together on a page, and this investigation is an assay to gather together the similarities I have recognized in association with those marks. What I present, therefore, cannot be "knowledge." It cannot be knowledge, because there is nothing to ground these similarities, no essence or substratum of Liszt. Liszt provides an opportunity, however, for reflecting on the philological dread that the unity of "Liszt" does not *mean* anything at all, that writing only asserts by technical composition. But how, then, is it possible to consider Liszt as a historical individual, that is, as a referent, at all?

There are many biographies of Liszt, most notable, perhaps, the current volumes by Alan Walker.[4] Here I will present only a brief list of the standard events in Liszt's life. Liszt was born in Raiding, Hungary, in 1811; his father was Hungarian and his mother German. His musical career began with a recital in 1820 at the Esterhazy estate, where his father was employed. He then went to Vienna, where he studied with Czerny, an interesting detail to anyone familiar with Czerny's exercises, in light of Nietzsche's remark: "*Liszt*: oder die Schule der Geläufigkeit—nach Weibern" ("Liszt: or the school of fluency—with women") (2: 991). Nietzsche's comment says much of what there is to say about Liszt. Liszt was engaged in what were considered scandalously open sexual relations throughout his life and never married. Accounts of his life tend to be organized around his two major relationships with women. The first was with the Parisian countess Marie d'Agoult, also known by the pen name Daniel Stern, who was "well connected" in the salon circuit. They had three children, one of whom was Cosima, who later married Richard Wagner. His relationship with d'Agoult, which ended during Liszt's years of intense traveling and performing (1841–47), was followed by a long relationship with the Polish princess Carolyne von Sayn-Wittgenstein. After his retirement from the concert platform at the height of his fame in 1847, at the age of 35, Liszt became conductor of the court at Weimar, where he lived for many years with the princess. After his retirement from performance, Liszt concentrated on transcription, composition, and conducting.

In 1823, when Liszt was 21, his father brought him from Vienna to Paris. Cherubini denied him entrance to the conservatory, since it did not accept foreigners. This event is typical; much of Liszt's energy throughout his life was spent trying to gain entrance where he was a foreigner and above all to be included by the aristocracy. "Since he was deprived of this equality [with the aristocracy]," writes one biographer, "he was determined to gain recognition through style of living and princely behavior" (Seroff, 70). Liszt's "social climbing" and "grotesque reverence for titles" of course become a major theme for caricature; he is often depicted bearing the jeweled "Sword of Honor," a sabre presented to him by Hungarian noblemen in 1840 at Pest, following a performance of, among other works, his *Grand Galop chromatique*. The title of this composition, by the way, continues to resound in visual caricatures of Liszt, which typically represent him riding his piano.

Liszt's desire to attain "natural" nobility through artificial means was largely a stylistic enterprise. Liszt's description of the presentation of the sword in his correspondence clearly links his concerns about aristocracy, fame, money, and clothes. These obsessions are the ostensible reason for much of the ridicule and criticism received by the virtuoso Liszt. Walker notes:

> It has to be observed here . . . that not only the newspapers but also some of
> his biographers started to believe the myth they had created. It became manda-
> tory to call Liszt at this juncture of his life an actor, a poseur, a vulgar charlatan,
> even . . . [Liszt's letters to Marie d'Agoult] describe the honours showered on
> him, the adulation of the crowds, the homage paid him by titled aristocrats,
> the large fees earned, and the sum of money (a thousand francs) he had to pay
> for the privilege of decking himself out in Magyar costume. (329)

Liszt was considered to be extremely attractive and was always concerned with his physical appearance. "To make the most favorable impression on English society, he asked Marie to send him immediately from Paris his fur-trimmed Hungarian overcoat, his white dressing gown, also fur-trimmed, and his gray jacket" (Seroff, 67).

The offensiveness of Liszt's preoccupation with clothes and aristocratic style becomes more acute with regard to his "conversion," which led to his move from Weimar to Rome in 1859. The Wagners, who were increasingly estranged from Liszt during these years, attributed Liszt's interest in both religion and religious music to the influence of the princess, who was a devout Catholic. Liszt's motivations for taking minor orders in 1865 are ambiguous. Some suggest that he did it to avoid marrying the princess, to retire from social demands to concentrate on composition, or to gain a musical post at the Vatican. Interestingly, Liszt's taking orders in the Church does not seem to have interfered with his lifestyle in any significant way, including his sex life. He himself writes:

> I have just carried out in all simplicity of purpose an act which by deep conviction I have been preparing for a long time. On 25 of April I entered the ecclesiastical state by receiving minor orders. . . . This modification—or, as one person of high rank expressed it—this transformation of my life does not mean a sudden change. In a short time I shall resume my composing. . . . Since my new state imposes no demands upon me, I am confident that I can live like this quite normally, observing the rules without any more disturbance to the mind than is caused physically by my soutane, on which subject I am being complimented that it fits me as though I had always worn one. (Merrick, 77)

For Liszt, religious orders are but a garment that can be changed at will if only one has the fashionable elegance to wear them properly. Even in Rome, clothes make the spirit, just as the instrument makes the music, as Liszt proved to the world in his early years.[5]

Accounts of Liszt's life, then, include the "scandalous" impropriety of the virtuoso's station. These scraps of Liszt's biography, grounded in a naive empiricism, commemorate his bad taste and sum up his life as "bad style." The anecdotal quality of Liszt's very identity both invites and forbids his absorption into a unifying schema. Schlegel comments in his notebooks: "Point of view of common virtuosity, a mixture of formal and material virtuosity." Virtuosity spins in a common mix, extending into the anecdotal material that philology collects, turning to be reduced and refined toward its formal side, its reconnection with a shape or character. The disintegration of Liszt's life is registered in the commemoration of his character. Virtuosity syncopates life, tracing the philological rhythms between evidence and speculations, between what is found and what is made.

Traditionally, Liszt's personal incoherence is rendered comprehensible as it is enlisted to elucidate the general incoherence between whole and part, general and particular, popularized as "Romanticism." Indeed, Romanticism is the unity constantly called in to explain Liszt, the unity that refigures Liszt the deviant as Liszt the originary exemplar. Not only Liszt, but music in general, tends to be read against a background of Romanticism. In his widely cited *Music in the Romantic Era*, a lively and informative work, Alfred Einstein outlines the argument that understands music to be the "strongest expression" of the Romantic spirit, the key to a whole segment of European Romanticism. Given this presupposition of an ultimately unified Romantic spirit, Einstein analyzes various musicians in terms of their Romantic traits. At the same time, he suggests that what is properly Romantic in fact breaks the continuity between a general spirit and its particular manifestations:

> The Romantics . . . struggled against tradition. Not only did they cease to avoid originality, they actually sought it, and esteemed their work all the more highly the freer of presuppositions it appeared to be. Romantic music, that of the 19th century, seems filled with a more colorful procession of personalities, a more sharply defined group of profiles, than does that of all the earlier centuries; and it is a difficult task to draw the line of development neatly. (17)

For Einstein, music exemplifies an extremity of Romanticism that reveals its essence; conversely, the essence of Liszt shows up not in his particularity, but only insofar as this particularity is coopted to reveal Romanticism. It is thus in his manner, his performative deviance from the generality "Romanticism," that Liszt can be taken as a starting point for constructing this same generality. So, there is a point at which the particular example precedes, exceeds, and founds the general structure that is used to explain the particular. The virtuoso's job is to ground the generality of which he himself is supposed to be a product.

Liszt functions as an emblem of the embodiment of a general spirit in a particular figure whose idiosyncratic virtuosity lends breath to the Romantic whole he acts out. This emblem is constructed with a double origin in a conceptual totality and a singular deviant; the struggle between these two origins parallels the arguments between Wagner and Liszt, composer and virtuoso, and, in the end, between language and music. What is at stake is the very capacity to *give voice* or *shape*, that is, the tropic art of figuration and specifically prosopopoeia.[6] If the trope of prosopopoeia is properly linguistic, its musical incarnation as Liszt stands and persists as its improper double, the mirror of its own impropriety and inability to hold its own identity. The transfer and exchange between composer and virtuoso, while based on a logocentric model, hands its linguistic center over to music to perform and make real.

The historical dialectic that has been sketched between Liszt and Romanticism duplicates the tensions among style, meaning, and authorial control and integrity that arose in the previous discussions of Heine. The valorization of style in both Heine and Liszt is characteristic of a certain turn from a Classical to a Romantic aesthetic. This turn ruptures the adherence of textual expanse (style) to the unity of a conceptual structure, a signified meaning or a referent, and produces digression. Romanticism recovers the uselessness of the stylistic arabesque and debilitates its autonomy by reattaching it to a particular subject, interpreting it as an "expression." The subject that these styles are said to "express," whether psychological entities or historical totalities, would logically need to precede the idiosyncratic mark of style it produces and subtends; but of course the subjects that the style shows—Heine, Liszt, or Romanticism—have only been gathered and derived from the texts and extended contexts in which the style smiles. These subjects' identities are unstable, fluctuating with style and the readings of style. The subject's proper name is just another interpretive name, an economic and reductive metaphor, for describing a style, a text. The recognizability of authorship does not attest to authentic inscription of a subject there, but only to a certain consistency, a more or less regular and regulated recognition of similar traits.[7] These patterns, drawn and articulated in critical texts, fissure the background they allow to come forth, marking out their historical landscape by scratching characters, names, ciphers, memories, and messages on the pages of the past. The consistency of texture, constructed out of similarities, is to be located as the holding together (con-sistence, *Zusammenhang*) of a (con)text, always interpreted and interpretive. The life of philology syncopates itself between its "material" and "formal" sides. It is an epistemology of simile, noting and connecting its likes and unlikes, its likes and dislikes, separatings its unities and etching its dream life of reading. Consistency is experimental and random, traditional and singular, unreliable and necessary: it is the ground that makes the recipe hold together or fall apart, succeed or fail.

The ambiguity of style means that it is impossible to determine the difference between expression and digression, a difference parallel to that between style and manner. The same difference structures the inevitable distinction between "good" and "bad" style. The stylistic arabesque either is enlisted in the service of a referent or a meaning—or, in a different turn, retains validity in returning to the particular subject it is supposed to express. "Good" style either presents what it is destined to present (that is, it arrives at its address, returns home, or reaches its addressee) or expresses and thus solidifies the identity of the subject whose mark it is. This expressive swerve of signification is a Romantic ideal that opens itself to censure from the "Classical" perspective as manner. Manner, like "bad" style, is digressive verbiage. In Heine, the deflection from "Classical" to "Romantic" "good style" passes through digressive verbiage; critical reception has accommodated most of this digressiveness and recovered it as "particularity" or "subjectivity." In this sense, "bad style" is a stylistic device of "good style," thus a means toward an end and part of a teleological structure. "Bad style," however, "really is" digression, encapsulated in isolation and no longer related to any path in terms of which it is defined as digression.

These evaluations of meaning and representation clearly subtend judgments about Liszt and structure the selection of material narrated as his life. Here, I would like to examine the tenuous link between the bad taste of Liszt's lifestyle and the problems of style in Liszt's text, *F. Chopin*, published in 1852 following the Polish pianist's death. This text shows how the "scandal" of digressive verbosity engages the issues of the integrity of an authorial subject and problems of philological authority, shaking the possibility of evaluation right where one can hardly bear to do without it.

This rather odd, indeed, one might say very bad, book "still remains unread and ignored. Why? Probably because a legend of misunderstanding and nonappreciation has grown up around it" (Waters, 5). Liszt and Chopin were intimate friends in their early twenties—virtuosi together in the Parisian salons—but later had a falling out. In his introduction to a recent English translation, Waters attributes to them "an early intimacy cooling off as both men were subjected to feminine influence" (6). The "disturbing factors" of women—here George Sand and Marie d'Agoult—are consistently invoked in the biographical tale of Liszt and Chopin. In a certain parallel, the "feminine influence" of d'Agoult and Sayn-Wittgenstein, Liszt's two longtime partners, has direct bearing on the critical reception of Liszt's writing, including critical attempts to validate it, despite its highly problematic style and questionable authorship and its utterly noncanonical nature.

Before considering the strange reception and philological difficulties of Liszt's book, I turn first to a passage in which Liszt describes a performance by Chopin. The performance, told and retold throughout the literature of the era, is the very same that Heine attended. Chapter 3 has shown how Heine's description of Chopin's performance detaches and distances itself from a referent and how the musical "spectacle" installs and makes possible this lyrical excursion or digression. Heine's description of the musical scene draws on a newly established commonplace that places the meaning of music in its impression or trace. As narrator, Liszt performs the same duties as the virtuoso, staking out and instituting the musical topos and setting up its representational self-effacement. Liszt describes the same scene as follows: "His apartment . . . was lighted by only a few candles gathered around one of those Pleyel pianos. . . . Corners left in darkness seemed to remove the limits of the room and to extend it into the shadows of space" (173–74/90). In Liszt's description of Chopin's apartment, narrative verisimilitude gives way to allow the fantastical figure to emerge. As the literal lights of this historical stereotype are extinguished, spatial boundaries dissolve to allow the figure of musical transmission to step forth. While this scenario promises a description of "the music itself"—that is, of Chopin playing—and to lead the reader into its thematic center, this theme never arrives; Chopin never comes into focus. Instead, Liszt fabulously narrates the presumed reactions of the various auditors. The shall we say imaginative quality of the narrator's portraits of these reactions is most flagrant in the following description of Delacroix:

> Eugène Delacroix remained silent and absorbed in the specters that filled the air, their rustlings seemingly audible to all. Was he wondering what palette, what brushes, what canvas he should have chosen to quicken them into life by his art? Was he pondering on a fabric woven by Arachne, a brush made of fairy eyelashes, and a palette covered with rainbow mists that he would have to unveil? Was he pleased to smile inwardly at these fancies and to surrender himself wholly to the impression that gave them birth, through the attraction that some great talents feel for others of contrasting nature? (180/95)

The rhetorical questions allow Delacroix to reflect the very problem of this narrative: that of the relation between a received impression (registered in description) to what makes or causes the imprint (the thing described). Liszt lets Delacroix ask the question of the possibility of translation; the question asks whether a translation can reproduce the relation of the means to the end effect, of the performance to the impression. Can a text even pretend to translate the impressions of music? Can one take up another material and medium and render again these impressions? These questions, attributed to the proper name of Delacroix, stand in the place of reception itself. Reception of or affection by music is presented as the quest for a translation, a re-saying, an appropriation into one's own medium.

This manipulation of Delacroix allows Liszt to give vent to his own phantasms. Liszt's installation of Delacroix is a sort of pseudoprosopopoeia, the insertion of a mouthpiece that "personifies" a person through a fictionalized attribution of questions and statements. While the insertion of a proper name suggests a narration of "fact," the double rhetorical question—was he asking a rhetorical question?—underscores the narrator's inability to know what he is telling. Liszt's conjecture is not a report. His ornamental rendition does not signify; instead, the relation between narrator and narrated subjects (Liszt and Delacroix), through the narrator's hypothetical invasion, destroys any clear distinction between observer and observed. The disintegration of a narrative boundary between Liszt and Delacroix that allows Liszt to float in and out of Delacroix's consciousness resembles the subjective absorption in the temporal experience of performance, the loss of the auditor's autonomy into the maelstrom of music.

The reaction to Chopin that Liszt attributes to Meyerbeer suggests a way to read Liszt's text: "Harmonist of cyclopean structures, he passed long moments of rare delight as he followed the detail of the arabesques enveloping Chopin's thoughts as in a light translucence" (179/94). The musical ear follows the curve of its improvisational experience, presses the outside of the envelope but does not tear it open or reveal an interior. Liszt's text seems to support Heine's suggestion that proper writing about music provides neither a concept nor an analysis of technical form but consists instead of the poetizing of the individual receptive subject. Since Liszt is indeed a technical specialist, one cannot suspect a lack of expertise here. For both Heine and Liszt, this petition is a deferral of the referent—a deferral that is digression. The fact that Liszt does not simply gush forth, but rather distributes and attributes this gushing to other elocutionary subjects, brings out the fatal citability of lyric presence. Insofar as the interiority of the subject has been expressed—displaced onto a subject of the *énoncé*, either *I* or Delacroix—the writing subject is nothing but the editorial technique, the *metteur en scène* of the spectacle to which he adds (almost) nothing. The author, dispersed and dissimulated in his text, is an editor and a plagiarist, neither origin nor original. He is a journalist, cutting, editing, and juxtaposing, a maker of sentences—not a poet.

Heine, too, is included in Liszt's presentation of Chopin's performance:

> Assembled around the piano in the lighted area were several figures of brilliant renown: Heine, saddest of humorists, listening with the interest of a compatriot to the tales that Chopin told him, tales about the mysterious land that also haunted his airy fancy since he had explored its most delightful parts. By mere suggestion of word and tone [*à demi-mot et à demi-son*] he and Chopin understood each other, and the musician answered with surprising phrases the questions that the poet softly asked about those unknown regions, even about that "laughing nymph" (3) of whom he sought news, inquiring "whether she continued to drape her silver veil over her green-hued hair with the same saucy coquetry?" During the chattering and amorous accounts about those places he wanted to know "if that sea-god with the long white beard still pursued a certain pert and roguish naiad with his ludicrous love?" . . . Chopin would reply, and both, after talking long and intimately of the charms of that aerial country, would fall silent in the throes of nostalgia that affected Heine so much that he compared himself to that Dutch captain of the *Phantom Ship*. (174–76/91–92)

This dialogue between Heine and Chopin disappears into the very center of this narrative—along with the music played and Heine's reception of it, the exchanged *demi-mot* and *demi-son* that suggest or solicit questions but give no answers: this murmuring talking without a topic. Liszt's elision of this reported dialogue, as in Heine's passage, defers the idealized communication it presents. Heine's version joins in the Romantic topos of the dialogue, adjoining historically divided subjects in an eternal poetic homeland. But Liszt's version, in its explicit citation, enacts dialogic fusion as mere citation; or, in the case of Delacroix, it exposes the very technique of the attribution of speech to replace the experience of an object. This second arabesque does not itself break from reference to establish metaphoric communication through figurative fusion; for Liszt is not himself included in the spectators whose impressions he reports. Indeed, Liszt characteristically excludes himself from what he narrates and makes no attempt to simulate his own subjective presence in his texts. For Liszt, lyric presence is always somebody else's and somewhere else; that is, lyric presence is never lyric presence. Liszt installs others instead of *I* and withdraws from what he relates. Liszt's writing composes through editorial techniques and citations, exposing the prosopopoeia allowing a subject to speak in its dependence on the horizontal juxtaposition of subject and predicate, quotation marks, spacing, and the mechanical reproduction of already produced speech. What Liszt adds to the interchange between Heine and Chopin is the represented presence, or simulated actuality, of the conversation—the seemingly inessential supplement of the virtuoso's presence, the mere report, in the mise-en-scène. This supplement is marked by Liszt's indiscriminate shift from fantastical dialogue to quoted text. Unlike those of Delacroix, Heine's words here are not Liszt's invention; Liszt himself provides the footnote to Heine's *Salon*, the "(3)" referring to the passage quoted from the tenth letter in *Über die französische Bühne* (On the French stage).

In Heine's text, Chopin, as poet, allows a lyrical interruption in a journalistic text through which Heine makes contact with the synaesthetic homeland, repeating and adjoining himself to a Romantic topos. The power of communication remains fundamentally poetic, performing substitutions between interior and exterior that are productive of metaphor. Liszt, however, is much more a virtuoso than a composer and tends to recall that very connection that Chopin makes us forget. In his citation of Heine, too, Liszt makes blatant the fictional device whose illusion is destined to obfuscate its mechanics. His addition—his narrative fiction, the illusion of cited speech, his prosopopoeia of Delacroix—is fact; that is, he really is quoting Heine. For he not only describes the evening of Chopin's performance with the verisimilitude of an "objective report" but he also explicitly quotes Heine, including a footnote; and at the same time he cannot help dramatizing the communication of his own reporting text with the lyrical text (of Heine) he cites. This dramatization, too, takes on the form of a reported dialogue. As Heine becomes a mouthpiece, he receives Liszt's addition, the answers he could not give himself:

> Well-informed on all the glorious enchantments that are seen *yonder, yonder*, he [Heine] would ask "if the roses there still glowed with so proud a flame? if the trees there still sang so harmoniously in the moonlight?" Chopin would reply, and both, after talking long and intimately of the charms of that aerial country, would fall silent in the throes of nostalgia that affected Heine so much. (175–76/92)

Liszt retemporalizes into sequential discourse—"literal" conversation—Heine's lyrical interlude; he thus recontextualizes it in precisely the technical sphere of division that it was supposed, for a moment, to overcome. Moreover, his juxtaposition of the questions he fantasizes for Delacroix with those he quotes from Heine debilitates above all the believability of his report, and by extension, of quoted speech. In this way suspicion is thrown not simply on this particular report but on the form of the reporting document, including citation, in general. The distance thus grows between what Liszt reports as the impression left on the auditors by Chopin and whatever might be imagined to somehow correspond to "Chopin." Liszt tends to exaggerate, to the point of blatancy, certain narrative techniques that are not so very different from Heine's. These techniques become obtrusive to the point at which their function—to efface themselves and to give forth a signified—begins to fail. Liszt's display of technique openly exposes the dependence of the end on the means and consistently broaches the threat of hyperimmanence. This is what has already been described many times and in the words of many, in terms of both Liszt and Chopin, as the disappearance of the instrument into the revelation of music.

But, as it is, Chopin never arrives. It is hard to say in what sense Liszt's *Chopin* has anything at all to do with "Chopin." In his introduction, Waters writes: "It is regrettable, perhaps, that Liszt more than once referred to the book as a biography. . . . Page after page after page is devoted to fanciful improvisations, and the reader (far from being entertained) wonders when he will again encounter the composer hidden behind all this verbiage" (27). It is interesting, and not haphazard, that the translator describes Liszt's text with the musical phrase of "fanciful improvisation," a term that perhaps also describes Heine's deflection into fairyland by way of Chopin. But perhaps too much credence has been given to Heine's conversation with Chopin and the lyrical expedition into the Romantic homeland. The break with referentiality, the reunion of the divisions of language and history that the lyrical passage attempts to enact, could be described less politely and quite simply as digression. The deflection of indicative narrative through Heine's subjunctive opens a digression no longer determined by the assumed or presupposed referent Chopin, a digression that enjoys its self-designation as "subjective expression." Like the self-interested autonomy of the virtuoso, this digression runs in the circuit of deviance; and Liszt's *Chopin* can only be classed as a biography *sui generis*.

In *Chopin - par François Liszt*, it is not necessary to go far in search of stylistic deficiencies. Charles-August Sainte-Beuve's oft-cited response to Liszt's request for editorial assistance was: "I have glanced through your interesting and generous appreciation [of Chopin], and it seems to me that, to give it form in the French language as I understand it would have required a revision and rewriting of the entire course of the work and that, at that time, I was in no condition at all to apply myself to such a task" (49).[8] And although Baudelaire described this book as "delicious," another critic remarked: "His numerous volumes, piled up one upon the other, would form a literary tower of Babel that would menace the heavens and which, like the other one, moreover, would collapse by the confusion of languages; it is German in French" (58). Liszt's language is an improper admixture—and what else could be expected from one who, if we are to believe his biographers, had no native, no proper or first, language? "By the time Franz had reached maturity, he had forgotten Hungarian, his mother tongue. . . . Although he never learned to write correctly in either French or German, he had nevertheless become a man of the world" (Seroff, 2–3).[9] In illustration of Liszt's tendency to allow his associations to flow forth unbridled, I quote the following somewhat lengthy passage for which Chopin's *Polonaises* are a sort of *Invitation au voyage*:

> In listening to some of Chopin's *Polonaises* the imagination hears the heavy even more than determined tread of men, boldly valiant, who brave all that fate can offer of injustice. At times the imagination views the passage of magnificent groups such as Paul Veronese depicted, and the mind clothes them in the rich costume of past centuries: golden brocades, velvets, flowered satins, soft and flowing sables, sleeves casually tossed over the shoulder, inlaid sabers, rich jewels, boots red with trampled blood or golden yellow, sashes with sinuous fringes—restraining tuckers, pearl-encrusted bodices, rustling trains, headdresses sparkling with rubies or verdant with emeralds, slippers embroidered with amber, gloves perfumed with the scents of a harem. These groups stand out against the dim background of vanished times, surrounded by sumptuous Persian rugs, by filigreed furniture from Constantinople, by all the ostentatious lavishness of those grandees who, with their crimson goblets embossed with medallions, drew upon the fountains of Tokay. They shod their Arabian steeds with silver and topped their escutcheons with the same crown which, through election, might become royal and which, leading them to scorn any other title, was worn alone as a badge of their glorious equality. (108–9/44–45)

It is undoubtedly passages such as this, which abound in Liszt's text, that inspired Emil Haraszti (a great apologist who has devoted much work to Liszt's texts) to write of *Chopin*: "A deluge of pompous words and the use of expressions that are repugnant to the spirit of the French language make this text largely unenjoyable" (228).

Liszt's improper relation to language takes bad style to the extreme of error and improper use, and it is, as always, these qualities that offend. For Liszt, all language is assumed. The display of the artificiality of his connection to language presents a threat, not only to the heavens, but above all to the ground of a "native language," a notion positing a natural relation between a language and a geographical territory. Liszt, his language, his music, and everything he does destabilize the idea that a work reflects identity, just as a "native" language would "naturally" reflect an origin and a national identity. Liszt problematizes at once this relation between ground and articulation, and, in turn, any symmetry within the horizontal order of the "sister arts."

In "Liszt Problems," a 1936 text published in a collection entitled *Essays*, Béla Bartók takes up this question: "With what justification do we regard Liszt as a Hungarian?" (508). This question becomes debatable precisely because of the disparity between the fact that Liszt was born on Hungarian territory and was a Hungarian citizen and yet did not really know Hungarian. Bartók points out especially the indeterminacy of Liszt's relation both to national languages and to national aesthetic paradigms in his music:

> Liszt's mother-tongue was German, for his mother knew only German in his youth. . . . He went to Paris, and French became more or less his second mother-tongue; moreover—and this is very important and characteristic—he knew French better than German, and preferred to speak French. He also wrote his books in French. Therefore, on the basis of language, we should consider him French, but nobody would think of doing so, for apart from the early years spent in Paris, he had no great cultural connection or affinity with France. His mature years were spent mostly in Germany, at Weimar. Why was this? Simply because there, there were opportunities for the propagation of contemporary music. But what about the style of Liszt's works? One can say anything of it rather than that it is German. His art is the antithesis of the excessive density and laboriousness so characteristic of the works of the outstanding German composers of the nineteenth century; it is rather the clarity and transparence of French music that manifests itself in every measure of Liszt's works. (509)

The musician in his art, therefore, does not stand in a proper relation to a native language that would ground the expressivity of musical *parole*. Identification with national models is made unsteady, for the ground of national space and geographical location is determined, for Liszt, by commercial interest, manipulated to a purpose; it is not naturally determined. Liszt, it would seem, is simply an artificial subject. The spectacle of such a person is dangerous and troubling, for he cannot be included in any canon. Bartók concludes: "Obviously, if one maintains, in spite of all this, that Liszt was not Hungarian, one is forced to call him a homeless cosmopolitan" (509). Bartók resolves this problem by looking at what Liszt says about it himself: "It is public knowledge that Liszt himself maintained . . . that he was a Hungarian. And it is the right of such a great artist as he that the whole world should take note of his wishes in this matter and not dispute them" (509–10). Bartók suggests that nationality can be established by a mere claim. And it is this that is consistently so very peculiar about Liszt: that he so thoroughly developed the technical art of becoming himself, over and over, simply through claiming to be what he was always yet to become.

Liszt's appreciators consistently rescue his text on Chopin from criticism by interpreting digressive passages like the one quoted above as the mark of musical lyricism. One critic writes: "Liszt's work [*F. Chopin*], imprinted with the marvelous melodic and harmonic qualities of *the author* [my emphasis], produces the effect of a magnificent musical improvisation on a given theme. Liszt executes diabolical variations and overcomes enormous *difficulty*, yet without ever taking leave of the principle motif" (72). Thus, the authentic mark of Liszt elevates his text to a Romantic topos inspiring the same lyrical ecstasy as Chopin's performance inspired in Heine. It is important to note the strong use of musical terms in this critical elevation and justification of Liszt. Another critic writes: "Chopin, by Liszt!—This title alone evokes a whole world of thoughts. . . . Here, the soul of the living sings a divine duet with the soul of the dead" (70). And another writes that this work "deserves more to be called a funeral symphony than a biography" (66). These critics use these terms to compensate for Liszt's text's lack of sense; I note this because musical terms continue to perform exactly this function in all sorts of critical texts to the present day. But what they imply here is that the writer Liszt is not a writer, that he maintains his status as first of all a musician even as he writes. The true author would not be the elocutionary *I* of the pen, but someone else. The enunciated, stylistic *I* is not *I*, and in this Liszt consists. He consists in his inconsistency; and who but Liszt would write of himself: "The poor musician has the least responsibility; for he who bears neither sabre *nor pen* can surely give himself up to his spiritual curiosity without too much of a bad conscience, and turn to all sides where he thinks he may have noticed light" (2: 201, my emphasis).

Inconsistency, or self-contradiction, like digression, is a mark of "bad style." It endangers the very idea of the recognizability of the author in its mark; for how could inconsistency—dispersion and dissimulation—gain the consistency by which it can be remarked and recognized? According to the philological habits of the rhapsodic tradition, a system is devised by which what is consistent with a unified "idea" is attributed to the author (determined to be the interior as essence and source of intention) and what is digressive (determined as what is extraneous as such, superfluous, contingent, mere material expanse) to someone (or something) else. For what sort of writer is it of whom one can ask, and it has been asked: "Is Liszt a writer? Yes and no" (74).

This question of Liszt's authorship does not ask, did Liszt literally write this book, was Liszt an author; but rather, was Liszt a *good* author, was the pen his proper medium, one in which he essentially expressed himself? Or is his writing merely a frill to his real work (music), merely a historical addendum in which we do not glimpse the essential artist Liszt (the author)? The title of authorship already expresses a judgment of the style and quality of writing. But the question of Liszt's authorship addresses not only the idealized relationship between artist and work but also the more mundane issues of signature. In the introduction to *Chopin*, Waters explains:

> Curiously enough, though the book appeared under Liszt's name, the amount of his authorship is unknown, for there seems to be good reason for doubt that he wrote any of the essays to which his name is attached, and we have the phenomenal situation (or possibility) of a great musician issuing reams of material, not a word of which came from his own pen! Marie d'Agoult is charged as being his first ghost writer, Carolyne Wittgenstein the second. Both women became prolific authors in their own right after serving this apprenticeship, but why they were willing to work in such obscurity remains an unanswered riddle. (17)

In the essay to which Waters refers in this passage, "Die Autorschaft der literarischen Werke Franz Liszts" (The authorship of Franz Liszt's literary works), the music historian Emil Haraszti attempts, through "methodical historical research" (*methodische historische Forschung*), to establish "what is" really Liszt and what is not. Haraszti has devoted more work than anyone to the question of Liszt's authorship. His efforts to establish authorial origin are dominated by gendered distinctions between "idea" and "style," duplicated in the difference between "good" and "bad" style and "style" and "manner." Haraszti's work displays contradictions of historicism that are still at work in most philological writing today. These contradictions show how difficult it is to avoid presuppositions about unity, authorship, idea, and style in efforts to historicize literary research.

Through the comparison of manuscripts, correspondences, and notebooks, Haraszti presents a great deal of evidence to support his claim that Liszt's two amorous partners were largely responsible for his written work. These demonstrations rely on a notion of the propriety of ideas as the ground of authorship — a criterion that undermines the authority of the signature (as handwriting) and of the manuscript that serve as his evidence. For the "true author" is not the literal hand in which the manuscript is written but rather the (figurative) place of origin, the proper owner, of an idea. Haraszti concludes that Liszt's earlier writings (previous to *Chopin*) ought to be attributed to Marie d'Agoult as an author in her own right. Haraszti awards d'Agoult authorship on the basis of stylistic and thematic consistency of texts written in her hand or signed with her name: "The Countess is the fully entitled author of the Liszt-writings from the Paris era. The themes of these articles are Mme d'Agoult's own, personal ideas; we also find them in the Countess' other works" (202). This concept of authorship defines the author as the origin of content. Yet at the same time, this feminized authorship adheres not to "ideas" but to style or "ideas" that are stylistically gathered and presented. In the very same paragraph, Haraszti writes: "The content of the articles that appeared in the *Gazette et Revue* did not originate with Liszt; rather, the Countess composed it [*hat ihn zusammengestellt*] from the works of other writers. The form and the tone are in the style characteristic of the Countess" (202). How can these be "Mme d'Agoult's own [*eigensten*], personal ideas" any more than they are Liszt's, when, after all, Liszt published them and they were read under his name in the public sphere of the musical journals? Haraszti preserves Liszt as the one who does not plagiarize, while Mme d'Agoult is permitted to appropriate the language of others. Liszt's ideas, according to Haraszti, are either his own or not his; but Mme d'Agoult's "own ideas" are borrowed items and cultural citations. Haraszti thus tries to save Liszt (the man) as an integral subject, delimiting the crossing of property lines to feminine writing.

As an individual author, the countess comes to be known by her style: "Rhetorical fire is the fundamental element of her personality. She sometimes composes brief sentences, sometimes lets them march by in periods that seem to never want to end. They are exhaustingly bombastic; this is the style typical of the time" (217). Her individuality thus is no individuality at all; it is homogeneous with what is undoubtedly the critic's "general impression of the period." That is, Mme d'Agoult's particularity, her style, does not distinguish her. For "the Countess's style, by the way, is by no means unusually individual," or rather, it is composed, stitched together, from the works of other writers. But what, then, can guarantee the stability of d'Agoult's character or style, such that it can be used as the criterion of difference from Liszt? Haraszti uses d'Agoult to stand as the author of texts of which Liszt is not the proper author, to stand in the place of Liszt as an improper author. Liszt is negatively defined as the unique character which, were it present, would exceed and distinguish the average stature of d'Agoult's style.

The Duchess von Sayn-Wittgenstein, Liszt's other other, is likewise known by her rather less flattering style: "The Duchess' letters show the author to be an educated woman, but a rhapsodic chatterbox who loved all sorts of gossip" (277). She, too, is granted the responsibility of authorship, although here we have more a situation of "reworking" (*Bearbeitung*). It is indeed lucky for Haraszti that Liszt had two women friends. For here, although Liszt may be the originator of the theme, the duchess is nevertheless granted the autonomy of author—but as the author, therefore pseudoauthor or deviant author, of *digression*:

> The literary works from the Weimar era originated thus: Liszt gives the
> Duchess some idea or theme, but sometimes the thought to be executed be-
> longs to the latter. The Duchess then works up the theme with a rare loquacity,
> often very confused—but always in such a way as to display her great erudition.
> In this way, she pulls together a material that no longer has anything to do with
> the object, as for example in her study of the *Harold Symphony*. The explicitly
> musical part, the thematic analysis, is naturally Liszt's work. (224)

The duchess's working over of *Chopin*, as evidenced in the comparison of the second edition (which she expanded) to the first, too, separates out the "bad" digression from a Liszt imagined to be present. "In its broad bombastic presentation it [*Chopin*] lost precisely the immediacy of Liszt's recollections" (227).

This exposition was meant merely to point out the disruptive effect that Liszt apparently has on the unifying, but ultimately inoperable, notions of consistency and authorship. There is generally a difficulty in trying to understand a "historical individual" at all when the difference between consistency and inconsistency is itself inconsistent and fails to hang together. Haraszti describes the problem of Liszt: "Behind the strange sequence of his seemingly incoherent [*zusammenhangsloser*] actions there is hidden a plenitude of complicated motives which are difficult to discover" (177). The same argumentational circularity is at work here: from a series of disconnected and incoherent actions, the principle of a subjective identity is sought by which to give order and meaning to the same series. Following this logic, there must be a "real" and unified Liszt beyond or outside of the disjointed actions available to view. Where, then, is this historical individual, this Liszt, to be sought? For Haraszti, the "real Liszt" is ultimately authorized by yet another subject—the transcendental unity of periodization, or a Zeitgeist. It is not coincidental that Haraszti should take recourse to a musical figure at the very point at which he presupposes the unity that remains to be demonstrated: "This is why the Liszt-problem is so complex and indivisible—just as a unified *fundamental tone* [*Grundton*] determines his character" (177, my emphasis). It is finally "the spirit of the times" that explains the contradiction, the "riddle" that is Liszt. Regarding the reported "spiritual crisis" of the young Liszt, Haraszti writes: "Later he could easily be brought out of balance; but this is no longer an individual crisis, but rather the general psychic crisis of the René generation" (211). A fictional character, Chateaubriand's *René*, is thus the ground of generality against which the facts of Liszt are determined and set off from "legend." "Liszt himself" comes to be figured as what is left after subtracting the various fictional devices structuring virtually all the formations of his transmission through history. His biography figures prominently among these fictions, although its narration is fairly consistent in many sources. The basic outline of his life was first published in 1835 in the *Gazette musicale* under the signature of Joseph d'Ortigues, an important music critic and friend of Liszt. Haraszti describes this biography: "The fundamental tone [*Grundton*] of the short life-story is novellistic" (196). Once again, the Countess d'Agoult is held responsible for this fictional work, which, he says, she based on the *Second Scrapbook* belonging to Liszt's father: "Adam Liszt began by collecting and pasting in newspaper clippings. . . . From the correspondence it is certain that this life-story is the Countess' work, who used the Versailles Second Scrapbook, which she had in her possession" (196–99). It is strange that Liszt's life should be both the authentic imprint of a Zeitgeist and this peculiar mélange of plagiarism and fiction. Liszt is forged out of scraps of writing cut out of a journalistic discourse whose only generality is that of universal distribution—spatial ubiquity. This biography gives a name and a mouthpiece to a vague generality, an abandoned newspaper lying in the gutter, drifting in the breeze.

Still, can "Romanticism" be used as a unifying principle to explain what dissimulated, dispersed, and distributed itself in the first place in order to appear to be Romanticism? "The Countess originated the idea of the mystical crisis which fits so well with the atmosphere of Romanticism" (198). Haraszti's mode of argument itself requires the establishment of this atmosphere that will debilitate the basis of his own claim of objectivity. *René* is the reality against which the reality of Liszt is measured; but to the very same extent, Liszt is a reality against which any phrase of *Grundton* and variation, rhapsody, and virtuosity, must also be measured. Liszt is himself as much a component of the "atmosphere of Romanticism" that forever clouds its "essence" as a concept.

"Liszt is indeed a being with a thousand faces," writes Haraszti, a grammatical subject in syntactical contiguity with a thousand different aspects. It is in this contiguity that he consists, in the performance, and not in the nameable synchrony of a physiognomic portrait. This subjectivity *is* its distribution for which there is no unifying principle but this very process of partition. Rather than look behind the curtain,[10] perhaps one should side with Heine: "Perhaps the solution to the question does not lie in such deep and strange mysteries, but rather on a very prosaic superficial surface" (*SS* 5: 533).

# 6. Poetic Originality and Musical Debt: Paradoxes of Translation

The nineteenth-century tension between music and language often issues in a struggle for priority and originality. Amid efforts to determine what belongs "properly" to music and what to language, the trope of prosopopoeia emerges at the center of the antagonism. *Prosopopoeia*, an important term in the texts of Paul de Man, is a term for personification or animation. Literally, it means to make (or give) a face or mask (from the Greek πρόσωπον [*prosopon*] + ποιεῖν [*poiein*]).[1] It is thus a trope implied along with other tropes, such as apostrophe, for example, which presupposes animation in what it calls upon.[2] Carolyn Abbate has characterized writing about music as primarily a mode of prosopopoeia precisely in order to highlight the difference between language and music. She outlines as follows her vision of a critical language to describe music's multiple voices based on prosopopoeia:

> I prefer an aural vision of music animated by multiple, decentered voices localized in several invisible bodies. This vision proposes an interpretation of music shaped by prosopopoeia, the rhetorical figure that grants human presence to nonhuman objects or phenomena, and one that traditionally entails a strongly visual fantasy in which we imagine faces and eyes upon nonhuman forms. (13)

By underscoring the rhetorical aspect of critical language, Abbate hopes to pre-serve a region of autonomy for music that is not covered by language; the more critical language is seen to be "merely figurative," the more music will appear as "other." Music, Abbate writes, "exists in present time, as physical and sensual force, something beating upon us. The text of music is a performance. Thus music is fundamentally different from the written texts that have for the most part shaped critical theory. (Poetry retains vestiges of live performance, and me-diates between the extremes of live and unperformed written texts)" (12). These comments assume a basic difference between poetry and critical prose that is parallel to that between music and text and imply that prose has *no* "physical" or "sensual" force and no performative aspect. It is unclear what "vestige" of the musical might be found in poetry, especially if prosopopoeia, traditionally a po-etic trope par excellence, is to be the model for critical prose.

According to Abbate, the term *prosopopoeia* is a constant reminder of the de-gree to which language projects predicates upon objects that cannot "speak" for themselves (18). Her efforts to free music from linguistic domination have much to contribute to the self-awareness of both literary and music criticism, but she continues to affirm the oppositions between subject and object, lan-guage and music, and literal and figurative. Though she concedes that language codes and cultural histories help constitute the musical work as it is experienced, she is less interested in how linguistic and cultural norms and conditions might determine the possibility of the production of music "itself." The antagonism between composer and virtuoso offers precisely such a point; it displays how linguistically determined oppositions structure debates about the origin of mu-sic and intrude on its production, reception, and evaluation.

De Man, Barbara Johnson, and Jonathan Culler all suggest that apostrophe and the prosopopoeia it implies are virtually synonymous with "the lyric" itself and constitute its most performative moment.[3] This highly poetic trope comes to be mixed up with music whenever music is made into a subject, made to act something out or to carry certain predicates. In *Resonant Gaps: Between Wagner and Baudelaire*, Margaret Miner points to the interrelation between problems of predication and personification in various antagonisms and identifications between writing and music. Defining her project's theme of "writing on mu-sic," Miner writes:

> Especially with respect to Baudelaire, this "on" hints at the effort of all these authors to superimpose some of their writing so directly onto music that the two might become fused—inseparable, if not indistinguishable, from each other. In specific instances, that is, Baudelaire and the others try to make their readers take the preposition much more literally than usual. . . . The writing on

music to be considered here, then, aims to put its figures at the service of the letter and thereby to render the letter profoundly, essentially musical . . . ulti-mately . . . the writing in question fails to reach its goal . . . fails to overcome the gap separating it from the music toward which it is directed. (2–3)

Much of Miner's text is organized by the difference between personification, un-derstood as a "rhetorical embellishment" or a *figurative* personification, and the *literal* embodiment or incarnation through which music physically affects audi-tors. Miner argues: "Literal embodiment and figurative personification in the end reveal not only their intermittent incompatibility, but also the threat they pose both to Wagner's music and to Baudelaire's writing" (76). But how can this distinction between a literal and figurative trope be maintained? The trope of prosopopoeia itself obscures the distinction in question between literal and figu-rative, for it animates the "object" and allows it to be taken for a "subject." Miner allies "literal embodiment" with anthropomorphism, referring to de Man's es-say "Anthropomorphism and Trope in the Lyric." But in that essay, anthropo-morphism does not establish a clear border between "literal" and "figurative"; instead, it points to that moment of (mis)reading in which the grammatical sub-ject is interpreted as the agent of its verb: "Anthropomorphism seems to be the illusionary resuscitation of the natural breath of language, frozen into stone by the semantic power of the trope. It is a figural affirmation that claims to over-come the deadly negative power invested in the figure" (247). Anthropomor-phism allows letters to speak and things to resound; it is the forgetfulness of prosopopoeia and thus not an alternative to personification. Anthropomor-phism stands in a relation of blindness and insight, just as the terms *literal* and *figurative* only duplicate the ambivalence between signification and reference.

This oscillation of prosopopoeia is articulated through the competition, among the arts, for the dominant position and origin of the power of figura-tion and embodiment as the very power of art itself. Lacoue-Labarthe has ad-mirably delineated the struggle for priority between poet and musician in Baudelaire's essay "Richard Wagner et *Tannhäuser* à Paris" (Richard Wagner and *Tannhäuser* in Paris).[4] In the drama of recognition, self-loss, and appropriation, Baudelaire attributes the prize to music insofar as it delivers the sensation of space itself. "What it offers first of all," writes Lacoue-Labarthe, "is the pure form *a priori* of sensual intuition—space, here depth—which is in effect neither material nor spiritual. Music, in other words, carries *aisthesis* to its limit: it gives the sensation, infinitely paradoxical, of the very condition of all sensation . . . that is to say the pure possibility of presentation itself in general" (*Musica ficta*, 77 / 31). These characteristics, however, are not those of the limited and specific referent "music"; rather, they are features of excess aligned with *écriture* (81/34):

that extension that carries over, forth, and between. With this step, though, Baudelaire's Wagner ceases to be Wagner: "And thus in the end, his Wagner is not Wagner" (77/31). Anthropomorphism (Wagner) reveals itself to be trope (Wagner).

This aporia between signification and reference structures Baudelaire's relationship to music in his 1861 essay on Wagner, and it is thanks to this essay that Paul Valéry attributes central importance to music in Baudelaire's poetics. In his essay "Situation de Baudelaire" (The place of Baudelaire), Valéry analyzes the Baudelairian project primarily as one of *distinction*. He locates the historical singularity and importance of Baudelaire in the project of self-constitution of a poetic idiom that would distinguish a particular poet from historical precursors or influences. "Baudelaire's problem," Valéry writes,

> might have—indeed, must have—posed itself in these terms: "How to be a great poet, but neither Lamartine, nor Hugo nor Musset." I do not say that this matter was consciously formulated, but it was necessarily in Baudelaire—and it even was essentially Baudelaire. This was his *raison d'Etat*. In the domain of creation, which is also the domain of pride, the need to distinguish oneself is indivisible from existence itself. (1: 600 / 8: 195)

The poet's project to distinguish himself in a unique idiom at the same time distinguishes poetic from "everyday" language: "The duty, work and function of the poet are to bring to light and to utilize these powers of movement and enchantment [*charme*] . . . which, in ordinary language, are confused with signs and the means of communication of ordinary and superficial life" (1: 611 / 8: 209). As poetic language separates and makes evident what in ordinary life is confounded or blurred, it distinguishes itself from that ordinary domain. "This extraordinary speech [*parole*] is known and recognized by [*par*] the rhythm and the harmonies which support it and which must be so intimately and even so mysteriously bound to its generation that sound and sense can no longer be separated, and correspond to each other [*se répondent*] endlessly in the memory" (1: 611 / 8: 209).

Valéry uses explicit musical terminology to describe the indivisibility of sound and sense characteristic of poetic language. These musical terms mark simultaneously the unique quality of Baudelaire's poetry (versus other poets) and the difference between poetry and prose: "Baudelaire's poetry owes its durability and the empire it still exerts to the plenitude and singular clarity of its timbre . . . it almost always keeps and develops an admirably pure melodic line and a perfectly sustained sonority that distinguish it from all prose" (1: 611 / 8: 209–10). Valéry describes the excellence and singularity of Baudelaire's poetry with a semitechnical vocabulary borrowed from the domain of music—that is, with a figurative use of musical terms. At the same time, he places the distinction of Baudelaire within a historical context by shifting the musical register back to a literal thematics of music, to music *proprement dite*: "It is noteworthy that the same man to whom we owe the return of our poetry towards its essence is also one of the first French writers to be passionately interested in music itself [*proprement dite*: properly speaking]" (1: 611–12 / 8: 210). The unique excellence of Baudelaire's poetry, to which Valéry attributes no less than a return to an originary essence of French poetry, is indissolubly related to an interest in music—not merely a musical aspect of language, but to music *proprement dite*.

Valéry invokes Baudelaire's writing on Wagner as evidence of his authority both to speak about music and to speak musically. And yet Baudelaire's ignorance of music is well known. In a letter to Wagner, Baudelaire describes himself as someone who "*does not know music*, and whose entire education is limited to having heard some beautiful pieces of Weber and Beethoven" (*OC*, 2: 1452). Like Heine, Baudelaire is a poetic dilettante in music, whose authority comes to exceed his technical expertise. If Baudelaire's essay tells us anything about music, it is from the point of view of a poet whose perspective is limited by the historical condition of the division of labor and the separation of the arts. As he himself presents it, Baudelaire's experience of music is not direct and originary, but fragmentary and limited to morsels of a few composers. His version of Wagner has its beginning much more in the pages of the Parisian *feuilletons*; his own essay, too, was first published on April 1, 1860, in the *Revue européenne*. For Valéry, Baudelaire's individuality, uniqueness, and originality are inextricably associated with musical qualities. Baudelaire's ability to speak musically is thus presented as part of his particular historical experience of music, as if it derived from the empirical reality of music itself. Valéry thus posits a continuity between the historical experience of a particular subject and its transposition into poetry. The shift toward the referential sphere, while increasing Baudelaire's authority about music, also suggests that Valéry's characterization of Baudelaire's poetry is denotative and referential, that the pure melody and other musical features he notes are objective traits of the text rather than interpretive metaphors. Musical terms are the identifying markers of poetic language that seem to mediate between the text's discursive extension and its reception or recognition by a reader.

Valéry presupposes a model of adequation between language and things. Musical traits—rhythm, harmony, and so on—announce themselves out of the "object" text; they are traits of the *parole*'s self-revelation and self-articulation, remaining bound to their origination in the text. By deploying these musical terms, Valéry evades any formal or technical specification of the effect he attributes to texts; instead, he practices a turn from technical detail to mystifying suggestion when he writes:

> A short while ago I spoke of the production of *enchantment* [*charme*], and I have just now pronounced the world *miracle*. These are doubtless terms which must be used with discretion because of the force they possess and the ease with which they are employed; but I could only replace them by an analogy which would be so long, and perhaps so debatable, that I will be forgiven for sparing [us]. . . . I will remain vague and confine myself to suggesting what it might be. (1: 611 / 8: 209)

The use of musical terms in critical language, too, can be facile, eliminating the necessity of specification and replacing it with a vague and suggestive sense or impression of a text. The interjection of the terms *charme* and *miracle* in the passage above performs a critical obfuscation that Valéry describes as abbreviation. The suggestive neutrality of abbreviation allows the critical text to maintain a referential dimension; in the same way, Valéry refers the musical dimension of Baudelaire's poetry to his contact with music within the sphere of biography and history. But the condensation of space implied by abbreviation also opens a difference between the musical terms crystallized in Valéry's text and the Baudelairian lines from which they have been culled. This difference points to the addition of the critic, the additions of reception and reading.

Valéry's use of musical terms in describing poetry implies a referential relation between text and experience held stable precisely by Baudelaire. In his essay, Baudelaire dramatizes a certain relation to history as it is mediated and shaped by literature. According to Valéry, Baudelaire's interest in music "properly speaking" is significant because of the role it plays in interrupting the sphere of history and deflecting music into literature: "I mention this taste, which was manifested in the famous articles on *Tannhäuser* and *Lohengrin*, because of the later development of the influence of music upon literature" (1: 612 / 8: 210). These articles themselves perform the translation of music into literature and stand in the stead of music itself. Valéry's text continues with the following citation, the source of which is not provided: "*'What was baptized Symbolism may be summed up very simply in the aim common to several groups of poets of taking back from music what belonged to them [leur bien]'*" (1: 612 / 8: 210). Lent the typographical authority of citation and italics, this sentence implies that the power of music is, "properly speaking," a poetic power that has wandered astray, dispersed itself, and been usurped by music. Music is thus the improper place for the musical traits of poetry, "the rhythm and the harmonies which support it and which must be so intimately and even so mysteriously bound to its generation that sound and sense can no longer be separated, and correspond to each other [*se répondent*] endlessly in the memory" (1: 611 / 8: 209). Rhythm, harmony, and melody are understood as properly *poetic* and not musical characteristics, properties of poetic language that can be borrowed, lost, stolen, usurped.

Music, therefore, stands as the improper place—ground or subject—of poetic predicates. The experience of music leads poetic essence out of itself into the dispersion, loss, and depropriation, the chance circumstances of finitude. Music leads poetry into history, a nondifferentiated sphere that is not accessible to understanding. Valéry calls this—the region of finitude constraining and determining the emergence of an individual—"Romanticism." Romanticism is, for Valéry, the ill-defined mass of a historical situation marked above all by imperfection. Among its "vices," Valéry mentions "the relaxation of formal requirements . . . the poverty and impropriety [*l'impropriété*] of the language . . . impassioned facility . . . inconsistency of style . . . bizarre and puerile excesses" (1: 601 / 8: 197). These terms all point to the threatening impropriety of the predominance of the materiality of writing over an intelligible sense. Valéry invokes a concept of Classicism to contain, order, and rationally control the impenetrable mass of historical precedence:

> All classicism presupposes a romanticism that went before. . . . The essence of classicism
> is to come after. Order implies a certain disorder it has come to reduce. Composition, which is artifice, follows some primitive chaos of natural intuitions and
> developments. Purity is the result of endless labors on language, and care for
> form is nothing but the considered reorganization of the means of expression.
> The classical then implies conscious, voluntary acts which modify "natural"
> production in conformity with a clear and rational conception of man and art.
> (1: 604 / 8: 201)

Composition appears as a departure from nature and not its extension, an artifice engendered by and subordinate to the conception of a knowing subject. Like the poetic subject, this subject of criticism has an interest in lifting itself above the sphere of dispersion and purifying itself of bodily admixtures, historical influences. The relation of Romanticism and Classicism Valéry puts forth here parallels that between music *proprement dite* and literature. To mediate between them—between history and poetry or music and letters—Valéry calls on Baudelaire who, "although romantic in origin, and even romantic in his tastes, can sometimes cut the figure of a *classic*" (1: 604 / 8: 200). While Baudelaire allows the figure to emerge out of a vague mass, the movement is cut short; the clear character falls back on its ground to which it remains attached: "Baudelaire, in the milieu of romanticism, makes us think of a classic, but he does no more than make us think of one" (1: 605 / 8: 201).

Valéry, it seems, does not himself wish to fall back into Romanticism. In the same way, he does not wish to display the fact that the musical words he attributes to poetry originate not in music but in language. The terms *must* appear to belong properly to music; for if they have not been usurped, they cannot be reappropriated. What emerges here is another kind of music that sounds quite like the *musique proprement dite*—Romantic—but ought not to be collapsed with it. For it is a linguistically produced "music," a metaphor, a dummy figure sent out to carry linguistic predicates that they might return to their home, acting in the service of a linguistic *I*—poet and knower, stable, apart. This "music" names not a concrete art but a general power. In "L'Existence du symbolisme" (The existence of symbolism), Valéry describes it as follows:

> Among all the modes of expression and excitation, there is one in particular that imposes itself with unmeasured power: it dominates and devalues all the others; it acts upon our whole nervous being, overstimulates, penetrates . . . and submits it to the most capricious fluctuations . . . it is master of our conscious time, of our nervous tremblings, of our thoughts: this power is *Music*. (1: 698–99 / 8: 230)

This power, Valéry says, happened to be manifested at the time in the music of Wagner, thus allowing a momentary identity of music and Music. The poetic power, it would seem, happened to have wandered over to music: it is given by music to be restored as Music. Valéry attributes the restorative poetic project to Mallarmé: "The problem of Mallarmé's whole life, the perpetual object of his meditation, of his subtlest researches, was, as we know, to return to Poetry the same empire that the great modern music had seized from it" (1: 700 / 8: 231). The essence of poetry Valéry supports in his Baudelaire essay thus depends on its dispersion in history via music, just as the constitution of a unique and original poetic subjectivity depends on its predecessors. On the one hand, Valéry attributes the singular importance of Baudelaire to the musical qualities of his poetic language (recall *timbre*, *melodic line*, for example), presented as the proper qualities of Baudelaire's verse. Yet Valéry's essay is organized by a double register; he does not simply investigate the proper qualities of Baudelaire's poetry but he also sees his importance in a certain relation to history already suggested by the title, "Situation de Baudelaire."

Baudelaire develops a subtle literary strategy for dealing with his "situation" in the struggle between music and poetry. In "Richard Wagner and *Tannhäuser* in Paris," Baudelaire situates himself explicitly as a particular and limited reader and writer within a specific context. The essay begins:

> Let us go back, with the reader's permission, some thirteen months, to the beginning of the question; and further I must beg to be allowed in the course of

this appreciation to speak frequently in my own personal name. This *I* . . . implies a great modesty; it imprisons the writer within the strictest bonds of sincerity . . . it is hardly necessary to be a consummate judge of probabilities to convince oneself that this sincerity will find friends among impartial readers; there is clearly a reasonable chance that, in relating no more than his own impressions, the candid critic also relates those of some unknown sympathizers. (*OC* 2: 779 / *Painter of Modern Life*, 111)

The journalistic writer, Baudelaire declares, speaks about music here only with the limited expertise of a writer. What he has to offer are not general truths but only his "own [*propres*] impressions." His remarks, directed toward an indeterminate audience, are emitted into the haphazard sphere of journalism. The journalistic writer thus takes the chance that his own particular comments will be received by unknown readers, with the hope that their limitations will be overcome in resonating with those of others.[5] By means of his text, Baudelaire strives to add his personal voice to the more general dialogue about music current in the Parisian press. But at the same time, Baudelaire begins not as a distinct personality; rather, he picks up the general and abstract form of the first-person pronoun, "this *I*," "ce *Je*." This *I* is not Baudelaire, but the monotonously uniform sign of the journalistic reader: the indefinite public, the members of the crowd. Baudelaire's articulation of his experience of Wagner allows the empty convention of the word *je* to be appropriated, to differentiate itself from the commonplace language of the journalistic sphere in which it is made available, and to become individual. This transformative appropriation takes place through an intricate process of reading, writing, and rewriting—an elaborate philological exercise.

The first few pages of Baudelaire's essay convey the announcement of Wagner's music through gossip and journalism: "Thirteen months ago, then, there were uproarious rumors in Paris . . . we knew vaguely that on the far side of the Rhine there was much agitation about the question of reform in lyric drama" (*OC* 2: 779 / 111). This vague knowledge presupposes and is a consequence of geographical and national separation. To some extent, journalism succeeds in making Wagner present for Baudelaire. But insofar as journalism depends upon conditions of absence, it continues to transmit and reinforce the imperfection of the world over which it travels. The marks announcing Wagner become obscured in their spatiotemporal extension in the press. Baudelaire writes: "But these various documents, appearing as they did at long intervals, simply glided over the spirit of the crowd [*la foule*]" (*OC* 2: 780 / 112). Journalistic readership is troubled by forgetfulness, by the difficulty of holding together the many texts it receives spread out over time and space. The daily readings of an indeterminate readership—the crowd—do not come together to form certainty or knowledge. On the contrary, this kind of reading is itself the haze of rumor and vague intimation, the cloud of day-to-day life, reading punctuated by all sorts of other activities, the picking up of a text at a certain time of day. This chance of communication that Baudelaire seeks, then, is also the constant chance of loss, of eluding notice and not being read, of being forgotten.

The activation of the word *je*, as Baudelaire recounts in this essay, occurs through the movement from his intimation of music through texts to his actual experience of performance. At the same time, the essay is structured by a trans-formation of reading that draws into relief this *je* as a distinct reader, a *poetic* reader differentiated from the crowd. The essay thus enacts an alteration of reading that interrupts and reorganizes the kind of journalistic reading de-scribed above. Baudelaire restructures the experience of reading newspapers—a quasi-physical action connected to bodies enmeshed in the passage of time.[6] But initially, Baudelaire himself is one of those readers who buys a ticket and picks up a program.[7] Baudelaire, too, undergoes the journalistic initiation into Wagneriana and becomes aware of Wagner first through the journalistic incan-tations that influence through frequent repetition. But through writing, Baude-laire attempts to extricate himself from the crowd and to instead express his own impression. How does Baudelaire differentiate himself from the repeti-tious mimesis of the crowd? How does he cut the figure of a unique and origi-nal poet among the mass of poets? For Baudelaire, both critical and poetic dis-tinction proceed by way of relating a historical expanse to a subject as its origin and structural ground. This involves an act of interpretive reading, of produc-tive repetition asserting difference through editing: selection, reproduction, re-ordering. Baudelaire, too, is a philologist.

The journalistic generation of text upon text itself provides the material or background out of which a unified character can be gathered. The same jour-nalism draws the musical performance into closer readings of the historical context of Wagner's life: "The general curiosity drawn to Wagner gave rise to a spate of articles and brochures which introduced us to his life, his weary struggles and all his sufferings," Baudelaire relates (*OC* 2: 787 / 119). Baudelaire begins to organize his reading by focusing on the subject Wagner. Concentrat-ing on the character of Wagner as the expressive origin of his works, Baude-laire's text edits and selectively reproduces a particular sequence of journalistic texts: "Among these documents, so well known today, I want to extract only those which appear to me the most suitable [*propres*] for clarifying and defining the nature and character of the master," he explains (*OC* 2: 787 / 119). This edit-ing, which proceeds according to the standard of a genuine relationship be-tween the artist-subject and his work, gathers together a horizontal series of texts. Baudelaire presents his selection not as an original statement but as the selection most suitable or adequate (*propre*) to the object itself, the subject Wagner.

Yet Baudelaire has gained a foothold through the *me* in "*ceux qui me paraissent*" (that which appears to *me*), through which he inscribes himself as the recipient of what appears as an affected and impressed subject. Baudelaire's selective reading, once initiated by its journalistic past, disengages the banal subject of the horizontal expanse of texts—of literal writing and reading—releases the receptive subject from the bonds of finite linearity, and establishes a vertical relation between subject and text, artist and work, or between writer and reader, *I* and *you*. In reorganizing the time of reading, Baudelaire shifts from recounting his experience of reading to performing it as he establishes a new present in his own text. The *je* begins to perform with the introduction of the present tense, accompanied by a direct address to the reader. The present instance of discourse implies a simultaneity of writer and reader, a cotemporality and proximity inscribed in dialogue. This bond between subjects is figured first of all through the relationship of reading.

Baudelaire quotes from the opera program, introducing it in the present tense: "I read from the program *distributed* during that period at the Théatre-Italien" (*OC* 2: 782 / 114, my emphasis). He picks up a piece of print distributed in the context of an experience and imports it into his own text with the addition of italics scattered throughout the passage. Baudelaire's selection of passages already lends emphasis to them, lifting them out of the broader text that is left behind. The addition of italics underscores this implicit addition of emphasis that covertly begins a new program; Baudelaire gives only the following hint: "The reader will shortly understand why I italicize these passages" (*OC* 2: 782 / 115). The present tense draws into relief the activity of citation, a split in the temporality of experience that leaves its trace in the *emphasis* given to the received text in its repetition by another—an emphasis made explicit in the graphics of *italics*.[8] As the graphic performance of citation and italics allows an *I* to emerge, an oblique relation of address is established between *I* and *you* or reader and writer. While the origin and the destination of the message are connected in the present on the page, they are still held fast in an irreversible sequence, as *you* is addressed in the third person: "the reader will understand" but does not yet understand. Baudelaire's italics prepare and perform the "other" standard of selection, namely phenomenal similarity noted through the senses. At first, the finite reader still in the dark must begin by noting the similarities destined to be gathered into a unified picture.

The present tense of "I read," *je lis*, is amplified by the explicit reference to the ghostly hands of a literal reader as Baudelaire introduces a long citation of

Liszt: "I now pick up Liszt's book and open to the page where the imagination of the illustrious pianist (who is an artist and a philosopher) translates in his own way [*traduit à sa manière*] the same piece" (*OC* 2: 782–83 / 115). The citation of Liszt here occurs at the point of substitution between the literal activity of reading in the present of Baudelaire's narrative and what is read, a substitution marked by the empty space between the colon and the quotation marks. This is where the imagination takes over the technical work of the letter. Liszt narrates, for Baudelaire, the hidden principle of repetition. The passage Baudelaire quotes from Liszt describes the overture to *Lohengrin*:

> This introduction contains and reveals that *mystical element* which is always present and always hidden in the piece. . . . To teach us the unnarratable power of this secret, Wagner first shows us *the ineffable beauty of the sanctuary* . . . [my elision] He makes glitter before our eyes the temple of incorruptible wood, with its sweet-smelling walls, its doors of *gold*, its joists of *asbestos*, its columns of *opal*, [its vaults of onyx: omitted by Baudelaire], its partitions of *cymophane* . . . [my elision] It does not make it perceptible to us in its imposing and real structure, but instead, as if managing our feeble senses, he first shows it to us reflected in *some azure wave* or reproduced *by some iridescent cloud*. (*OC* 2: 783 / 115, Baudelaire's emphasis)

Liszt narrates here the very substitution of the "letter" of music by metaphor, by that which is perceived by the receiver who is not in a position to understand or see clearly what is yet to be revealed. One begins, perhaps, to understand not only Baudelaire's assemblage of quotations but also the figure of italics. The italics Baudelaire has added to Liszt's text bring out the *mystical element*; this consists of the concealment of compositional strategy, a rational plan or structure, hidden and "reflected" in the opaque metaphoric materials as they are experienced over time by a sensible subject, a member of the audience. The artist's calculation organizing the work is both present and absent to the receiver; it functions precisely by not being evident in its real structure, which is covered over by a vaguely sensible mass, wave, and cloud of color. This experience of an immediacy that is not immediate might be compared to the vague intimations of journalistic rumor—or the suggestive effect, in a first reading, produced by Baudelaire's italics.

Like Heine, Liszt diverts attention away from an "object" or the "objective" or technical structure of music and directs his view instead toward a dreamlike metaphor of reflection. In quoting Liszt, Baudelaire strengthens this diversion; he mentions Berlioz's "magnificent eulogy in the technical style" but does not cite it or refer to any of its contents. In other words, Liszt describes the diversion from the referential linearity of narrative to metaphor, from the horizontal extension of letters on a page to their metaphoric animation. The signifying body becomes agitated.

For Baudelaire, Liszt consistently stands as both agent and instrument of the substitution of metaphor for reference, or of reading for writing. "Liszt" is a proper name drawn from the sphere of historical reference, his texts part of a historical intertextuality preceding and exceeding Baudelaire's text. Baudelaire incorporates Liszt's text and appropriates it to the degree that Liszt serves as a mouthpiece for what Baudelaire himself would, but cannot, say: my translation translates the original in such a way that for you, reader, it is the condition of possibility of your experience of the original; my translation partakes in and is part of the original; I am the origin. In his capacity as virtuoso, this is, in fact, just what Liszt does say. In Liszt's status as virtuoso, there is a fusion of and confusion between original composition and translating performance simulated by Baudelaire's citational practice, which slides from the active to the passive and enacts a fusion of writer and reader: "I read in the program . . . " Here, the reader is forced to read along with the writer, and, for an instant, will have been controlled by the ruse of the first-person present tense in which the copying of a passage, the transcription of a citation, and the incorporation of a foreign text are called "reading." In succumbing to the *mystical element*, we read not Baudelaire, but Liszt. If the reader momentarily reads along with Baudelaire, Baudelaire is also read along with Liszt, and he has left his editorial mark in the added italics. In quoting Liszt, Baudelaire is speaking *improperly*, as a translator: he is cutting and pasting, technically manipulating language of which he is not the origin or author; he is not speaking in his own idiom. These, of course, are the characteristics of Liszt's use of language: erroneous, borrowed, plagiarized. In compelling the reader to read along with him and to be drawn into the present tense of his text, Baudelaire sets himself up as both interpreter and obstacle. Moreover, in communicating through the gesticulating manipulation of the space of the page, translating Liszt into his own text and own idiom, Baudelaire insinuates himself, the one quoting, a fraction of a space ahead of Liszt.

In the passage Baudelaire has quoted from Liszt, Liszt explicates how the composer's intention—the "imposing and real structure"—is disguised in various material metaphors that arrive to the auditor entrenched in the sense experience of music. The power to displace a compositional structure is attributed to Wagner, who, Liszt says, gradually "teaches" us by showing the ineffable secret. This pedagogical series is locked in a temporal sequence separating origin, message, and destination. The composer knows the plan; the addressee, still in ignorance, can only receive its marks over time and space, which gradually direct him toward the sense conveyed.[9] The cloudy vagueness of Liszt's metaphors allows the secret structure to remain concealed as it works. The imprecise, indefinite aspect of Liszt's writing style both describes and performs the distribution of a sense in a multiplicity of sensual terms, the diffusion of a definite meaning in a variety of material metaphors that cannot be simply deciphered into a single represented sense. Through Liszt, the lack of precision in this repetitive performance comes to signify the musical more generally. Here, the musical aspect of language is located in the adherence of communicated sense to the material expanse of its signifiers in general. Music points to a sense experience that cannot be absorbed in its reception. This materially bound level of experience affects the one who receives it; it does not communicate conceptually or lend itself to paraphrase. This sense of music thus characterizes not only poetic language, but more generally, the persuasive action of text on reader. Baudelaire's italics, spacing, and quotation marks operate musically; they are "prosaic" counterparts to the "musical" traits of language (melody, rhythm, rhyme, sonority, and so on) traditionally identified with poetry.

Music, in part, means for Baudelaire the priority of a history, a past, preceding and exceeding a particular subject in the present. It means that the subject must receive its language from another, that *je* is not self-originating but rather is provided by a world that predates it. This history exceeds the experiential capacity of the particular individual "Baudelaire"; and we have seen him attempt to gather up a dispersed extension of time and consolidate and contain it in a digestible form. Indeed, this is why, in his article, he is compelled to assemble a list, a collection of examples of a pattern that he has picked out on the basis of similarity—this is why he does not begin with a logical standard of selection. What is at stake, finally, is the origin of the theory of correspondence or indeed, of "Correspondances" (Correspondences). Liszt's passage gives a synaesthetic presentation of the theory of correspondence, and in Baudelaire's text, it comes *before* his own statement of it. In Liszt's translation, he can be read as the elocutionary subject of synaesthesia that makes possible the induction of correspondence. His text is the example or singular case that grounds the general principle.

In the same way that Liszt's translation precedes Baudelaire's, Baudelaire's list precedes the demonstration of the theory of correspondence that would ground it. Following his collection of citations, Baudelaire introduces his own translation of the same overture to *Lohengrin*:

> May I also be permitted to tell [*raconter*], to render in words the inevitable translation my imagination made of the same piece when I heard it for the first time, eyes closed, feeling, so to speak [*pour ainsi dire*], lifted away from the earth? I would certainly not dare to speak smugly of my *reveries*, if it were not useful to join them to the preceding *reveries*. (*OC* 2: 782 / 116)

In this rhetorical question, Baudelaire's historical narrative—the journalistic report caught in a diachrony—splits and pluralizes itself, glazing its simple "telling" with a layer of translation, turning from narrative to poetic rendering. At this ambiguous point, the chance narrative of the particular *je* introduced at the beginning of the essay is drawn into a relationship with other speakers through the unifying category of "translation." As Baudelaire adjoins himself to the group of translators, he puts repeated emphasis on the word *reverie*; the translations are lent the dignity and elevation as well as the generality of a literary genre and a poetic topos. He aligns these *reveries* with the preceding *translations* so that the "original" object—the musical work—will resound in all of them.[10] This double alignment (between translations, between translation and *rêverie*) enacts the systematic programming that has been attributed to the Wagnerian leitmotiv; the secret plan is revealed as translation, and covered up, clouded over, by the *rêverie*, its poetic counterpart. In thus arranging his citations, Baudelaire has already assumed what he then states as his purpose:

> The reader surely knows what goal [*but*] we are pursuing: to demonstrate that the true music suggests analogous ideas in different brains. Besides, it would not be ridiculous here to reason *a priori*, without analysis and without comparison; for what would be truly surprising would be that sound *could not* suggest color, that colors *could not* give us the idea of a melody, and that sound and colors were unsuitable [*impropres*] for translating ideas, seeing that things have always found their expression through reciprocal analogy ever since the day when God uttered the world like a complex and indivisible totality. (*OC* 2: 784 / 114)

In this linkage of the arts and media, conceptual exactitude increases with each linking element: "suggest," "give the idea," and finally, with the combination of sound and color, "translate ideas." At the level of suggestion, material elements communicate with each another; they are not directed toward an independent signified but point only to their own communication. This is the level of synaesthesia; its sense resides in the specificity of its terms—sense images—that say nothing, really, but their own intercommunication on the page, their linkage in a concrete text. The culminating phrase in the passage above transposes a horizontal relation between the arts (sound suggests color, and so on) to a vertical substitution of sensible materials for intelligible ideas that are clearly distinct from their aesthetic presentation. The final step, explicitly called translation, fixes the transcendent opening between the senses in Baudelaire's theory of correspondence; it indicates the point of contact between the horizon of the arts and a thinking subject. Here, synaesthesia gives way to the *theory* of correspondence that grounds it. In the *Salon of 1846*, Baudelaire writes that this point of contact characterizes all the arts: "Since they are all always the beautiful expressed by the feeling, the passion and the reverie of each person, that is to say, variety in unity, or the diverse facets of the absolute—criticism, at every instant, touches upon metaphysics" (*OC* 2: 419 / *Art in Paris*, 45). The universality of the aesthetic cannot be simply deduced but rather must be induced from the historical expanse of its individual and varied specifics; the adjoinment of what is spatially and historically distended establishes a "unity" that is not Hegelian sublation. In the same sense, the theory of correspondence does not exist separately from its articulation in figures of synaesthesia that point ineluctably to the dependence of such a fusion on the sensual elements in which it takes place.

The principle of correspondence thus gives a key for understanding a work, for gathering together and unifying what is disparate under a named structure. Baudelaire pursues this unity singlemindedly throughout the paragraph; the goal is to reduce the variety of analogous translations to a single unifying source and thus to demonstrate the principle of correspondence. Baudelaire's list itself, then, serves as the model of this resonance; music (Wagner's overture) stands as the ground of this unifying correspondence. In the same way, music—"the true music"—stands as a figurehead for the origin and subject of the theory of correspondence. Liszt, in his translation of Wagner, is the synaesthetic speaker who proffers that out of which the theory of correspondence can be induced, gathered, and read. The impropriety of Liszt's language presents a parody of the *Gesamtkunstwerk*; it is the mere mixing together of worldly languages that ironically suggests but does not attain to a metaphysical totality.

As Baudelaire adds his own translation to the list he has assembled, he sets up a communicative community between a plurality of speakers, unified by a musical referent as its origin or ground. On a philological plane, the various elements of journalistic print that Baudelaire has gathered up are unified by the literary topoi of *rêverie* and translation. The agreement of the various speakers is initially coincidental; it comes forth, by chance, in individual attempts to represent private opinion within journalism. Their coincidence, however, becomes more compelling when Baudelaire identifies the individual utterances as translations that share a common bond with the "original." The literal or conventional sense of translation implies the existence of an already composed text that is then rendered in another natural language; in this horizontal transference, the position of origin is relative within a historical series. The subject of literal translation is finite, existing within the worldly conditions of the dispersion of languages, the division of nationalities, and the separation of the arts. The term *translation* remains embedded in an irreversible temporality, the historical sequence that maintains the priority of the original and the ordinal position of particular translations.

In noting the resemblances between these haphazard utterances, Baudelaire grounds and thus lends necessity to the similarities he finds, locating them in the single source of Wagner's overture. The more Baudelaire condenses the "sameness" of the translations, looking away from their individual divergences, the greater the emphasis on translation in its artistic function. In this expanded sense, translation performs the substitution between the intelligible (or invisible) and the sensible (visible): sounds and colors translate ideas; Wagner, in his capacity as artist in general, translates "the tumult of the human soul by thousands of combinations of sound"; and the arts in general are said to be means of translation that bring the supersensible into their worldly media.[11] Translation thus stands as a metaphor for artistic production in general, for that activity that brings about a vertical substitution incarnating the spiritual in the materiality of a signifier. The point of substitution can be located in the combinatory aspect of the organization or composition of a work. While translations precede and follow one another, the act of substitution places each in an equal relation to the original. Artists are united in this equality, historical sequence obliterated, division and specialization superseded. The structural model of substitution replaces the sequential priority characteristic of the journalistic "Daily Times" with the logical priority of origin over extension, structure over particular articulation or example. Baudelaire's translation reverie parallels Heine's elevated city of poet-artists.

In introducing his own translation of Wagner, Baudelaire recounts the transport from the temporal distention of horizontal narrative (past and present) into the present of an experience of vertical dislocation, pointing specifically to its figurative quality: "I felt . . . *so to speak* [ *pour ainsi dire*], lifted away from the earth" (my emphasis). Baudelaire then quotes the first two verses of the famous "Correspondances." But the detachment from prosaic ground continues to expand in the narrative that follows the two verses:

> Vaste comme la nuit et comme la clarté
> Les parfums, les couleurs et les sons se répondent.

> Vast like the night and like light
> Perfumes, colors and sounds correspond.

> So—I continue. I remember that, from the very first bars, I underwent one of those happy impressions that almost all imaginative men have known, in their dreams, in sleep. . . . Next I involuntarily pictured [ *je me peignis*: literally, painted to myself] the delicious state of a man in the grip of a profound reverie, in an absolute solitude. (*OC* 2: 784 / 116–17)

The painting of the lyric state—the detached isolation of a subject dissolved of its earthly boundaries—is involuntary, forced or compelled by that (music) to which the transport is a reaction; the subject undergoes an impression from without. As this submission is transformed into involuntary painting, the dream is replaced by the *rêverie*, referring no longer to a literal bodily condition of sleep but to its literary simulacrum or semblance. The transposition from literal to figurative passes from the closing of physical eyes to the figurative opening of an infinite dreamlike space.

In this reading, I answer to the invitation extended by the discontinuous passage passing over the empty space between the end of the verse and the recommencement of the prose text: "So—I continue." Baudelaire is still translating and fuses the presence of his verse with the narrative present reinstated following the citation. A change in the language of the essay has taken place. The historical narrative has been interrupted, the subjective *rêverie* isolated and detached from its prosaic frame. The spatial emptiness surrounding the citation of the verses, like the brief blank space introducing the citation of Liszt, causes the reader to experience the same detachment and isolation Baudelaire describes. This lacuna in his text is not "reproduced" or imitated or translated; if it occurs, it can only occur in a singular, nonrepeatable movement (of reading or experience). This animation of reading, the invisibility of rhetorical contact, transposes the "reader" into an "auditor" who receives the message exceeding the visible typeface. In the experience of music recorded here, Baudelaire appropriates certain transmissions of historical influence in such a manner as to establish his own isolation from them. In the same way, the verses of Baudelaire's poem, *the text directly cited*, indicate the difference of Baudelaire's translation from all others, that aspect of a text that cannot be paraphrased or translated. In spatially performing, rather than simply stating, Baudelaire persuades by forcing the reader to act along with him, to momentarily cohabitate the place of *je* in reading the present tense, in crossing the space between poetry and prose. "So—I continue": I have thus done it, mistakenly, in reading it. Passing from the singularity of the poetic text to the continuation of translation in prose, and thence toward generalization, I concentrate not on the stated content but on a certain material extension of writing holding them together on the page.

In imitating and partaking in the act of translation, Baudelaire, like his predecessors, performs the action of substitution through which the dream takes the place of music. This act translates from one sphere of language (prosaic, everyday, or literal) into another (metaphoric, synaesthetic, poetic); the experience of listening to music *proprement dite* is replaced by a text. The connection among the various translators is thus made by a concentration on the synchronic structure of substitution. This synchrony, grounded in the assembled similarities of many examples, can only be induced. That is, it is noted in the recurrence of similar terms that must be gathered together and cannot be found first.

Baudelaire borrows Liszt to prepare his own "Correspondances," whose originality would not be possible without the prior models and the prose introduction from which it deviates. This is not the first time that Baudelaire uses the words of another, indeed of one biographically closer to music than he, to enunciate synaesthesia. In the *Salon de 1846*, Baudelaire writes:

> I recall a passage from Hoffmann that perfectly expresses my idea . . . "It is not only in dreams, or in that mild delirium which precedes sleep, but also when awake, when I hear music, that I find an analogy and intimate reunion of colors, sounds and perfumes. It seems to me that all these things were engendered by a single ray of light, and that they must reunite in a wonderful concert. The smell of brown and red marigolds especially produces a magical effect on me. It makes me fall into a deep reverie, and then I hear as if from far away the deep and profound sounds of the oboe." (*OC* 2: 425–26 / *Art in Paris*, 51)

The coincidence of stated content in a variety of speakers produces truth by probability, not by necessity; it is this kind of philological veracity that Baudelaire hopes to attain in his critical edition of remarks on Wagner. Recall: "There is clearly a reasonable chance that, in relating no more than his own impressions, the candid critic also relates those of some unknown sympathizers" (*OC* 2: 779 / *Painter of Modern Life*, 111). The journalistic—or prosaic—message, presupposing only an indistinct addressee, is emitted into a sphere of chance and probability that governs rhetorical success: "The more eloquent the music is . . . the greater the *chances* that sensitive men will conceive ideas in affinity with those that inspired the artist" (*OC* 2: 782 / 114, my emphasis). Such sympathetic communication would mean the gathering together or recollection out of the dispersed hazards of prose that would connect speaker and addressee.

Baudelaire's repetition of Hoffmann repeats an action of substitution, that is, of translation. The communicative filiation Baudelaire establishes between himself, Hoffmann, and Liszt does not place Baudelaire in the position of epigonal imitator; it suggests instead a coparticipation in artistic language, where priority is not determined diachronically or metonymically but rather synchronically or metaphorically, in terms of the synchronic pattern of similarity connecting them. The "absolute principle" shared by all the arts consists of the differentiation occurring at the point of substitution between these two axes. Originality comes to mean not historical priority but the uniqueness of each position in its isolation from the sequence.

In other words, in repeating the topos of the reverie, Baudelaire subscribes to the view that the truth of music lies in its reception and not in its "objective" structure. The emphasis on the originality of subjective addition privileges vertical substitution over horizontal transference in a hierarchized relation of value and control. When he quotes E. T. A. Hoffmann's *Kreisleriana* to articulate his own theory of synaesthesia, Baudelaire thus suffers nothing in saying, "I recall a passage from Hoffmann that perfectly expresses *my idea*" (*OC* 2: 425, my emphasis). As the *I* claims possession of the idea of which the externally given is an expression, the historical priority of one writer over another is invalidated. The foreign text is only another expression, and not the origin or source of, the idea expressed in the "native" text. In a single blow, the present text joins a fraternal order and is thus raised to the level of an equal translation of the same original as the prior text. In the same way, Baudelaire's own and authentic translation of Wagner's music is said to reflect his own experience of the event itself, of the original object. As telling (*raconter*) or rendering in words is separated from the more genuine activity of translation, the hearsay experience announced in the journalistic texts Baudelaire has read passes into his own experience of the musical performance.

Or so he says. The closing of the eyes can be read both as the extreme border of the literality of the letter from which the reverie detaches itself or as an instance of metaphor, as herald or prelude to the reverie. If we forget about or look away from whatever historical influences might have informed this figure of the closing eyes, we read the metaphor to which it gives way. In the same sense, if we ignore the rhetorical devices at work in Baudelaire's presentation of his originary lyric translation, we are persuaded by what is said, by the isolated verses. Through this persuasion, Baudelaire hooks into a figurative dialogue with the other translations he cites. In this persuasion of reading, Baudelaire will have momentarily played the role and fulfilled the function of Liszt. In a text about Beethoven's piano sonatas, Berlioz describes the task of the virtuoso as follows: "It is absolutely necessary that the virtuoso efface himself before the composer, just as the orchestra does with respect to symphonies; there must be complete absorption of the one by the other. But it is precisely in identifying in this way with the thought he transmits to us that the interpreter is elevated to the greatness of his model" (*Oeuvres littéraires*, 83 / *Art of Music*, 38). Here, the virtuoso functions much the same way that the subject citing others does: as a subject that, through identification, disappears into what it transmits, but to the degree that it disappears is expanded and elevated. In disappearing, the virtuoso is all the more present, his existence utterly indispensable, though it be thoroughly evacuated for the sake of the thought transmitted to us through him.

Berlioz goes on to contrast a performance of Liszt that he recalls from thirty years before writing his essay, in which, he says, Liszt disfigured Beethoven's piano work in an overly decorative rendition. Returning to the present, Berlioz describes another occasion on which Liszt performed the same piece, yet this time with the opposite effect. According to Berlioz, Liszt's performance in the dark raised Beethoven from the dead, leaving the audience in tears (quoted in Chapter 5).

If we are crying, then Ion is surely laughing, and perhaps Baudelaire as well.[12] Successful virtuosity effaces its techniques; forgetting the manipulative action of citation, we can read simply Liszt in Baudelaire's quotation just as, according to Berlioz, Liszt brings to life the ghostly voice of Beethoven himself. Animation—the prosopopoeia allowing the work to speak as an expression of the artist—emerges in the erasure of the techniques of citation.

Once more, we run up against the contention about animation—about the originary position or place of origin of enunciation. Baudelaire has used Liszt to narrate the replacement of the literal experience of music by metaphor, a replacement he performs again himself. He does this by inserting a quote, by putting Liszt (among others) in the position of the *sujet d'énonciation* in his own text. Interestingly, this literary or philological act, too, is already given by Liszt. For whether or not Baudelaire had read Berlioz's text, there is another quite similar scene, familiar by now, at which Heine, too, was present; Baudelaire refers to a description of it in Liszt's book *Chopin*, where we find Liszt playing Baudelaire: "In his delicious study of Chopin, Liszt puts Delacroix among the poet-musician's most assiduous visitors, and says that he loved to fall into deep reverie at the strains of that airy and impassioned music which resembles a brilliant bird hovering over the horrors of an abyss" (*OC* 2: 761 / *Painter of Modern Life*, 60). In his capacity as narrator, Liszt effects the passage from an outward description of a literal scene to the interior effect, the reverie, which he renders forth in the words of a simile. He places a figure in a scene or atmosphere and attributes imaginary poetic speech to that figure. The painter is the last dummy figure, the opacity of the narrative mouthpiece itself, doubled by the contingency of the historical reference of the proper name. If Baudelaire's centrality is lost as he hands the word over to Liszt, it is drawn in again insofar as Liszt speaks what Baudelaire would have him say, just as Liszt (like Heine) ventriloquizes through Delacroix—or, like Hoffmann, perfectly expresses Baudelaire's idea.

# 7.   Rivalry Among the Arts and Professional Limitations

It seems, at first, that Baudelaire's essay "Richard Wagner and *Tannhäuser* in Paris" is about Wagner. As Baudelaire's text concentrates on the character of Wagner as an author, the similarities he notes between the texts he quotes are exchanged for objective properties or predicates of a subject. The program instituted in the alignment of translations in the first section of Baudelaire's essay, the role assigned to them in selective editing, is ahead of the reader. This gap underscores the secondary position of the receptive subject, who will be manipulated and controlled by what it is given. The apparent claim of objectivity of Baudelaire's interpretation of Wagner presupposes a community of response between selective organization and the recognition of similarity, a communicative community characterized by the nonsimultaneity and division of the two extremes of this rhetorical chain.

The nonsimultaneity of the origin and the destination of the communicative message refers us to the contingent and historical division of the arts as a division and specialization of labor. Quite banally, what does Baudelaire know about the particular art of music, except insofar as it partakes in the general structure of art? Baudelaire's interpretation of Wagner replaces a particular process by a generalized metaphor as its universal sense—that is, Wagner's work can communicate universally, even to those who do not know music, because he expresses or translates the generality of "the human soul." Baudelaire points this out explicitly in his famous letter to Wagner in which he tries to communicate a certain "correspondence" in spirit transcending the professional boundaries, the individual bodies, of divided artists. He writes: "At first it seemed to me that I knew this music . . . it seemed to me that this music was *mine*. . . . For anyone but a man of spirit, this statement would be immensely ridiculous, especially when written by someone like me who *does not know music*, and whose whole education is limited to having heard a few beautiful pieces of Weber and Beethoven" (*OC* 2: 1452). The emphasis on the metaphoric effect of music as its essence strives to distance the bodily aspect of musical sense, the finite and corporeal origin of a subject, so that it can be replaced by a nonsensual interior as subject.

It is possible that Baudelaire, like Heine, locates the meaning of music in its metaphoric translation merely because he is ignorant of and has no access to its technical generation. He certainly does not attend to any of the musical details, indicated only vaguely as "thousands of combinations of sound" in Wagner's translation of "the tumults of the human soul." As a writer, Baudelaire can only read music as a foreign language that exceeds his own specialization. As an undistinguished member of the public, he needs a translator who can give the foreign work a wider distribution and open it to public access. But if Baudelaire does not "know music," surely Liszt must know something about it! To Liszt, Baudelaire confides the duty of presenting the departure of imagination, or the separation of metaphor, from the literal or objective structure of the musical work. Remember how Baudelaire picks up Liszt's text, "open to the page where the imagination of the illustrious pianist (who is an artist and a philosopher) *translates* in his own way the same piece" (*OC* 2: 782–83 / 115, my emphasis). As translator, Liszt brings about the transition from the specialized idiom of musical letters to its more generally available metaphoric sense. Baudelaire needs Liszt to read Wagner, just as the master composer ultimately needs the virtuoso. Sticking to his peculiar mannerisms and bizarre idiom, Liszt ends up exceeding Wagner; the compositional figure represents "the artist in general," but Liszt is both artist and philosopher. Baudelaire evokes Liszt at textual junctures stressing the primacy of difference and division. His relationship to Liszt is characterized above all by historically determined difference: quite simply, Baudelaire is not Liszt.[1] In contrast, the relationship between Baudelaire and Wagner is much more one of identification or similarity based on the structure of authorship. The difference between the roles of Wagner and Liszt for Baudelaire bears upon the division between composition and performance, conception and execution, or between the figures of poet-composer and virtuoso.

The specialization of activities as socially distinct professions implied by the division of labor indicates a limitation to the capacities of a particular individual subject and thus to its fundamental finitude. For Wagner, this division, held responsible for the inadequacy of the particular arts, is the ground provoking the theory of the *Gesamtkunstwerk* (the "total work of art").[2] The poet must hand over the task of musical description to a musician, just as for Wagner each art should hand over the expressive task to its neighbor as it reaches its limits. Baudelaire's ignorance of music is not called in here as a biographical fact to explain his text; rather, it reflects his status as poet and thus the finitude of particular subjects of enunciation in general. If in no other way, this limitation is given by the fact that a writer writes in a particular language and not in language in general. The separation from totality implied in the division of languages means only that mediation is necessary or that finite subjects require a tool in the discovery of truth. If such an instrument divides and separates the subject from truth, it also makes such access possible at all.

Baudelaire begins his investigation of Wagner from the point of view of the finite poet, the reader of *feuilletons*, and a member of the undifferentiated public. The experience of Wagner's music, "this ardent and *despotic* music," overpowers Baudelaire, who occupies the ignorant position of the nonspecialist. He describes his reaction thus: "From that very moment, that is to say at the first concert, I was possessed by a desire to enter into a deeper understanding of these singular works. . . . In what I had experienced, there was . . . something new that I was powerless to define, and this impotence caused me a rage" (*OC* 2: 785 / 118). Baudelaire determines to master this condition of ignorance precisely through reading; his ignorance begins to give way as the marks of method become recognizable in their repetition. Baudelaire begins to identify the mnemotechnic of the leitmotiv, the hidden workings of which Liszt has intimated or suggested metaphorically but has not explicitly named:

> Nevertheless, frequent repetitions of the same melodic phrases in pieces extracted from the same opera seemed to imply mysterious intentions and a method which were all unknown to me. I resolved to inform myself of the why and the wherefore, and to transform my pleasure into knowledge, until a stage-production should come to provide me with a perfect elucidation. . . . I gnawed at M. Fétis' indigestible and abominable pamphlet. I read Liszt's book. (*OC* 2: 786 / 118)

In reaction to the "despotic" quality of Wagner's music, Baudelaire reverses the chronology of reception so that the performance will now appear as a repetition in compliance with a knowledge that precedes it. With this same gesture, the thinking aesthetician will have brought under control the new and unique experience presented by music.

Baudelaire has described Wagner's music as "ardent and *despotic*." This artistic despotism consists of a technological attitude of control that posits both chronological and structural priority of conception over execution. This is part of the logic of *unité de but* (unity of purpose) that subsumes individual cases under the generality of a concept, which in turn is connected to such cases by application. Baudelaire locates the despotic tendency in the Wagnerian opera by stressing the dramatic text, the synchrony of the *mythos*, as the origin of its significance. Baudelaire writes of Wagner:

> This absolute, despotic taste for a dramatic ideal in which everything, from a declamation so meticulously noted and underlined by the music that it is impossible for the singer to deviate from it in a single syllable—a veritable arabesque of sounds sketched out by passion—down to the most scrupulous niceties in matters of decor and production, in which every detail must ceaselessly concur in a totality of effect—it is this, I say, that has moulded Wagner's destiny. (*OC* 2: 790 / 122)

Thanks to the priority of the dramatic ideal over its externalization in music, where it is "noted" and given affective emphasis ("underlined"), Wagner emerges as a unified "hero" of a destiny. At the same time that the composer determines the musical performance to be a realization of his conception, authorial control is exerted over the temporal expanse of the work in a way that obscures the technical operations of detail in order to produce a general effect. This hierarchy, installing a teleology that relates history to a suprahistorical end, is itself historical insofar as its metaphorics belong to a political—indeed, an imperialistic—paradigm. Baudelaire says explicitly that Wagner "has marched on, without deviating by an inch, towards this imperious ideal. . . . I have found in those of works as have been translated . . . an excellent method of construction, a spirit of order and of division that recalls the architecture of the tragedies of antiquity" (*OC* 2: 790 / 122). This architectural metaphor suggests that art originates in the rational and technological constructions of a subject or spirit. The political relation that binds this spirit to its work enacts a technological transference from the blueprint or design to its realization in the actual building. Such transference produces an immanent duplicate of the prior calculation of a subject; as Baudelaire remarks here, the method is evident within the *ouvrage*.[3]

Epistemological mastery is gained over the dispersion of a diachronic experience precisely by establishing a synchronic view or a mythic simultaneity of what is temporally extended in experience. This is, indeed, how Baudelaire comes to interpret Wagner's operas:

> The *Tannhäuser* overture, like that of *Lohengrin*, is perfectly intelligible, even to one who does not know the libretto . . . this overture contains not only the original idea [*l'idée mère*: literally, the mother-idea], the psychic duality which constitutes the drama, but also the principal formulae, clearly accentuated, destined to paint the general sentiments expressed in the course of the work. (*OC* 2: 797 / 128–29)

This thorough accomplishment of technological repetition, according to which the synchronic "mother-idea," controls the performed work, conflicts with the notion of art as the expression of sentiment or the work of passion. The *veritable arabesques* of sentiment add nothing to the work and operate strictly under the control of a master architect. In this aspect, Baudelaire's poetics share in the despotism of the ideal attributed to Wagner; the model of technical and rational calculation divides meaning and its means of transmission in such a way as to assure priority to a subject as master and origin, and at the same time guarantees a general knowability to which particular cases are subordinate.[4]

The Wagnerian work can become intelligible because it bears immanently the systematic markers placed in it by the composer. Through this transference, the work gains a certain autonomy; it can speak by itself in the stead of its producer. In this respect, the musical work is assimilated to poetry as the art of linguistic combination producing an autonomous whole.[5] Thus, as Baudelaire gains intellectual mastery over Wagner's work, the domain of music is colonized by poetry as the originary division of art and non-art of which all other divisions, resulting in the various arts, are repetitions. Poetry is the essence of art: "In fact," Baudelaire writes, "without poetry, the music would still be a poetic work, endowed as it is with all the qualities that constitute a well wrought *poesie*: self-explicative, so well are all things well united, conjoined, reciprocally adapted and, if it may be permitted to use a barbarism to express the superlative of a quality, prudently *concatenated*" (*OC* 2: 803 / 134). The capacity of a work's autonomous and immanent structure to disclose its intelligibility suggests that its meaning in fact originates in its material, technical ("objective") dimension. As the work attains autonomy, it will function necessarily in accordance with mechanical laws. The mechanical relation of cause and effect operates within a homogeneous plane of objectivity ("nature"); this is why for Baudelaire, all art, like poetry, must be highly explicable. But if the effect of the work is said to originate not in a subjective interior but in technological laws, the work will have absorbed the place of the transcendent subject it was meant to express. The mechanics of the work of art induce the danger of hyperimmanence yet also ground the possibility of critical knowledge. After all, Baudelaire advocates an aesthetics of genius, inspiration, and originality, and not one of mechanistic determination. To counteract the tendency of mechanization, attention must be diverted away from the rationally calculated technical details toward the metaphor of their effect. This deferral occurs precisely through the mystification of eloquence. Terms like *charm* and *magic* intervene to obscure the technical structure of linguistic tropes and to turn attention toward their metaphoric effect.

Eloquence cannot display the law of its dependence on the letter to transmit its persuasion; for in this displaying, it would have transgressed itself as letter and communicated a meaning. The poetic law of influence and repetition cannot state itself, since by obscuring itself and failing to be noticed, it works on a finite and sensible subject, and not a conscious and knowing one. Eloquence, in contradistinction to the dictating voice of a pure rational subject, naturalizes consciousness as it literalizes it; it reaches its limit and hands itself over to another, delivering itself over from the orientation of a rational *I*. The prescription of this delivery, however, can itself be rational, or prudent, as Baudelaire puts it in the Wagner essay:

> To construct the ideal drama in full liberty, it will be wise to eliminate all difficulties that might arise out of technical, political or even too positively historical details. I will let the master [Wagner] speak for himself: "The only portrait of human life which may be called poetic is that in which motives which have meaning only for the abstract intelligence give way to the purely human impulses [*mobiles*] which govern the heart. This tendency (relative to the invention of the poetic subject) is the sovereign law which presides over poetic form and representation. . . . Rythmic arrangement and the (almost musical) ornament of rhyme are means available to the poet to endow his lines and phrases with a power which captivates as though by a charm and governs sentiment to its own taste. Essential to the poet, this tendency leads him to the very limit of his art, a limit that touches music directly; consequently, the poet's most complete work would be the one which . . . would be a perfect music." (*OC* 2: 791 / 123–24)

In the quoted Wagner text, the governing law of intelligibility is displaced onto the horizontal, immanent arrangement of the work. This law transfers its sovereignty to the sensible aspects of rhythm and the ornament of rhyme. In a hierarchical reversal, Wagner takes universality away from conceptual language and gives it to the sentiments of the heart, to a language of sensibility. This transference, which Wagner allies with music itself, raises music to the supreme art, or the veritable image of the essence of art.[6] Thus, in a single blow, Wagner's statement subordinates meaning to its material articulation at the same time that it subordinates this articulation as a case to a general law. The universal extension of his theory vies with that of his art. Wagner seems to evade this contradiction by claiming, in his identification of himself as *musician*, to articulate a theoretical position that would not be commanded by the logical controls or the conceptual obstacles of language; but in doing so, he claims for *his own* art the ability to do what he cannot say. The claim for music thus proceeds out of and is dependent upon a hierarchical division of means and end that interprets the material aspects of poetry as servants or tools to a commanding subject-general, as something external to and separable from poetry, which can be confused with *ornament*.

Wagner's attention in the text cited to the origin and essence of art in its material body—the musical *corps sonore*—immediately follows Baudelaire's directing attention away from "technical, political or even too positively historical details." In focusing on the fundamental status of the materiality of the signifier, Baudelaire hands the word over to the master himself, and, in quoting, renounces the ability to speak. If we take the content of Wagner's text at its word, it is the contiguity of Baudelaire's text—the space between the colon and the quotation mark—that assures Wagner his persuasive power. It is perhaps in this quotation that the poet indeed reaches the limit of his language and "touches music": not in Wagner's sense, but in the literal contact on the page between writing and the theme of music or between Baudelaire's text and that of "the Musician."

Baudelaire seems to gain authority by citation right at the point at which he recognizes his own professional limitation and calls in assistance. His authority is increased by the forgetfulness of citation, the illusion that another person is really speaking. The obfuscation of the prosaic concatenations enacted by citation populates Baudelaire's essay with textually divided literal, historical subjects. Wagner's generalization of music to encompass poetry, along with Baudelaire's subsumption of painting and music under the general rubric of writing or poetry, suggests that the articulation of art's essence is influenced by the particular art of which the speaker is said to be the master. What these determinations share is an essentializing relation to *one's own art* or to one's own or proper instrument.

Citation, in contrast—a prosaic technique par excellence—parcels out and distributes speech; it does not collect, but rather disperses and increases the availability of speech, repeating without expressing what the cited language is said to express. As Baudelaire carries out this transcription or scriptural translation of a piece of a foreign text into his own text, thus deflecting from the voice of a *je*, the device of quotation is obscured and we seem to read Wagner; Baudelaire seems to say, to add, nothing. At the same time, we forget the unreliability of speech as the first person solidifies into a third person. Citation mimics prosopopoeia in allowing a narrative mouthpiece to come to life and to speak in its own voice.

The effacement of the rhetoric of citation replaces narrative structures by musical metaphors as it puts the musician in the narrating poet's place. For Baudelaire, this replacement or substitution is the poetic activity par excellence, the essential activity shared by all the arts, which makes possible the expression of a subject in its work. In the following quotation, he makes explicit the role of musical metaphors in the passage from rhetorical technique to the mystical effect of the metaphoric dream. The paragraph refers to the work of Delacroix:

> One might say that this kind of painting, like magicians and hypnotists, can project its thought at a distance. This singular phenomenon pertains to the power of the colorist, the perfect accord of tones [*tons*], and the harmony (pre-established in the painter's brain) between the color and the subject. It seems as if this color, if one will pardon me this subterfuge of language to express extremely delicate ideas, thinks by itself, independently of the objects it clothes. Further, these admirable chords of color often make one dream of harmony and melody, and the impression one takes away from his pictures is often quasi-musical. (*OC* 2: 595 / *Art in Paris*, 141)

The technical extension of linguistic structures is replaced by the metaphor of their effect: the musical dream or the metaphor of reading. Delacroix's painting embodies, first, the ability to affect from afar by means of immanent relations between colors, tones, and their principle of composition (harmony). The autonomous work, through its combinations and concatenations, disseminates the thought of its creator by a substitution of agency: "It seems as if this color . . . thinks by itself." The material opacity of color *seems* to think by itself; its illusory autonomy is gained through a linguistic *subterfuge*. Language *goes under* in pretending to hand itself over to another medium. As the improper subject takes up its grammatical position, displaced linguistic powers take on musical shape and evoke *dreams* that are metaphors, musical substitutions that mark the impression left by the painting. The metaphoric function of musical terms here both describes and obscures the process of communication. Neither music nor painting can explain the rhetoric that allows them to come to the surface of this text. But nor can the linguistic subterfuge operate without calling in neighboring terms from the other arts to occupy grammatical positions. These mark, too, the limits of language's sovereignty.

In his defense of a rational aesthetics, Baudelaire goes so far as to claim: "A painting is a machine, all of whose systems are intelligible to a practiced eye; in which everything has its *raison d'être*, if the painting is good" (*OC* 2: 432 / *Art in Paris*, 57). This principle of perfection defines the knowable as the repeatable, just as for Wagner, the musical execution should be the repetition of the compositional conception. Likewise, Baudelaire accounts theoretically for the event of error. Describing Delacroix's painting, the passage continues:

> An occasional error in drawing [*dessin*] is sometimes necessary to avoid sacrificing something more important. This intervention of chance [*hasard*] in the business of Delacroix's painting is all the more improbable since he is one of those rare beings who remain original after having drawn deeply from all the true sources, and whose indomitable individuality has borne and shaken off the yokes of all the great masters in turn. (*OC* 2: 432 / *Art in Paris*, 57)

In this analysis, Baudelaire translates what may seem to be *hasard*, the "occasional error" implicit in the imperfection of matter, into a theoretical necessity, a necessity because it belongs to the essence of art to enter into materiality. The same imperfection allows for the deviance from historical precedent that constitutes artistic originality. This kind of error is the law governing the "*veritable* arabesque of sounds drawn by passion." Error and arabesque are veritable as long as they can still be related to an authorial source, just as particular performances—good and bad alike, faithful or disfiguring—are referred to the musical composition that precedes them.

Baudelaire's theorizing outlines a general structure describing the dependence of a general synchrony on its particular diachrony. He strives to find an ideal proposition that escapes the dependence it names. Baudelaire chooses Wagner as the representative of the synchrony of duality under the mark of theoretical necessity: "It was impossible for him not to think in a double manner, poetically and musically, not to catch sight of every idea in two simultaneous forms" (*OC* 2: 787–88 / *Painter of Modern Life*, 120). The approach to simultaneity overlaps with Baudelaire's efforts to make certain general ontological statements such as: "Every well-formed brain carries within it two infinities, heaven and hell" (*OC* 2: 795 / 127). In this kind of universalizing statement, Baudelaire attempts to comprehend cases in compliance or conformity with a prior conceptual unity.

Baudelaire compares Wagner's work, in its symmetry of interior and exterior, conception and execution, to ancient tragedy. But like Delacroix, every contemporary artist must emerge in a specific historical circumstance. "Romanticism" lends clothing and character to the specific apparition:

> The phenomena and the ideas which occur periodically throughout the ages always, at each resurrection, assume the complementary character of the variant

and the circumstance. . . . In the same way Wagner's poems, while revealing a sincere taste for and a perfect understanding of classical beauty, are also imbued with a strong dose of the romantic spirit. (*OC* 2: 790–91 / 122–23)

The break with the Classical ideal of the past marks the point at which the material circumstances of the work exceed the control of the subject as artist; the Romantic (or modern) work is coconstituted by its timely specificity. This same break establishes the originality of a particular artist, located in the singularity of manner viewed as an essential determinant of the work, which makes any particular rendition differ from whatever influences or models it may presuppose.

Baudelaire's theory itself oscillates here as it momentarily places the particular, spatiohistorical manner, the arena of production of a specific work or utterance, at an equal value with whatever intelligible or eternal idea may be read in it. This side of Baudelaire's thinking suggests that technical labor and the historical chance in which it occurs are not simply instruments of a spiritual commander. The spiritual commander, the *I* of language, cannot, of course, simply say this without controlling the instrument it uses to do so. The point of surrender is indicated by the replacement of a human grammatical subject by an oblique indication of agency (indicated by *par*). In the disappearing space of this displacement, a moment is passed through in which conception and execution stand on a par, stand *side by side*; but the moment is indeed passed through. It can only be said in the synaesthetic multiplication of terms extending into space, which is nontranslatable. Baudelaire writes:

> One can always momentarily abstract from the systematic element which every great willful artist inevitably introduces into his works; it remains, then, to seek and verify by what personal and proper quality he distinguishes himself from others. A man truly worthy of the great name of artist must possess something essentially *sui generis*, thanks to which he is *himself* and no one else. From this point of view, artists can be compared to different flavors in the realm of cooking. (*OC* 2: 806 / 137)

The tension between the symmetry of Classicism and the excess of Romanticism is set in the inversion of value of composition, as an ideal, and of performance, as both the expression of that ideal and the inevitable deviation from it:

> It is true that an ideal ambition presides over all of Wagner's compositions; but if in choice of subject and dramatic method he comes near antiquity, in his passionate energy of expression he is at the moment the truest representative of modernity. And to tell the truth, all the science, all the efforts, all the permutations of this rich spirit are no more than the very humble and zealous slaves of this irresistible passion. (*OC* 2: 806 / 137–38)

Baudelaire's *sui generis* brings together many of the paradoxical tensions between history and the eternal ideal of poetry notable throughout his work. In naming the quality that cannot be named, the "mysterious *je ne sais quoi*" (*OC* 2: 744), the "proper quality" by which one individual is distinguished from others, criticism initiates the distinction between nature and its representation, of the hero from the crowd. *Sui generis* functions as a critical category for that which cannot be subsumed within any given category; the cases collected under the name of *sui generis* cannot be understood as particular examples of a higher generality, for they are defined precisely as that which exceeds the logic of application and subsumption. The unity of the category of *sui generis* can only be inductive, a sort of abbreviation or association of what has been abstracted from amassed data. The artistic "elevation" that is not quite transcendent thus provides a model of truth that is not conceptual and ideal but only comes forth as it is historically performed. *Sui generis* exceeds the logic of technical repetition precisely at the point at which the musical relation between composition and performance must be understood as *something different from or other than* the relation of conception and execution belonging to a logic of identity and compliance.

Baudelaire's aesthetic prescribes an excess, an overflow, through translation, from an ideal position of origin into the hazards of singularity. In his essay on Victor Hugo, Baudelaire writes: "For what, then, is a poet (and I take the word in its broadest sense), if not a translator. . . . In the work of excellent poets, there is not a single metaphor, simile or epithet that is not adapted with mathematical precision to its circumstance. For these comparisons are drawn from the inexhaustible depths of *universal analogy*" (*OC* 2: 133). The poetic victory over circumstance (*circonstance actuelle*) is, at the same time, a necessary error, a fall, a capitulation before time and materiality. Once this structural flaw is introduced, it becomes very difficult to hold apart necessary and contingent mistakes. But to give up the attempt to do so would collapse the very structure of poetic distinction—"excellence"—into the confusion and causal determination of hyperimmanence. For Baudelaire, the artist's technical ability and relation to his tools assure the subordination of the work (as an execution) to the originary conception:

> If a very neat execution is necessary, it is so that the language of the dream may be translated as neatly as possible; if it should be very rapid, that is lest anything may be lost of the extraordinary vividness which accompanied its conception; if the artist's attention should even be directed to the material cleanliness [*propreté*] of his tools, that is easily intelligible, seeing that every precaution must be taken to make the execution agile and decisive.
> (*OC* 2: 625 / *Art in Paris*, 160)

Holding fast to this ideal origin of art as a general principle, Baudelaire distinguishes the "cleanliness" of the region of artistic technique from its deviant double: something "secondary," something "lower," which might be a bit dirtier, something like printing. Every necessary deviant implies the possibility of a faulty deviant; the very structure of adaptation and translation bears with it the errors that can never be foreseen or overseen:

> Obviously, all of these precepts are modified more or less according to the various temperaments of the artists. Nevertheless I am convinced that what I have just described is the surest method for those with rich imaginations. Consequently, if an artist's divergences from the method in question are too great, this is testimony that an abnormal and undue importance is being given to some secondary part of art. (*OC* 2: 626 / 161)

But how to determine the exact quantity of this deviation, this "too great," given an ideal of deviation and excess? How to assure the abasement of what is "abnormal and undue"?

The difference between the literal and the figurative aspects of inscription relies on the reassertion of the principle of authorship. Baudelaire stresses that rational calculation guides the artistic mastery of instruments. The principle of calculated control directly follows from and doubles the despotism of the ideal as it is operative in artistic expression. Again about Delacroix, Baudelaire writes:

> Now this is the principle from which Delacroix sets out—that a picture should first and foremost reproduce the intimate thought of the artist, who dominates the model as the creator the creation; and from this principle there emerges a second which seems at first sight to contradict it—to wit, that the artist must be meticulously careful concerning his material means of execution. He professes a fanatical regard for the cleanliness [*propreté*] of his tools and the preparation of the elements of the work. In fact, since painting is an art of profound ratiocination, and one that demands an immediate concurrence of a host of different qualities, it is important that the hand should encounter the least possible number of obstacles when it gets down to business, and that it should accomplish the divine orders of the brain with a servile rapidity: otherwise the ideal escapes. (*OC* 2: 433 / 58)

Technical proficiency masters the instruments and materials of expression by reducing them to a unified effect; in this compression of elements, the agent of the medium—the hand—is subordinated to the brain in the same gesture that renders the work a reproduction of the intimate thought of the artist. The artist becomes "present" in his expression to the degree to which the technical means of accomplishment are effaced and forgotten, to the degree to which the signifier becomes transparent for the signified. The work is received as a metaphor of the artist's subjectivity, a metaphor replacing the literal (material) elements of the work. In other words, the metaphor of expression is the very means by which attention is diverted from the letter so that this metaphor can emerge. The critical difference drawn between the expression of a subject and the "objective" (material, formal, technical) manner of its articulation, mystifies and subordinates the technical operations it simultaneously draws into focus. The technical principle, Baudelaire says, must follow from, and not precede, the law of expression, although in the chronology of communication, the effect must precede the expressive telos: "The effect produced on the spectator's soul is analogous to the artist's means" (*OC* 2: 433 / *Art in Paris*, 59). The metaphor of the effect, therefore, twists the term *analogy* from the letter of the work toward the metaphor of expression; it is hard to imagine how the impression produced by a painting would in any sense be "analogous" to the action of a brush or palette or the rational calculation of technique.

The key *rapidity* enacts the rhetorical shift from the technology of the letter to the rhetoric of metaphor; it indicates the origin in technical proficiency of that which exceeds it. In technical terms, it describes the technique of effacing technique—the very principle of virtuosity: "There is no chance [*hasard*] in art, any more than in mechanics. A happy invention is the simple consequence of a sound train of reasoning whose intermediate deductions one may perhaps have skipped" (*OC* 2: 432 / 57). The rapidity of eloquence abbreviates by excising certain steps, by editing out a certain history or context; the passage from a preexisting conception to its execution—its "literalization"—omits the explicit laws governing the produced "letters," giving only what has been deduced from them.

The absence thus inscribed by the rational producer places the receiver in a position of ignorance vis-à-vis the work, at the same time allowing for its possible reappropriation by a knowing subject. This ignorance refers both to the secondary position of the receptive subject, the epigone in a pedagogical diachrony, and to the finitude of one subject's knowledge enforced through the division of labor. Again we are reminded of the finitude of "Baudelaire" as a writer. With respect to painting or music, it is not possible to know whether the lack of attention to technical form issues from theoretical necessity or the chance lack of expertise. This "chance lack of expertise" does not mean that Baudelaire simply did not know what he was talking about; much more, it indicates the point at which the writer's generalities cannot penetrate another medium, where the letter of the arts is needed to complete the speech of the theorist.

The "despotism of the ideal," though it be conceptual master, is only one aspect of Baudelaire's aesthetics particularly evident in the assimilation of Wagner's method to that of Baudelaire's essay. Baudelaire progresses from an indistinct reader of the *feuilleton* to a distinguished critic and poet, from the angry ignorance of his historical experience of Wagner's music to its synchronic explication. At the same time that Wagner becomes an exemplary representative of Baudelaire's more general aesthetics, music is assimilated and subordinated to poetry, which occupies the position of the general principle of art.

The division of the positions of the rhetorical origin of the artwork and its destination (artist and receiver) — the difference between Wagner and Baudelaire — extends over a temporal expanse in which Wagner's production of the work precedes Baudelaire's reception of it. This temporal disparity draws the division of the arts, and thus Baudelaire's particular limitations as poet (rather than musician), into focus. That is to say, from the point of view of the receiver, the "first" in a diachronic series of experience cannot be known or understood. We have seen how Liszt presented this receptive ignorance in his description of the overture, the beginning of the opera. He uses heavily metaphoric language to describe the oscillating presence/absence of the artist in his work, thanks to which the principle of repetition can function without being known. Liszt functions as a mediator or translator for Baudelaire, both in his status as an author whose texts describe the unknown and in his function as virtuoso, whose job it is literally to transmit the musical message.

It is significant that in the first quotation of Liszt, he does not name the technical device of the leitmotiv; instead, he suggests its effect metaphorically. Baudelaire's delay of the specification of this device imitates the operation of the leitmotiv itself. The mnemotechnic of the leitmotiv, the calculated method by which immediacy will be produced and transferred, divides the positions of composer, in control of them, and audience, inevitably taken by surprise. It is a device that cannot possibly be noticed the first time it occurs, since it takes effect only in its repetition; to notice it does not dispel the effect but in fact forces the association it enacts. By means of the recognition it compels, it produces the unity of a character out of the temporal dispersion of music. The noting of the leitmotiv, at the same time, signals the systematicity, that is, the hand of the composer, in the work as his expression.[7]

Baudelaire's essay relates a certain history of the passage from ignorance to knowledge that occurs as a reordering of time; cognitive mastery is gained by a reorganization of a diachronous experience into a synchronic structure. The naming of the leitmotiv signals the transposition of a temporal expanse into a principle of repetition. In the passage in which Baudelaire specifies this principle in Wagner's music, he explicitly draws attention to the layering of repetition in his own essay:

> I have already spoken of certain melodic phrases whose relentless return
> [*retour*] . . . had intrigued my ear at the first concert given by Wagner. . . .
> We have observed how, in *Tannhäuser*, the recurrence of the two principle
> themes . . . served to wake up the public and put them into a state analogous
> to the situation at that moment. (*OC* 2: 801 / *Painter of Modern Life*, 132)

The overlapping of synchronic structures adjoins the poetic principle of repetition with the extension of musical performance. The compression of temporal disparity in the alignment of similarities in this paragraph of Baudelaire's text simulates, yet demystifies, the rapidity of musical eloquence. For Baudelaire, music, distended in resonating bodies, remains limited by division and chance. The speed of music tries to overcome the discursive distance and difference between origin and destination: "The more eloquent the music, the more rapid and accurate the power of suggestion, the greater the chances that sensitive men will conceive ideas in affinity with those that inspired the artist" (*OC* 2: 782 / 114). As Baudelaire masters the Wagnerian theory of the leitmotiv, music accelerates and begins to catch up with poetry—that is, with the *direct address* of lyric apostrophe and personification.

Immediately following the reference to his own series of repetitions, Baudelaire continues to explicate the principle of repetition in Wagner: "In *Lohengrin* this mnemonic method is applied much more meticulously. Each character is, *so to speak*, heraldically blazoned by the melody which represents his moral character and the role that he is called to play in the fable" (*OC* 2: 801 / 132, my emphasis). How, exactly, is force or voice lent to a figure? Baudelaire's explicit *pour ainsi dire* turns out of rhetoric into another medium, again by the term *par*, and thus hands over to musical melody the very power of prosopopoeia. Yet is power located in melody—its placeholder—or in the one who sends it forth and gives it direction? To articulate the poetic power of prosopopoeia, Baudelaire turns not to Wagner, its figurehead, but to the expert and specialist in handling, turning and trading, to the writer who is no writer, who has no language:

> Here I will hand over the word to Liszt, whose book (*Lohengrin et Tannhäuser*)
> I recommend to all those who love profound and refined art, and who, despite
> the somewhat bizarre language he affects—a species of idiom [*espèce d'idiome*]
> composed of extracts from several languages—knows how to translate with
> infinite charm the full range of the master's rhetoric. (*OC* 2: 801 / 132)

Baudelaire not only quotes Liszt, the performing artist par excellence, on points extremely important to his own aesthetics, but he also points explicitly to Liszt's privileged status as a translator of Wagner. Called in as an expert, the translator is nevertheless a servant to the master-composer, something like the actual printed matter that carries forth the rhetorical force of the enunciating subject as its origin. The impropriety of Liszt's language presents a parody of the *Gesamtkunstwerk*; it is the mere mixing together of worldly languages that ironically suggests but does not attain to a metaphysical totality. Above all, his *manner* of translating remains bound to the idiosyncratic determinants of Liszt as a contingent historical individual speaking his peculiarly savory *espèce d'idiome*.

We know the impropriety of Liszt's language, which is neither "original" nor native. In every sense, he writes incorrectly, offending all standards of authorship. Similarly, the language of translation does not claim an "originary" relation to meaning but rather presents the spectacle of the production of meaning by language in dissociation from a subject; the passage or "externalization" from an originary intention to expression is not the translator's task. Liszt's *espèce d'idiome* presents him as an aberrant from general rules of genre and language. This aberrance, made evident in the abstract autonomy of writing or musical performance, is of course a distinguishing feature of virtuosity for which it is often criticized. In the long citation of Liszt that follows, Liszt explicitly compares the Wagnerian leitmotiv to the poetic trope of prosopopoeia:

> His melodies are as it were *personifications of ideas*; their recurrence announces that of the sentiments which the words uttered do not indicate at all explicitly; it is to them that Wagner confides the task of revealing to us all the secrets of the heart. . . . Every situation or character of any importance is musically expressed by a melody which becomes its constant symbol. (*OC* 2: 802 / 134, Baudelaire's emphasis)

Liszt articulates the becoming-constant of the symbol through repetition in time, a force working beyond the clear contours of the semantics. Liszt both names the law of personification and exemplifies it in Baudelaire's text; he is the preferred mouthpiece for the repetition that finally, through accumulation, gives way to the idea of the *motif*. Liszt's opacity as an individual body, a specific alien text incorporated into Baudelaire's own, repeats the elusive persistence of melody itself.

In the same way that Baudelaire's text does not actually give forth melodies, Liszt never actually provides any content for the ideas, exactly, nor does he say precisely what it is that Wagner *confides* to his symbols. His descriptions tend to be extremely metaphoric, at times quite fantastic, for example, in the passage Baudelaire quotes: "There are phrases, the one, for example, in the first scene of the second act, which run through the opera like a poisonous snake, winding around its victims and fleeing before their holy champions" (*OC* 2: 802 / 134). It is hard to know in what sense Liszt is saying anything at all about Wagner's music. His writing consists precisely of this digressive style that wanders into metaphor at every turn and never arrives at its theme.[8] He thus keeps and reveals the artistic confession, is both key and lock to the secret.

"Liszt" plays a different role than does "Wagner," who imposes a decisive hierarchy through militaristic terminology. The conceptual focus on content in Baudelaire's citation of Wagner stands in contrast to the diversion into figurative language of Liszt's style. It is given to Wagner, this "artist in general," to speak the supremacy of music over poetry; but it is lent to Liszt to elaborate upon the poetic principle of music by virtue of which the content of sentiment is vaguely suggested—by virtue of which expression is confided to the work. Liszt is no conceptual despot, but only a stylistic aggregate. Baudelaire consistently designates him by a plurality of terms syntactically strung together: "an artist and a philosopher" (*OC* 2: 783 / 115). Liszt is a strange figure for Baudelaire, turning both inward and outward. At one end, he touches the public and the referential sphere of history, and at the other the texts into which he has passed. Liszt's famed virtuosity belongs, on the one hand, to the social conditions of performance that Baudelaire, too, considers to be extrinsic to the work itself. In this arena, the indeterminate public responds not to the work of art but to the virtuoso's rhetorical tricks focused on the specificities of instruments and proficiency. Baudelaire describes Wagner's concert in Paris: "The programme of his concert contained neither instrumental solos, nor songs, nor any of those exhibitions so dear to a public in love with virtuosi and their *tours de force*" (*OC* 2: 781 / 113). When the virtuoso puts himself forth as the particular individual he is, the public is persuaded by mere technical exhibitionism. Cleared of these distracting ornaments, Baudelaire says, the virtuoso's tours de force fall away as the work is redirected toward the thought-expression of the author-composer: "The public . . . took fire at certain of those irresistible passages in which it found the thought more clearly expressed, and Wagner's music triumphed by its own force [*propre force*]" (*OC* 2: 781 / 113). Liszt, as always, is both the protruding ego of the self-willed concrete performer and the self-effacing operator of the work of another.

As the *thought* of the work emerges, for Baudelaire, the absence of these "tours de force" translates into the work's "own force" (*propre force*). While this may appear to be a different force, as it passes through musical instrumentation, the composer's thought is indistinguishable from the virtuoso's persuasive powers. The work, Baudelaire says, must operate as the placeholder of the composer; as his representative, it is bestowed with a *propre force*, its own proper force. This force, said to proceed directly from the thought of the composer and not from the hands of the virtuoso, nevertheless exercises the very same rhetorical powers on the addressee; for the intelligibility of the piece is brought home to the audience by means of the "forced returns [*retours forcés*] of the melody"

(*OC* 2: 797). Baudelaire at once describes Wagner's despotism of the ideal as in-scribed in his work and practices it himself in subordinating the musical articu-lations to a single controlling idea, one which is intelligible. The particular mu-sical elements, "the principal formulae," for example, are not self-originating but are destined by another to carry out the material task of painting. The embod-ied melody thus has no *propre force* but works by *retours forcés*—repetitions of the composer's conception that invert the rejected "tours de force" of the virtuoso.

Baudelaire gives a one-sided reading here that manipulates material to direct it toward a single idea understood as the thought of a subject. To counteract this stated (Wagnerian) privileging of ideal and intellectual control, Baudelaire calls upon Liszt, at the same time allowing his own particular position to ex-plicitly come forth:

> The overture, *I say* [*dis-je*], sums up the dramatic thought in two songs, the religious song and the sensuous song, which, to use Liszt's phrase, "are placed here as two terms which, in the finale, find their equation." The *Pilgrims' Cho-rus* appears first, with the authority of the supreme law, as though to mark at the outset the true direction of life . . . that is to say, God. But as the intimate sense of God is soon drowned in every consciousness by the lusts of the flesh, the song representing holiness is gradually overwhelmed by the sighs of volup-tuousness. (*OC* 2: 794 / 126, my emphasis)

With the superfluous "I say" (*dis-je*), Baudelaire recalls his own finite status, mingling with the similar finite voice of the musical performer. His citation of Liszt is notable here precisely because the expression he borrows is not strik-ingly imaginative or insightful. It restates *first* the difference of two terms, and *then* their fusion: not in a vertical substitution, in a metaphor or idea, but rather, further along in the sentence, in the last temporal segment, technically named, of a musical composition ("finale"). Baudelaire draws on Liszt's ability to manipulate the technical aspect of music, and, remaining within the tempo-ral expanse in which it occurs, to adjoin it to the ideal, yet still remain himself, Liszt, and not sublate disparity within the simultaneity of an idea.

Insofar as Liszt is a virtuoso, he is himself the obstacle to the idea that he pre-sents; he is the chance element in Baudelaire's phrase "the more eloquent the music, the more rapid and accurate the power of suggestion, the greater the chances that sensitive men will conceive ideas in affinity with those that inspired the artist" (*OC* 2: 782 / 114). Recalling Delacroix's demand that his tools per-form with a *rapidité servile*, it would seem that "rapidity" takes on a figurative meaning for the accuracy of address, the *netteté* allowing the author-composer to be disclosed in his work. The notion of rapidity thus gives a material ana-logue to the exactitude of diction implying an adequacy of the expression to the idea. Because it is a term remaining within time, it approaches asymptotically but does not arrive at spontaneity or the simultaneity of the ideal. In the same way, the lyric symbol may function more efficiently—faster—than the drawn-out concatenations of Baudelaire's prose poems or criticism; but the exactitude or rapidity of diction, the eloquence, is not therefore less. Conversely, the eloquence of the symbol is no less calculated than the well-chosen citation. Expansion can seduce as well as lyric compression; neither can reliably "demystify."[9] Art does not stand, as inspiration, in opposition to the technological but rather is its double, though as we recall it may tend to abbreviate and edit out certain steps of reason.

It is with "rapidity" that the poet and the virtuoso part ways; for there is no common measure of time with which to compare the accuracy of the transposition of the synchronic structure of *langue* into an instance of *parole*, of myth into legend, conception into articulation (a translation into time) with the rapidity leading out of time from the expression to the idea. Baudelaire probably does not mean that eloquence depends on the actual speed of the music, the speed with which figures are drawn, or how fast the poet writes his letters. (In this literal sense, the laser printer, or in Baudelaire's time, the printing press, would be the most poetic of all.) That is to say, there is no way to compare how long it takes to write these letters to the "time" of what they ought to convey, no way to say, really, "how long it takes" to write a text. "A month" does not mean a month of uninterrupted pen to paper, for without the interruption of space there would be no text, and it would be no more accurate a designation than ten years. There is no way to tell whether this literal time is commensurate with its figure, except in its "effect."[10]

But for Liszt, the virtuoso and producer of musical performances, this is precisely what "rapidity" does mean. The preoccupation with this literal rapidity is a common criticism of virtuosi; for it encourages the meaningless cramming of as many turns of the hand as possible in the smallest amount of time, producing superfluous ornamentation meant only to show off the particular virtuoso's skill. The virtuoso's rapidity cannot be taken figuratively, just as his texts are wandering digressions and not succinct expressions. The virtuoso's rapidity consistently marks the absence of the idea in the execution: its disfiguration, in Berlioz's words, the destruction, and not the animation, of the work.

While we have seen Baudelaire compare the painting to a machine and claim an equal technical rigor for art in general, it is Liszt, and not Baudelaire, who is in danger of becoming a machine. The virtuoso works as a body in direct contact with an instrument—that is, within the immanent field of mechanistic causality, occupying the position of the artist-composer's external instrument of repetition. Liszt, so often accused of mere technical show in his prodigious performances, clearly has much at stake in attempting to differentiate himself from the mechanical; he thus tries to distinguish himself in writing:

> What is, then, the virtuoso? Is he really only a machine devoid of intelligence whose hands are a couple of levers doing the business of a barrel-organ? Does he not need to think or to feel to take care of his mechanical task, like a machine? Is he only to provide the ear with a photograph of the notes he has before him? Alas! we know only too well how many so-called virtuosi there are who are not even able to render a complete idea of the original they have before them on the music stand without distorting it and mutilating its sense! Their number is legion! (*GS* 6: 331 / *Gipsy*, 264)

And Liszt certainly does know this complaint about virtuosi all too well, since he often was the very object of it. While the mere fact that Liszt writes this text would suggest a negative reply, he himself leaves these rhetorical questions fatefully open. Like Baudelaire, he strives to disengage the receptive doubling of reading from mimetic determination and to reformulate the status of musical performance as interpretive reading. Such a reading would both repeat and exceed the work, that is, it would be both receptive and productive. Yet because we speak of Liszt here, it is hard to know if he is competent to set the standard for the distinction between "true" and "false" virtuoso: if he himself is a "false" virtuoso, then his claim to distinction would seem to be an impotent and empty statement. Liszt obscures the self-interest inhering in the possibility of his utterances by way of the grandest Romantic mystifier of all: nature. He groundlessly asserts being grounded in nature:

> The rights of the virtuoso-poet, of the virtuoso with a calling, are of an expanse hardly suspected by a public ruined by illegitimate and ignorant rulers. As for the vulgar feats of these mountebanks on the violin, the piano, the guitar, and the cornet (!), after swallowing such bad stuff, the public can no longer distinguish them from the miracles performed by the true Masters in the name of a miraculous privilege granted by nature. (*GS* 6: 331 / *Gipsy*, 264)

In this text, Liszt attempts to join the aristocratic group of master poets, leaving behind the vulgarity of the technical plane. Liszt provides no standard for, but simply asserts, distinction, and in this assertion would distinguish himself. By denying the foundation of virtuosity in technical skill and relocating its essence in the position of poetic master endowed with a natural right, Liszt participates in and reinforces the political and value-laden distinction of the noble and the vulgar determining the servile position of performance. When Liszt tries to write, he cannot help enacting the egotism of compositional despotism in his very attempt to refute it.

Liszt's prose gives credence to the contribution of performance to meaning or expression, not in the arrival of a sense, but in its delivery. The suspension of meaning, which concentrates on expanse, delays the idea it ought to convey: that is, it digresses. The critical difference between Baudelaire and Liszt resides in their relation to rational technology; recall Baudelaire's dictum "A happy invention is the simple consequence of a sound train of reasoning whose intermediate deductions one may perhaps have skipped" (*OC* 2: 432 / *Art in Paris*, 57). The excising of the laws of production, an abbreviation lending "rapidity" to the product, is concomitant with the inscription or literalization of the work. Liszt's prose, on the other hand, is slowed down or delayed in its digressive manner; he describes the rapidity of eloquence not as an abbreviation of steps but as the mystical replacement of technique by metaphor:

> It is a faculty that rids those fortunate to possess it of the cumbersome baggage of technical science, sluggishly pushing toward the esoteric regions that they win to spontaneously—a faculty that takes wing far less in the secrets of science than in a frequent communing with Nature. It is in the practice of these tête-à-têtes with Creation . . . that one best catches the message it holds hidden in the infinite harmonies of its shapes and sounds, of lights, of tumult and twitter, of terror and of voluptuousness. (*Chopin*, 182 / 96–97)

Liszt says that art originates in a mythic dialogue with nature. With this anthropomorphism, prosopopoeia has been brought into play. If Liszt throws its origin back to nature, he opens without entering the terrain of the poet; mythic dialogue is displaced onto the inaccessible position of the third person. Liszt's answer to the machine is still the plant; Baudelaire, on the other hand, does not want to be considered a vegetable:

> "A man so given to reasoning about his art cannot produce beautiful works naturally," say some who would thus strip genius of its rationality and assign it a function purely instinctual and, so to speak, vegetable. I pity those poets who are guided by instinct alone; I regard them as incomplete. In the spiritual life of the former a crisis inevitably occurs when they feel the need to reason about their art, to discover the obscure laws in virtue of which they have created, and to extract from this study a set of precepts whose divine aim [*but*] is infallibility in poetic production. (*OC* 2: 792–93 / *Painter of Modern Life*, 125)

With this gesture of intellectualization, Baudelaire posits a crisis or gap within the artistic life that allows him to gain mastery for the position of the poet-critic. If Baudelaire sets up a new elite governed by the science of prosopopoeia, his addition to music criticism through which he joins the journalistic dialogue is still, perhaps, his desire to be included at the musical gathering, his manner of participating as an uninvited guest. It was, indeed, an illustrious group: "Assembled around the piano," Liszt writes in *Chopin*, "in the illuminated zone, were several figures of brilliant renown," among them Heine, Meyerbeer, Delacroix, George Sand—and of course, the narrator, Liszt—but no Baudelaire. For Baudelaire, this "primal scene" of musical performance has not been lived, but strictly read.

The arrival of animation through music, from the exterior of prior texts to the poet, resurrects the ghost of a history, a remnant that cannot be reappropriated. Liszt describes the famous scene of Chopin's intimate performance at home as follows:

> His apartment . . . was lighted by only a few candles, gathered around one of those Pleyel pianos. . . . Corners left in darkness seemed to remove all limits of this room and to extend it into the shadows of space. In a play of light and shade, clothed in a whitish slip-cover, a piece of furniture could be seen: vague in outline, it stood like a specter come to hear the sounds that had called it forth. The light concentrated around the piano fell on the floor, gliding over the surface like a spreading wave and mingling with the incoherent gleamings of the hearth where, from time to time, orange-colored flames, short and broad, shot up like curious gnomes summoned by words in their own tongue. A single portrait—of a pianist, an admiring, sympathetic friend— seemed called to be the constant listener to the ebb and flow of tone that moaned and growled, murmured and expired on and about the surface of the nearby instrument. By weird chance the responding surface of the mirror, duplicating the image for us, reflected only the handsome oval face and the silky blond curls which so many brushes have copied, which the burin has just reproduced for those who are charmed by an elegant pen. (*Chopin*, 173–74 / 90–91)

The piano, the material instrument, stands as the illuminating center animating sound and light, calling the furniture to life in this language of things. If the similarity of this passage to Baudelaire's translation in "Correspondances" lends the latter somewhat more historical reference than it claims to have, it can only be a reference to the division of language from historical referentiality. The metaphoric language of this passage by Liszt, the repeated use of the word *sembler*, "to seem," for example, detaches it from any distinct depiction of an actual event; the common historical ground can be only textual, the *lieu commun* of erudition and reading. The attribution of the power of animation to music can only occur by a linguistic enactment of that very power; it is impossible to decide whether language projects its own phantasm on the figure from which it claims to receive it. The piano is the necessary but only apparent ground of historical contingency by means of which figures are gathered and placed next to their means of production. Musical aura is the metaphor that arrives, the vague predecessor that gives subjectivity a medium in which "by weird chance" to find itself reflected. For, despite the blond curls, unmistakably Chopin, who else is portrayed in the chance portrait illuminated during Chopin's performance, what pianist and admirer but his sympathetic friend—and antagonistic rival—his biographer, Liszt himself?

# 8. Music, Painting, and Writing in Baudelaire's *Petits poëmes en prose*

Baudelaire's juxtapositioning of music, painting, and writing brings out the tension between technique and effect, the letter and its figurative animation, printed matter and the metaphor of reading replacing it. This tension can be described in terms of grammatical structure, in particular the establishment of a subject position and its animation through the attribution of predicates. The intervention of prosopopoeia leaves questionable the difference between a mechanics of cause and effect between message and receiver, on the one hand, and meaningful or sympathetic communication, on the other. The ideal of sympathetic adjoinment through communication is projected by a diversion from the technology of instruments, a diversion performed by replacing the technological by metaphor. This, too, is how translation is translated into reverie, sense experience into impression and reception, and graphic marks into meaningful carriers.

In this famous passage from the introduction to the *Petits poëmes en prose*, Baudelaire brings out the crucial role of music in his prosaic project: "Who among us, in his moments of ambition, has not dreamed the miracle of a poetic prose, musical without rhythm and without rhyme, supple enough and rugged enough to adapt itself to the lyrical movements of the soul, the undulations of reverie, the jibes of consciousness?" (*OC* 2: 275–76 / ix–x). This musical language stands as an external marker of the soul's movements, a point that emerges in a dreamy question that reaches out to an unconfirmed consensus. The musical resonance of the prose poems connects a community of readers, and, like the musical translations in "Richard Wagner and *Tannhäuser* in Paris," interrupts the sphere of division that subtends it. The interruption of reading that opens textual space takes the form, in this introduction, of a direct address that presumably interpellates Arsène Houssaye, to whom the collection is dedicated: "I have a little confession to make to you. It was while leafing through [*en feuilletant*], for the twentieth time, the famous *Gaspard de la nuit* of Aloysius Bertrand (has not a book known to you, to me, and to a few of our friends the right to be called famous?) that the idea came to me to attempt something analogous" (*OC* 2: 275 / ix). Once again, the infinitely repeatable leafing through the leaves of the *feuilleton* offers the beginning and point of departure for what will become original. This ultramundane reference, invoking the ghost of the hands that hold the text, is accompanied by a stilted list of divided and individuated but empty pronomial subjects: *vous, moi, nos amis*. Fame, too, is strangely emphasized as a predicate simply attached to those with whom we are familiar. This nonspecific group, echoing the partners in prose in the famous serpent metaphor, also recalls the alignment of translators and readers in the Wagner essay. Baudelaire's introduction to the *Petits poëmes en prose* names and calls upon the unknown pronouns we are left to imagine at the beginning of the Wagner essay: the "impartial readers" he invokes there through probability. The power of prosopopoeia allows a clearer *you* to emerge in the introduction to the prose poems; it becomes particularly distinct when it converges with the *I* in the project of musical translation: "You yourself, dear friend, have you not tried to translate into *song* the strident cry of the *Glazier* [du *Vitrier*]?" (*OC* 2: 276 / x). The song gathers up experience into a form compatible with both music and poetry; the italics indicate its separation from that experience. The example both joins and separates Houssaye's poem, "La Chanson du vitrier" (The glazier's song), dedicated to Hoffmann, and Baudelaire's own "Mauvais Vitrier" (The bad glazier). Originality is glazed over with multiple sources, references, recollections, and duplications.

## Absorption, Loss, and Metaphor: "Le 'Confitéor' de l'artiste"

In the prose poem "Le *Confitéor* de l'artiste," Baudelaire picks up the Latin name for a formulaic confession, institutionalized and outdated, already putting into question the possibility of a self-originating expression. The poem begins with a series of exclamations or exhalations describing the intrusion of nature, while no subject has yet been named: "Que les fins de journées d'automne sont péné-trantes! Ah! pénétrantes jusqu'à la douleur! car il est de certaines sensations déli-cieuses dont le vague n'exclut pas l'intensité" (How poignant are the late after-noons of autumn! Ah! poignant to the verge of pain! for there are certain deli-cious sensations which are no less intense for being vague) (*OC* 1: 278 / 3). The second paragraph depicts the "drowning" of the gaze in a natural exterior. The stillness of the tableau then becomes agitated as the eye focuses on a small boat, explicitly compared to the existence—that is, to the distended being-in-time and experiential extension—of a subject: "Une petite voile frissonnante à l'horizon, et qui par sa petitesse et son isolement imite mon irrémédiable existence" (a tiny sail shivering on the horizon which, by its littleness and its isolation imitates my irremediable existence). While the comparison is explicit through the verb *imiter*, the syntax of this paragraph is loose, stringing together phrases that are not grammatically bound together but that work through juxtaposition.

While the prose writer has deflated the metaphor by its explicitness, the ex-tension of juxtaposition counteracts this to veil its own action. The banal sim-ile is interrupted by a disconnected musical phrase, after which a curious ex-change takes place:

> Mélodie monotone de la houle, toutes ces choses pensent par moi, ou je pense par elles (car dans la grandeur de la rêverie, le moi se perd vite!); elles pensent, dis-je, mais musicalement et pittorresquement, sans arguties, sans syllogismes, sans déductions. (*OC* 1: 278)

> Monotonous melody of the waves, all these things think through me, or I think through them (for in the grandeur of reverie, the *I* is quickly lost!); they think, I say, but musically and picturesquely, without quibblings, without syllogisms, without deductions. (3)

The musical veil diverts attention from the explicit comparison and allows an exchange between the unspoken *I* and *things*, where each is the musical instru-ment of the other. The dual language resulting is poetic: musical, picturesque, alogical, the *I* is decentered and even the *moi* is lost.

The narrator has performed an ecstatic movement, exhaling and confiding himself to the marks on the page or the boat on the sea to take his place and trace his movement. The text has replaced the author, who has been stretched beyond the delimited space of the subject position. Suddenly, the musical lyre breaks and the strings revert to the nerves, the physical extension, that the mu-sic temporarily mystified:

> Toutefois, ces pensées, qu'elles sortent de moi ou s'élancent des choses, devien-nent bientôt trop intenses. L'énergie dans la volupté crée un malaise et une

souffrance positive. Mes nerfs trop tendus ne donnent plus que des vibrations criardes et douloureuses. (*OC* 1: 278)

These thoughts, whether they come from me or spring from things, soon, at all events, grow too intense. Energy in voluptuousness creates uneasiness and positive suffering. My nerves, strung too tautly, can no longer give out anything but shrill and painful vibrations. (3)

The nonpoetic pain of self-loss, extension, and dispersion reverberates through the taut nerve, where the subject is held and plucked by another: "Nature, enchanteresse sans pitié, rivale toujours victorieuse, laisse-moi!" (Nature, pitiless sorceress, ever victorious rival, let me be!). The Aeolian harp has another side, one less delightful, one of pain and loss. The music of poetic ecstasy reverses into the painful mechanics of a stretched nerve, a plucked string, a technical instrument. Correspondence and reciprocity snap into rivalry, tug-of-war, delusion.

### Painter Mouthpiece: Voice Lent ("La Corde")

In "Le *Confiteor*," the *I* enters temporarily into a flowing exchange: "ces choses pensent par moi, ou je pense par elles" (things think through me, or I think through them), where subject and things are alternately instrument and origin of the musical thoughts pervading and traversing the atmosphere. But as this aesthetic thinking becomes fixated on things, the speaking *I* marks itself out in explicit differentiation from the things it has deposited. At the same moment that the narrative lends animation to things, the *I* emerges as the hidden speaker, the grammatical manipulator, supporting the world of correspondence it projects: "elles [les choses] pensent, dis-je, mais musicalement et pittoresquement" (they think, *I say*, but musically and picturesquely [my emphasis]) without quibblings, without syllogisms, without deductions. Here, the *je* speaks actively and directly; in the relation of reciprocity, in contrast, agents think through oblique instruments. In such cases, the subject position is not the point of origin and control, but one position linked to others in a relationship of dependence. As the actively speaking *je* emerges, it breaks its bonds with its surroundings, the nerve snaps, the cry interrupts the harmony. Thus, through the extension of the narrative, the *je* undergoes a movement outward, a snap, a break, and a recollection inward, leaving a chasm—and indeed an antagonistic one—between the *je* and nature.

In "La Corde," the subject position stands in direct contiguity with sense experience. It is allotted strictly to the painter, who defines his vocation in these very terms:

Ma profession de peintre me pousse à regarder attentivement les visages, les physiognomies, qui s'offrent dans ma route, et vous savez quelle jouissance nous tirons de cette faculté qui rend à nos yeux la vie plus vivante et plus significative que pour les autres hommes. (*OC* I: 328–29)

My profession as a painter impels me to scrutinize attentively every face, every physiognomy that crosses my path, and you know what delight we get from this faculty which gives life more vitality, in our eyes, and renders it more significant for us than for other men. (64)

The painter experiences things directly, mediating that experience through a hypersensitive faculty of perception. The writer, in contrast, appears only briefly in the accusative case in the poem's first line, assuming the stance of a journalistic reporter. The entire text is quoted speech; the writing subject enters only once, graphically set off by dashes: "—me disait mon ami—" (—my friend said to me—). Never speaking in the first person, the narrator simply presents an anonymous story told to him (though based on fact).[1]

"La Corde" tells of the extended string that becomes the instrument of death, just as the ecstatic movement of the poetic voice leads to self-loss and dissipation. By means of the cord, the young model transforms himself into the "still life" that the painter habitually produces, just as "things" begin to think independently in "Le *Confitéor*." It is not coincidental that Baudelaire chooses a painter to be the narrator of this story of death, which is told obliquely through quotation that distances the reporter from any involvement in the events depicted. The dedication, "To Edouard Manet," remains a conventional address; this proper name is never explicitly merged with the painter-friend who is the quoted narrator. No animated dialogue occurs between this painter-speaker and the reporter-receptacle, who never enters into the nominative case, neither speaks nor replies, but simply renders a report, a tableau, a portrait, a "still life": a picture of death.

The address to Manet remains within the convention of a dedication and takes on no dialogic animation. In the penultimate paragraph, too, we find prosaic and lifeless versions of address and correspondence:

Je reçus un paquet de lettres: les unes, des locataires de ma maison, quelques autres des maisons voisines; l'une, du premier étage; l'autre, du second; l'autre, du troisième, et ainsi de suite . . . toutes tendant au même but, c'est-à-dire à obtenir de moi un morceau de la funeste et béatifique corde. (*OC* I: 331)

I received a bundle of letters: some from tenants in my own building, some from the neighboring houses; one from the first floor, another from the

second; another, from the third and so on . . . all with the same goal [*but*] in
view, that is to say, to get from me a piece of the fatal and beatific rope. (67)

These neighbors communicate by the dead letters of literal correspondence, all,
like the animated musical letters of the poetic work, *tending toward a single goal*,
though each presented in its own variation and style: "Les unes en style demi-
plaisant, comme cherchant à déguiser sous un apparent badinage la sincérité de
la demande; les autres lourdement effrontées et sans orthographe, mais toutes
tendant au même but" (some in a half-playful style, as if seeking to disguise the
sincerity of their request . . . others grossly brazen and misspelled, but all with
the same goal in view). In this poem, the famous lyric *I* is utterly effaced and
displaced onto another, a painter. As the origin of speech is placed elsewhere,
we find both a reciprocity and a reversed valuation of the structure of correspondence (*unité de but, variété de moyens*: unity of purpose, variety of means)
that Baudelaire attributes to artistic communication and production. Synchro-
nous communication through letters is transferred to the aggregation of divided subjects in the compartments of the apartment building. And of course,
with the cutting conclusion of the poem, one cannot help recalling Baudelaire's
remark in the preface to the prose poems:

> Mon cher ami, je vous envoie un petit ouvrage dont on ne pourrait pas dire,
> sans injustice, qu'il n'a ni queue ni tête, puisque tout, au contraire, y est à la fois
> tête et queue, alternativement et réciproquement. Considérez, je vous prie,
> quelles admirable commodités cette combinaison nous offre à tous, à vous, à
> moi et au lecteur. Nous pouvons couper où nous voulons, moi ma rêverie, vous
> le manuscrit, le lecteur sa lecture. (*OC* 1: 275)

> My dear friend, I send you a little work on which no one could say, without in-
> justice, that it has neither a tail nor a head, since, on the contrary, the whole
> thing is at once both head and tail, alternatively and reciprocally. Consider, I
> beg you, what admirable conveniences this combination offers to us all, to you,
> to me, and to the reader. We can cut wherever we please, me my reverie, you
> the manuscript, the reader his reading. (ix)

The convenience of the digestible commodity recurs in the mother's proposed
commerce. While Baudelaire's preface, also an open and conventional address,
speaks figuratively of the cutting and commodification, he takes advantage of
the muteness of painting to let the dead letters speak for themselves and to
show their ability to harbor the end of expressivity in the literalness of the material mark.

## Professional Specialization: "Les Vocations"

"La Corde" not only implies a covert historical reference, including a proper name, but also translates terms into the conditions of finite existence, including separation and division of labor. Painter, poet, musician, journalist, dreamer—these are all jobs. It is not surprising that "La Corde" and "Le Thyrse," which I shall suggest is a sort of inverse correlate to the former, are bridged by the short narrative entitled "Les Vocations." Here, the first three boys relate experiences of various degrees of absorption and relation to their environs. The first tells of the enclosure in the theatrical spectacle; the second envisions ecstatic correspondence and exchange between himself and nature, much like the speaker in "Le *Confitéor*"; and the third tells of his erotic experience in bed with his nurse, culminating with the immersion of his head in her hair, hinting at "La Chevelure." The fourth boy identifies himself as a placeless self, as an unstable movement of desire: "Je ne suis jamais bien nulle part, et je crois toujours que je serais mieux ailleurs que là où je suis" (I am never content anywhere, and I always think I would be better off somewhere other than where I am) (*OC* 1: 334 / 70). He describes his ideal existence as that of a group of musicians he has seen playing in a nearby village. These musicians present the spectacle of a self-sufficient and self-animating force, irresistibly compelling. The boy describes:

> Ils étaient grands . . . avec l'air de n'avoir besoin de personne. Leurs grands yeux sombres sont devenus tout à fait brillants pendant qu'ils faisaient de la musique; une musique si surprenante qu'elle donne envie tantôt de danser, tantôt de pleurer, ou de faire les deux à la fois, et qu'on deviendrait comme fou si on les écoutait trop longtemps. . . . Ils étaient si contents d'eux-mêmes, qu'ils ont continué à jouer leur musique de sauvages, même après que la foule s'est dispersée. (*OC* 1: 334)

> They were tall . . . with an air of needing no one. Their large somber eyes flickered brilliantly while they played music; a music so astonishing that first it made you want to dance, then cry, or to do both at once, and you would almost go mad if you listened to it for too long. . . . They were so happy with themselves that they kept playing their wild music even after the crowd had dispersed. (70)

The boy wishes to join this band of musicians who seem to answer to the stereotype of Gypsies, who move effortlessly from this musical and magical animation to the collection of money, sleep beneath the open sky, require no audience, and have no home. The boy wishes to join them, but in the end does not dare, "sans doute parce qu'il est toujours très difficile de se décider de n'importe quoi" (probably because it is always so hard to decide anything at all) (71) and also because he fears being apprehended at the French border.

The boy describes a fascination with musical performance not unlike the fascination that Liszt describes in his book on the Gypsies; the allure is great, yet the French boy cannot quite risk the boundaries of his identity and become dispersed in the placelessness of the unwritten life that, attractive as it is, seems to pose the danger of madness and loss of self. This boy, too, sends out an unaddressed message that happens, by chance, to be received by the narrator, who is coincidentally eavesdropping. The narrator concludes:

> L'air peu intéressé des trois autres camarades me donna à penser que ce petit était déjà un incompris. Je le regardais attentivement; il y avait dans son oeil et dans son front ce je ne sais quoi de précocement fatal qui éloigne généralement la sympathie, et qui, je ne sais pas pourquoi, excitait la mienne, au point que j'eus un instant l'idée bizarre que je pouvais avoir un frère à moi-même inconnu. (*OC* 1: 335)

> From the indifferent air of his three companions I decided that this little fellow was already one of the *un-understood*. I looked at him closely; there was in his eye and on his forehead that precociously fatal *je ne sais quoi* which generally distances sympathy, and which, I don't know why, excited mine, and to such an extent that for an instant I had the bizarre idea that I could have a brother unknown to myself. (71)

In this momentary identification, the narrator achieves an instant of being elsewhere, of losing and finding himself in an other, but in a manner controlled and reduced to the two, the pair of the boy and the narrator. The poetic instant does not drag the narrator away in a Gypsy band; it simply sparks and passes. As the sun sets, "les enfants se séparèrent, chacun allant, à son insu, selon les circonstances et les hasards" (the children separated, each setting out, all unconsciously, according to circumstances and chance) (71). They are reabsorbed into the crowd, "mélodie monotone de la foule." The *je* was touched indeed, for a moment, and resounded sympathetically. But it ends up safely protected by the quotation marks, remaining in the neutral position of reporter: though for an instant, the hand that quotes reached inside the frame.

## At Last: Voice Borrowed ("Le Thyrse")

In "La Corde" and "Les Vocations," we witness an oblique representation of speech. The narrator stands as an uninvolved onlooker, a reporter, while the speaker position is displaced onto an other. This other stands in direct contact with a potentially threatening experience that is both transmitted and held at a distance through the technique of reported speech. The figure of the painter in particular, like his medium, is a figure of opacity that protects the first-person narrator from the spectacle of death in "La Corde" and from the desire for self-loss in "Les Vocations." The insertion of mouthpieces is a protective device, especially in the hyperbolized form of the painter whose canvas stands between the eye and nature, who stands as both nerve and *corde* connecting and separating. The poet-writer manipulates the painter's mouth, displaces the painful movement between extension and retraction seen in "Le *Confitéor*" and makes available a sensual world that is simultaneously a temptation and a threat. The narrative distance installed through displaced speech holds apart the *sujet d'énonciation* and the *sujet d'énoncé*, allowing both for momentary identification: self-loss, ecstatic emptying, dispersion of voice, and retraction: concentration, recollection, and authorial stability. The dislocation between the narrator and the quoted narrator in "La Corde" is legible in the noncorrespondence between the painter in the dedication ("to Manet") and the "friend" quoted in the poem. Their identity is never made explicit, though a reader may hypothesize this substitution.

"Le Thyrse" also opens with a conventional dedication, "To Franz Liszt." But in this poem, the seemingly dead convention of oblique address will be animated, the letter opened as the poem twists inside the envelope and transforms the letter into a correspondence and correspondence by mail into direct address. This turn inside the addressed envelope parallels and offers a somewhat different perspective on the alternations between literal and figurative, center and periphery, inside and outside, unity and self-differentiation that are generally the objects of discussion in this poem.[2]

"Le Thyrse," too, exhibits the tensions between centered control and decorative dispersion that are by now quite familiar. The poem begins with the seemingly straightforward question "Qu'est-ce qu'un thyrse?" (What is a thyrsus?) (*OC* 1: 335 / 72). The dictionary-like response is both mythological and analytical:

> Selon le sens moral et poétique, c'est un emblème sacerdotal dans la main des prêtres ou des prêtresses célébrant la divinité dont ils sont les interprètes et les serviteurs. Mais physiquement ce n'est qu'un bâton, un pur bâton, perche à houblon, tuteur de vigne, sec, dur et droit. (*OC* 1: 335)

> According to its moral and poetic sense it is a sacerdotal emblem in the hand of priests or priestesses celebrating the divinity of which they are the interpreters and the servants. But physically it is just a stick, a simple stick, a staff to hold up hops, a prop for training vines, straight, hard, and dry. (72)

While this dried-up and lifeless physical instrument is erected as a central prop, digressive decorations are allowed to circle and unfold about it: "Autour de ce bâton, dans des méandres capricieux, se jouent et folâtrent des tiges et des fleurs, celles-ci sinueuses et fuyardes, celles-là penchées comme des cloches ou des coupes renversées" (Around this stick in capricious meanderings stems and flowers play and gambol, some sinuous and wayward, others hanging like bells, or like goblets upside-down) (*OC* 1: 335–36 / 72). The text maintains tight control, allowing only brief and oblique appearances of potentially endless and meaningless digression; it shows up but is granted only a limited territory on the page. Following this intrusion of digression, three questions reorient the text toward its definitional project. The first two questions establish a hierarchy in which the straight line serves as the center of control, although the negative form of the questions allows at least for a semblance of uncertainty:

> Ne dirait-on pas que la ligne courbe et la spirale font leur cour à la ligne droite et dansent autour dans une muette adoration? Ne dirait-on pas que toutes ces corolles délicates, tous ces calices, explosions de senteurs et de couleurs, exécutent un mystique fandango autour du bâton hiératique? (*OC* 1: 336)

> Wouldn't one say that the curvilinear and the spiral lines are courting the straight line and dance around it in mute adoration? Wouldn't one say that all these delicate corollas, all these calyxes, explosions of smells and colors, are executing a mystical fandango around the hieratic rod? (72)

The third question, which puts into question and ironizes the act of hierarchical organization itself, opens the possibility of the reversal of the hierarchy, leaving the questions unsolved, suspended, and undecidable: "Et quel est, cependant, le mortel imprudent qui osera décider si les fleurs et les pampres ont été faits pour le bâton, ou si le bâton n'est que le prétexte pour montrer la beauté des pampres et des fleurs?" (But what imprudent mortal would dare to decide whether the flowers and the vines have been made for the stick, or whether the stick is not a pretext for displaying the beauty of the vines and the flowers?) (*OC* 1: 336 / 72). These rhetorical questions end up delaying and subverting the search for an answer implied by the opening question.

While much attention has been devoted to the problems of the copula,[3] representation, equivalence, duality and unity, literal and figurative, structure and embellishment, I would like to focus here instead on Liszt's role in "Le Thyrse." In the center of the poem, the impersonal language of the opening is abruptly interrupted by an explicit proposition of representational equivalence that is also a direct address. The instance of address begins obliquely with the personal possessive pronoun: "Le thyrse est la représentation de votre étonnante dualité, maître puissant et vénéré, cher Bacchant de la Beauté mystérieuₓ sionnée" (The thyrsus is the representation of your astonishing duality, gₓ and venerated master, dear Bacchant of mysterious and passionate Beauty) (*OC* I: 336 / 72). Liszt is installed here as the unifying figurehead for all the dualities and pluralities of the poem, as both the unified anthropomorphic figure apparently supporting the predicate of duality and the constructed addressee of the poetic voice. Filling both these capacities, the name "Liszt" twists from a historical referent toward a poetic figure. With the direct address, verging on apostrophe, the poetic *I* emerges invisibly, yet audibly, in the unenunciated speaker position, amplifying the implicit voice inscribed in the previous rhetorical questions.

Liszt is addressed not as the Dionysian divinity himself, but as a "bacchant": mediator and link to the divine source, both servant and master, both thyrsus and the one holding it. Liszt's effect is compared to the intoxicating shaking of the Bacchic emblem on the heads of the followers. Both the bacchant and Liszt act directly on others through physical agitation, allowing the metonymic contact to flow from the Muse to the audience as in Plato's *Ion*. It is Liszt's particular power to agitate the instrument, resonate the string, in such a way as to transform it into a directed message, seducing and intoxicating the addressees. As the relation between Liszt and his audience is thematized, an *I-you* axis interrupts the third-person discourse of the opening. As the thyrsus is embellished, the dead stick comes to life, the distance between mythic history and the profane history of the Parisian entertainment scene collapses, and the reader of the *feuilleton* is drawn into the discursive present of direct address. At the same time, the distance between Liszt and Baudelaire is reduced as an unanswered literal written correspondence is translated into the animation of an intimate, though still unanswered, dialogue.[4]

After a long hyphen, the text begins, after all, to offer some answers about the thyrsus: "Le bâton, c'est votre volonté . . . les fleurs, c'est la promenade de votre fantaisie autour de votre volonté" (The stick is your will . . . the flowers the wandering of your fancy around your will) (72). As the text accelerates, its organizational logic loosens; the disparate elements of art are linked on the page, conjoined by spatial proximity with little help from grammar or syntax:

Ligne droite et ligne arabesque, intention et expression, roideur de la volonté, sinuosité du verbe, unité du but, variété des moyens, amalgame tout-puissant et indivisible du génie, quel analyste aura le détestable courage de vous diviser et de vous séparer? (*OC* I: 336)

Straight line and arabesque line, intention and expression, rigidity of the will, sinuosity of word, unity of goal, variety of means, all-powerful and indivisible amalgam of genius, what analyst would have the detestable courage to divide and separate you? (73)

Yet to whom does this "you" (*vous*) refer? Does it refer to all the preceding elements? To Liszt? To all who share the immortal name of genius? The following line, beginning "Cher Liszt," draws attention back to the specific situation of dialogic address. What began as an oblique interpellation of an other through possessive pronouns now becomes animated to the point of an explicit exclamatory apostrophe: "Cher Liszt . . . philosophe, poète et artiste, je vous salue en l'immortalité!" (Dear Liszt . . . philosopher, poet and artist, I salute you in immortality!) (*OC* 1: 336 / 73). Through the animation of this direct address, a hand is held out to Baudelaire, too, to step onto the Elysian field. As the envelope is turned inside out, Baudelaire has joined Liszt in the eternal city (*ville éternelle*) of artists.

It is odd that in the stringing together of terms in the poem's final paragraph, neither music, virtuoso, nor composer is specifically mentioned. Perhaps the poem is no more about a referent Liszt than it is about literal music, or music *proprement dite*. As the constructed addressee of this poem, Liszt is not master but a string on Baudelaire's lyre allowing his own voice to resound. Again we are confronted with the undecidability of the power of animation. While it is apparently lent to a musical personage, it actually emanates from the powers of prosopopoeia and predication, which place the figure and enact the transfer; the writer makes objects sing. The writer's power to animate through displacement comes out especially in the following juxtaposition of places in which Liszt stands as the one able to stand anywhere, able to displace his voice, and to transcend genre, media and geographical boundaries:

> Cher Liszt, à travers les brumes, par-delà les fleuves, par-dessus les villes où les pianos chantent votre gloire, où l'imprimerie traduit votre sagesse, en quelque lieu que vous soyez . . . improvisant des chants de délectation ou d'ineffable douleur, ou confiant au papier vos méditations abstruses. (*OC* 1: 336)

> Dear Liszt, through the mists, beyond the rivers, above the distant cities where the pianos sing your glory, where the printing press translates your wisdom, in whatever place you may be . . . improvising songs of joy or of ineffable sorrow, or confiding to paper your abstruse meditations. (73)

Liszt's historicized transcendence—the musical tournée booked from Moscow to London—strings territories together and does not rise above them; only its recording in the poetic metaphor, its textual substitution, detaches him from his geography. Similarly, the printing press translates his spirit as journalism spreads and communicates across nations and ground. The press stands as a metaphor for the language of expression: it is a socioeconomic machine that disseminates and distributes poetic voice, just as the mechanics of metaphor and enunciative positioning allow pianos to sing. Is it the virtuoso or the poet who makes his words legible or makes pianos sing his glory—the same glory laid out in the first paragraph of the poem: "Une gloire étonnante jaillit de cette complexité de lignes et de couleurs" (An amazing glory surges from this complexity of lines and colors) (*OC* 1: 336 / 72).

Baudelaire seems to give the poetic power to Liszt yet in the end takes it back through the figure of direct address. In the same way, opposed elements enjoy a passing equality as they lie side by side on the page. For a moment, hierarchical organization is open; but it is reinstated in this formulation privileging center over periphery:

> —Le bâton, c'est votre volonté, droite, ferme et inébranlable; les fleurs, c'est la promenade de votre fantaisie autour de votre volonté; c'est l'élément féminin exécutant autour du mâle ses prestigieuses pirouettes. (*OC* 1: 336)

> —The rod is your will, straight, steady and unshakable; the flowers, the wanderings of your fancy around your will; it is the feminine element executing its marvelous pirouettes around the male. (72)

Here, the text clearly privileges the male intention and will over the female execution and arabesques of expression in action. At the same time, through his address to Liszt, Baudelaire talks himself into posterity.

Some critics stress the unity of duality in "Le Thyrse," giving truth value to these final statements rather than to those passed over and claim that the poem establishes an equivalence of poetry and music. While another trend of criticism insists on the nonclosure of this poem, pointing to the ways in which its apparent symmetry and claims for unity in fact undermine the very concept of unity (or the opposition between unity and duality), both critical directions focus primarily on formal aspects of the poem. But there are two important problems in the poem that are usually mentioned but generally ignored: Liszt and Thomas de Quincey.

The address to Liszt is usually taken to refer to "music" in some nonspecified way. Barbara Johnson does not mention him at all. Richard Klein gives the following analysis of Liszt's role in the poem's final address:

> The text is a thyrsus and the thyrsus is the movement of the text, a movement which requires the fiction of a subject—a voice which announces itself in the very last line of the text: "I salute you in immortality." The genius of this poem raises a toast to a more essential one, one who appears now as the unique center towards which the entire piece is meant to tend. The narrative voice

assumes now the guise of one of those priests (or priestesses!) who shake the sacred emblem in celebration of the divinity of which they are the "interpreters and servants." And Liszt—of all people—has become the figure of genius itself, "mighty and revered master, dear Bacchant of mysterious and passionate beauty." Which is to say, the gesture of lifting a toast—the gesture mimed by the poem—has the structure of a thyrsus, as the narrator, lifting his glass, spins his phrases, shakes his emblems around the object of his praise. But nothing is more revealing of the paradoxical structure of the thyrsus than to examine that central object: Liszt, who is here simultaneously a fictional and a real man, present but absent, a musician and a philosopher, intoxicated but sober, romantic and classical—philosopher, poet and their paradoxical unity, *artiste*. Thenarrator salutes another who is the image of his own double self, torn as we have seen between the two poles. (84–85)

Why "Liszt—of all people"? The Liszt Klein reads here is strictly the Baudelairian Liszt, one amalgamated out of Baudelaire's own texts ("philosopher, poet, artist") and thus of course easily recuperable as the double of Baudelaire himself. This reappropriation is set up and prepared just as the philosophic narrator finally asserts the domination of the center (see Klein, 83). For Klein, in this context there is no Liszt but Baudelaire's; Klein reads him as a mere figure of the true subject of "genius itself." Klein translates the question of "Le Thyrse" as follows: "We might thus restate the question of the text: Is the figure of the thyrsus made to reveal the nature of Genius, or is Genius merely the pretext in the poem for showing the beauty of the thyrsus?" (84). If Liszt is nothing but an example of this generality, solely a *pretext*, Klein ends up relying on the subservience of the singular example to the general principle that his argument is meant to dislodge.

As we have seen Liszt functioning in a variety of texts, what he stands for is not simply "Genius," but rather the moment of reversal between general and particular, master and servant, center and elaboration, goal and digression. He appears in Baudelaire's texts not merely as a "figure," but as what he really is: an oscillating motion between figure and referent. Self-displacement, unstable identity, and traveling and mobility are Liszt's own improper qualities. Thus, he is always more than what can be contained within Baudelaire's transcription. Liszt is a limit and a lacuna that cannot be controlled. The fact that his power exceeds that of the writer can be read negatively in the peculiar omission of specific references to music in Baudelaire's poem. In "Le Thyrse," Liszt is never called musician, pianist, virtuoso, or composer. The only concrete references to the musical occur in the final paragraph. The reference to pianos lends human voice to wooden instruments in a catachresis that displays the animating power of metaphor: "where the pianos sing your glory." The second musical reference also centers on song: "improvising songs of joy or of ineffable sorrow." Baudelaire restricts his musical references to song, a controlled form easily intermingled with the poetic tradition of the troubadours and other poetic forms such as the ode and the ballad. The reduction of music to song exerts the control of abbreviation over the field of music, blotting out the vast noise, resounding bodies, and "sonorous texture" that exceed the term of "song."[5]

Besides the neglect of music per se and of Liszt's specificity, Baudelaire's borrowing of the figure of the thyrsus from de Quincey is also given short shrift in criticism. While critics take the "source" into account, they tend to foreground Baudelaire's "originality" rather than the foreign origin of the figure.[6] And indeed, what more could Baudelaire ask for than to have his own originary voice resound in dialogue with his precursors and pretexts? But the mastery of excess that Klein reads in "Le Thyrse"—and which is indeed enacted there, in a sense—has a darker shadow on its floor: a self-reference to Baudelaire as translator.

Baudelaire translated de Quincey's *Confessions of an English Opium-Eater* in serial form. While de Quincey's text is a straightforward first-person narrative, Baudelaire's translation is heterogeneous. Sometimes the first person is directly translated, sometimes in quotation marks and sometimes not. There are unmarked shifts between these passages, third-person paraphrase, editorial deletions, and outright commentary.[7] By referring to de Quincey, Baudelaire adds another strain to the "original" poetic voice enunciating "Le Thyrse": he adds a dose of the hand that repeats, translates, transmits, copies, steals, places, and animates—the hand that holds *Gaspard de la Nuit*. It is remarkable indeed how little the caduceus passage from *Suspiria de Profundis* is compared to Baudelaire's texts. Here is the relevant passage in de Quincey, a response to objections to his digressive style:

> I tell my critic that the whole course of this narrative resembles, and was meant to resemble, a *caduceus* wreathed about with meandering ornaments, or the shaft of a tree's stem hung round and surmounted with some vagrant parasitical plant. The mere medical subject of the opium answers to the dry, withered pole, which shoots all the rings of the flowering plants, and seems to do so by some dexterity of its own; whereas, in fact, the plant and its tendrils have curled round the sullen cylinder by mere luxuriance of *theirs*. . . . So, also, the ugly pole—hop pole, vine pole, espalier, no matter what—is there only for support. Not the flowers are for the pole, but the pole is for the flowers. (125–26)

Baudelaire does not simply refer to de Quincey's caduceus (which he translates into a thyrsus),[8] but indeed he also borrows many terms and much of de Quincey's imagery: the dry, withered pole, *les tiges et les fleurs*, the "ugly pole—

hop pole, vine pole, bells and blossoms round about the arid stock." Along with the quasi-plagiarism, there are some significant omissions and alterations. Baudelaire tones down the element of death implied by the straight line and the correlative function of animation by decoration that de Quincey describes as his literary task: "View me as one (in the words of a true and most impassioned poet) 'viridantem floribus hastas'—making verdant, and gay with the life of flowers, murderous spears and halberts—things that express death in their origin (being made from dead substances that once had lived in forests), things that express ruin in their use" (126). In borrowing and repeating, Baudelaire, too, attempts to revivify and reoriginate the dead currency of the already used language of the original. De Quincey, too, translates the Latin in an effort to bring to life the literal, the dead and naked stick and signs handed down through mythic tradition, precursor texts, and the dictionary. In contrast to Baudelaire, de Quincey's bias goes in the opposite direction, leaving no room for doubt: "Not the flowers are for the pole, but the pole is for the flowers" (126). For de Quincey, the power of centralization, allied with the literal, the physical, the bare and arid lexical term, the material but mind-altering chemical (opium), brings death:

> The true object of my "Opium Confessions" is not the naked physiological theme,—on the contrary, *that* is the ugly pole, the murderous spear, the halbert—but those wandering musical variations upon the theme—those parasitical thoughts, feelings, digressions, which climb up with bells and blossoms round about the arid stock; ramble away from it at times with perhaps too rank a luxuriance; but at the same time, by the eternal interest attached to the *subjects* of these digressions, no matter what were the execution, spread a glory over incidents that for themselves would be—less than nothing. (126)

Through this unequivocal valuing of the digression over the center, de Quincey's narrative meanderings exude and generate the very "glory" of the incidental event in time, as for Baudelaire; recall: "An amazing glory surges from this complexity of lines and colors, delicate or brilliant" (*OC* 1: 336 / 72). De Quincey, indeed, does get lost in his digressions, rambles seemingly uncontrollably, producing sometimes incoherent and certainly asymmetrical figures and analogies.

De Quincey gives Baudelaire an occasion for his famously contradictory *mot*: "De Quincey is essentially digressive" (1965: 444). In his treatment of de Quincey, Baudelaire has it both ways; the very phrase allows him both to focus on the essential and to name the digressive.[9] With this exemplary *fort/da* gesture,[10] Baudelaire tries to both partake in and avoid this excessive digression; he is and remains a master of abbreviation. In the introduction to *Un Mangeur d'opium,*

Baudelaire refers to the caduceus passage in this description of his own manner of transcription:

> Doubtless I abridged much; De Quincey is essentially digressive . . . in one place, he compares his thought to a thyrsus, a simple stick which takes its whole physiognomy and charm from the complex foliage [*feuillage*] that envelops it. So that the reader may lose nothing of the moving tableaux that make up the substance of his volume, the space I have at my disposal being limited, I will be obliged, to my great regret, to suppress many very amusing *hors-d'oeuvres*, many exquisite discourses that do not treat opium directly, but have simply the goal of *illustrating* the character of the opium eater. Nevertheless, the book is vigorous enough that it can be divined, even under this succinct envelope, even in the simple condition of an extract. (1965: 444)

The spatial restraints imposed by commercial concerns are clearly "real"; Baudelaire's translation was first published serially in the *Revue contemporaine* and had to conform to commercial editorial conditions. These enforced limitations seem to justify Baudelaire's critical procedures. Just as in his treatment of Wagner, Baudelaire performs a representational reduction, subordinating digressive predicates to a central character or subject. Indeed, Baudelaire states directly that the tortuously long and digressive *Confessions* have "un but facile à deviner" (a goal easy to divine), namely, the transcendent identity of the author as an expressive source and the center of metaphoric translation:

> The character must be known, he must make himself be loved and appreciated by the reader. The author, who has undertaken to interest the attention vigorously with a subject at first sight as monotonous as a description of drunkenness, insistently shows its excusability; he wants to create a sympathy for his personage, a sympathy that will profit the whole work. Finally, and this is very important, the narration of certain accidents, vulgar perhaps in themselves, but grave and serious by reason of the sensibility of the one who has undergone them, becomes, so to speak, the key to the extraordinary sensations and visions. (1965: 445)

Thus, reduction and subordination construct an interpretive grid relating digressions and predicates to a central author-subject that supports and, as a homogeneous shape or character, lends unity to the autobiographical disintegration over the time and space of writing. Baudelaire's reduction aims to unify what is dispersed and to halt the loss of self through the distance and spacing of writing. He exchanges de Quincey's digressive *envelope* with his own succinct one—the same envelope that is turned inside out by "Le Thyrse."

Through substitution, Baudelaire's *thyrse* becomes somewhat entwined in the italics of de Quincey's *caduceus*. Baudelaire performs a paradoxical gesture, at once thematically subordinating extension and representation to an originary subject and at the same time locating its value in the writing's expanding extensions: "Here . . . this thought is the *thyrsus* of which he has spoken so agreeably. . . . The subject has no other value than that of a dry and bare stick; but the ribbons, the vines and the flowers, in their demented interlacings, can be of precious richness for the eyes" (1965: 515). Indeed, it is safe to revalue in mentioning, but not himself actually performing or presenting the enticing yet threatening pleasures of opium and digression, self-abandonment and loss. Baudelaire gives the final word to digression only in pointing to the limits of his own language. The double-reversed movement is cleverly performed by the imposition of the *spiral*, a term not found in de Quincey's text. The spiral indicates the finite and discernible form destined to become Baudelaire's "Le Thyrse"; and by Baudelaire's exercise of the power of abbreviation, the act of subordination transforms forced limitation and inadequacy into success:

> De Quincey's thought is not simply sinuous; the word is not strong enough: this thought is naturally spiral. Besides, his commentaries and reflections would be too long to analyse, and I must recall that the goal of this work has been to show, by an example, the effects of opium on a meditative spirit inclined to reverie. I believe I have fulfilled this goal. (1965: 515)

Baudelaire seems to have achieved his goal, gained control of de Quincey's impossible disgressiveness, delivered the essence, and asserted himself along with what he transmits. Yet in de Quincey's caduceus passage, there is a predicate attached to the sinuous meanderings that Baudelaire has deleted, both in his translation and in "Le Thyrse": the "true object" defined by de Quincey as "those wandering *musical variations* upon the theme" (my emphasis).

Why no music? The strange antagonism between music and writing, digression and center, mechanical letter and spirit or meaning, arises again. For de Quincey, true legibility of character is musical; reading itself is defined as an analogy to music. What Adorno has called *Sprachähnlichkeit*, "language-likeness," is inverted here; language arises as "music-likeness":

> And if the reader has (which so few have) the passion, without which there is no reading of the legend and superscription upon man's brow, if he is not (as most are) deafer than the grave to every *deep* note that sighs upwards from the Delphic caves of human life, he will know that the rapture of life, or anything which by approach can merit that name, does not arise, unless as perfect music arises—music of Mozart or Beethoven—by the confluence of the mighty and terrific discords with the subtle concords. (208–9)

In other words, de Quincey here speaks of the nontranslatable, nonparaphrasable atmosphere or glory exuding from arabesques and digressions. He also grants the power of recollecting the past, the power of memory and self-gathering, not to literature, his own medium, but to music: "It is sufficient to say, that a chorus, etc., of elaborate harmony, displayed before me, as in a piece of arras work, the whole of my past life—not as if recalled by an act of memory, but as if present and incarnate in the music" (62). Finally, de Quincey suggests that the translation of the infinite variety of experience into organized legible forms will always entail a loss and a fading out of the remnant named "music":

> So thick a curtain of *manners* is drawn over the features and expressions of men's *natures*, that, to the ordinary observer, the two extremities, and the infinite field of varieties which lie between them, are all confounded—the vast and multitudinous compass of their several harmonies reduced to the meagre outline of differences expressed in the gamut or alphabet of elementary sound. (40)

Baudelaire is indeed a master of the kind of reduction that might be called writing. To cover up that which recedes as script is distinguished—music—Baudelaire adds and subtracts "music," translates and transcribes others, remains connected but differentiated, intoxicated by proxy, touches and returns: a member of the audience, a reader. In his preface to his translation of Edgar Allan Poe's "Raven," Baudelaire explains that it is impossible to reproduce the sonority of the original. Instead he recommends: "Listen to the singing in your memory of the most plaintive strophes of Lamartine, of the most magnificent and complex rhythms of Victor Hugo; mix in the memory of the most subtle and insightful tercets of Théophile Gautier . . . and you will perhaps obtain an approximate idea of Poe's talents as a versifier" (1928: 154–55). For Baudelaire, the recollection of the original is not musical, but literary; not a force arising "as perfect music," but a synthesis of reading, a literary amalgamation. Baudelaire invents a certain originality of recollection and transcription; and perhaps *that* is the "music" that, according to Valéry, Baudelaire deflected from the world into literature.

As he borrows and appropriates many of de Quincey's words in "Le Thyrse," Baudelaire retracts his poetic originality, blending his voice with those of Liszt and de Quincey, the lyric *I* and the commercial translator. In the cuttings, clippings, stitching, and magical touch that make the material traces of the past disappear and allows poetic language to resound, Baudelaire behaves, again, like the virtuoso, like Liszt himself, both genius and charlatan. Whatever subject performs this covert composition and execution of "Le Thyrse" is not the linguistic *I*, neither enunciating nor enunciated; much more, it is the skilled hands that work with tools, techniques, space, and print. The merger of and analogy between Baudelaire and Liszt are neither poetic nor complete, just as poetic animation and technical production and dispersion—expression, confession, publication, marketing—are never unified but remain juxtaposed. The subjects here are no longer Liszt, Baudelaire, Wagner, de Quincey, Poe, or Heine, or Delacroix. For their powers have been handed over, by the hand of the sentence maker, to the instruments, whether poetic or profane, as origin and carriers of expression.

In conclusion, I simply point out that the juxtaposition "où les pianos chantent votre gloire, où l'imprimerie traduit votre sagesse" (where the pianos sing your glory, where the printing press translates your wisdom) does not convey equivalence, does not equal [music = poetry]. What it says instead is that all are engaged in the process of handing over control to a mechanical device, whether it be predication, metaphor, musical performance, or translation. Expression is churned out by the printing press just as much as it exudes from the bare strings and keyboard. Juxtaposition on the page does not convey or enforce equivalence but holds apart the rhetorical ends of communication: the head and tail we might call Baudelaire and Liszt.

# Reference Matter

# Notes

## Introduction

1. Kierkegaard, *Either/Or*, trans. Hong and Hong (74–75). In another edition (1959), Swenson translates *genstand* as "subject" (i.e., of a proposition). In this quote, the word has the sense of an "object" in opposition to a subject; the roots mean literally "standing overagainst," comparable to the German *Gegenstand*.

2. *Premises* (186). I am greatly indebted not only here but throughout to Hamacher's unique work, especially on the relation between philosophy and literature. Happily, many of his essays are now available in English in this volume.

3. See Rowell, esp. chapter 4, for a good summary of Greek views on music; Warren Dwight Allen's *Philosophies of Music History*; and Neubauer.

4. *Republic* (7.531d, 532d). Plato's words are προοίμιον (*prooimion*) and νομοσ (*nomos*), in this context almost invariably translated as "prelude" and "melody," though the phrase can also be read as "preamble to the law."

5. Leibniz's concept of "pre-established harmony" is meant to explain how bodies can interact without consciousness yet with harmony. The motions of things are governed by the divine preestablished harmony, though it may not be available to knowledge in its details. See *De la monadologie*, esp. paras. 59–61 and 79–83; and *Nouveaux essais* in *Oeuvres*, 1: 15–18.

6. Kevin Barry and Downing A. Thomas focus rigorously on the texts of this period in France, also taking into account recent debates. See also Neubauer, Kramer, and Warren Dwight Allen.

7. Rousseau's *Essai sur l'origine des langues* is surely the most famous instance. In chapter 3, he claims: "As the passions were the first motives that made man speak, his first expressions were tropes. Figurative language was naturally the first" (*Oeuvres complètes*, 11: 223). In chapter 12, he argues for the original unity between language (poetry) and music (melody): "The first discourses were the first songs." (See also his *Dictionnaire de la musique*, *Oeuvres complètes*, vol. 14.) Rousseau's dis-

cussion of music is the well-known focus of de Man's discussion in *Blindness and In-sight* of Derrida's reading of Rousseau in *Of Grammatology*. For various treatments of this debate, see Barry, 9–10; Thomas, 86–90; Abbate, 16–19; and my own discussion in Chapter 2.

8. Kant, *Kritik der Urteilskraft*, 265–66.

9. See Chapter 1.

10. Hegel, *Ästhetik* (2: 261).

11. In *Music and the Origins of Language*, Thomas points out the tendency toward teleological language in discussions of music, especially when dealing with the "drastic changes" in the eighteenth century (6).

12. The following characterization of the Jena Romantics in Lacoue-Labarthe and Nancy's *L'Absolu littéraire* (*The Literary Absolute*) might also be said of music: "The word and the concept 'romantic' are indeed *transmitted* to the 'Romantics,' and their originality does not consist in inventing 'romanticism,' but rather, on the one hand, in using this term to cover up their own powerlessness to name and conceive what they invent, and on the other . . . in dissimulating a 'project' that exceeds, from all points of view, what this term transmits to them" (11/3).

13. Said gives a powerful presentation of modern musical performance in *Musical Elaborations* (2–34).

14. An early but undated English edition translates this as *The Gipsy in Music*.

## Chapter 1. Virtuosity and Journalism

1. Subotnik traces an intellectual history of the division of language and music, pointing to a rupture parallel to the "failing confidence in the indisputability of human access to general truth or knowledge" (175) in the modern period. See "The Cultural Message of Musical Semiology: Some Thoughts on Music, Language, and Criticism Since the Enlightenment" in *Developing Variations*. For an interesting and original discussion of literature in the age of journalism, see McLaughlin, *Writing in Parts*.

2. The story "Die Automate," for example, is structured around the anxieties and attractions of musical automata. Professor X, the notable collector of musical automata, embodies the anxiety-provoking reversibility between music and machine. Even his name inscribes the "crossing" of oppositions that destabilizes the boundary between them. "Don Juan," "Rath Krespel," and "Der Sandmann" are among the stories that bring up these same issues.

3. For this structural and historical analysis, see Habermas, *Strukturwandel der Öffentlichkeit*.

4. See also Duro, *Vocabolario della lingua italiana* (4: 1196); Robert, *Dictionnaire alphabétique et analogique de la langue française* (1007); Littré, *Dictionnaire de la langue française* (2504); and Grimm, *Deutsches Wörterbuch* (12: 372–73).

5. The relation between language and music has been taken up in musicology

with the most rigor by Subotnik, Neubauer, Dahlhaus, and Abbate. For a more philosophical approach, I am indebted to the work of Lacoue-Labarthe.

6. On these publishing figures, see James Smith Allen, *Popular French Romanticism* (123), which provides ample and detailed information about the state of printing, journalism, and the publishing industry in nineteenth-century France. In *The Dandy*, Moers draws interesting connections between the rise of journalism and the appearance of dandyism in France in the same period (126). Anderson gives an interesting analysis of the development of "print culture" in Europe in *Imagined Communities*. For conditions of the French press, see also Kracauer; Hohendahl; and Terdiman, *Discourse/Counter-Discourse*, especially chapter 2: "Newspaper Culture: Institutions of Discourse; Discourse of Institutions."

7. In *Heinrich Heine*, Preisendanz focuses on the inadequacy of traditional genre definitions for understanding Heine's texts, pointing out: "Feuilleton means, above all, a place in which texts are located" (28). Terdiman elaborates, suggesting that "the newspaper can be understood as the first culturally influential *anti-organicist* mode of modern discursive construction" (122). He stresses the role of a technical space in the composition of journalism: "The newspaper is built by addition of discrete, theoretically disconnected elements which juxtapose themselves only in response to the abstract requirements of 'layout'—thus of a disposition of space whose logic, ultimately, is commercial" (122). James Smith Allen gives a thorough review of how literary forms in the nineteenth century came to be influenced by technological conditions, such as the *cabinet de lecture*, the serial novel, problems of length, and illustrations. Beaujour analyzes brevity and spatial layout with respect to the prose poem in "Short Epiphanies."

8. These numbers are from Rarisch, *Industrialisierung und Literatur* (12–29). Consistent statistics with varying analyses can be found in Raabe, *Bücherlust und Lesefreuden*, and Kirchner, *Das deutsche Zeitschriftenwesen*.

9. Balzac provides tremendous insight into the journalistic climate in *Illusions perdues* (*Lost Illusions*) and in a fascinating "Monographie de la presse parisienne" (*OC*, vol. 21). This text presents in essay form text found almost verbatim in *Illusions perdues*. In the novel, Balzac especially testifies to the technological changes in printing and the division of labor between printing and writing, to the extent that Père Séchard, the old printer, does not himself know how to read.

10. On the tension between specificity and generality that informs the relation between journalism and the formation of national identities, see Anderson, *Imagined Communities*; Werner, "Crossing Borders Between Cultures: On the Preconditions and Function of Heine's Reception in France" in Hohendahl and Gilman's *Heinrich Heine and the Occident*; and my "Journalism and German Identity."

11. Lukács emphasizes the dialectical movement by which extreme subjectivity appears as an expression of the universal, by which isolation and idiosyncrasy are grounded in a generality ("Heinrich Heine als nationaler Dichter," 130). Therefore, for Lukács, Heine's position as "outsider" cannot be bound to his Judaism; Lukács

states unambiguously: "We believe that . . . as a poet and a thinker, Heine is profoundly connected to the development of Germany, and that his loneliness and isolation have nothing to do with his Jewish descent" (95).

The question of Heine's Judaism and how it affects his writing demands a more thorough treatment than can be undertaken here. To begin with, it would have to involve a rigorous examination of the relation between Jews and Germans at that time, especially in linguistic terms. Jews are often attributed an "improper" relationship to language, reflected in the tonality of Yiddish compared to German (see Gilman, *Jewish Self-Hatred*). This view was already voiced in humanistic debates about biblical translation; Richard Wagner states it with disturbing clarity in "Das Judenthum in der Musik" (Judaism in music) (*GS*, 5 / *WPW*, 3). In contrast to Lukács, Adorno, in "Die Wunde Heine" ("Heine the Wound"), traces Heine's alienated relation to language to his excluded position as Jew (98). He thus claims for Heine a prophetic rather than a representative role; Heine's particular isolation, as a Jew, is later fulfilled in a general disappearance of *Heimat*, or social groundedness (100). Arendt, in contrast, attributes the *success*, the natural groundedness—the "cheerfulness" and "volkish popularity" (*Heiterkeit* and *Volkstümlichkeit*) of Heine's language—to his identification with the figure of the Jew as pariah (53). In *Opfer Heine?*, Briegleb, too, gives Heine's Judaism a major role in his interpretation.

12. Habermas analyzes the change in this period as the point at which the "traffic in information" itself becomes a commodity, and in terms of the creation of a market-oriented public (*Strukturwandel der Öffentlichkeit*, 78–79).

13. For general discussions of style as constitutive of a materially grounded signifying process that exceeds propositional control, see Derrida, *Éperons*, *L'Écriture et la différence*, and *Marges de la philosophie*; Lacoue-Labarthe, *Le Sujet de la philosophie*; and Nancy, *Le Discours de la syncope* and *Le Sens du monde*. In *Heinrich Heine*, Preisendanz documents the attribution of innovation to Heine's journalism (21). He identifies this innovation as the engagement of style in producing meaning, linking this to the representation of a historical subject proper to the timebound form of journalism (see esp. the chapter "Der Sinn der Schreibart in den Berichten aus Paris, 1840–1844 'Lutezia'"). Briegleb, in *Opfer Heine?*, also focuses on the articulation of a temporal subject in a temporal medium. Referring to Benjamin's mention of Heine in his work on Baudelaire, Briegleb reads Heine as a "*flâneur*." On style, see Chapter 5, esp. 6.

14. In *Heinrich Heines Musikkritiken*, Mann gives evidence of both Heine's ignorance of music and the widespread influence his texts nevertheless exerted. Heine is a common source in music history; in *Jacques Offenbach und das Paris seiner Zeit*, for example, Kracauer quotes him often. In *The Virtuosi*, Harold C. Schonberg cites him as "a brilliant music critic." He is quoted in virtually every account of Niccolò Paganini, usually with no mention of the fictional status of Heine's text about him in *Florentinische Nächte*, *Sämtliche Schriften*, 557–615.

15. For "writing," I am relying on Derrida's *De la grammatologie*, where there is a thorough exposition of the Western association of writing with exteriority,

technology, and other traits that make it threatening to a metaphysical concept of meaning.

16. These poles were initially suggested by Jakobson in the famous essay "Two Aspects of Language and Two Types of Aphasic Disturbances" in *Language in Literature*.

17. This is, of course, a standard lament or celebration. For a good run-through of Heine's multiplicities, see Hohendahl and Gilman's introduction to *Heinrich Heine and the Occident*. See also Maierhofer, "'Die Sprödigkeit des Stoffes: Heinrich Heine als Erzähler." Interestingly, the undecidability about Heine interfered with the creation of a singular monument to him; Schubert analyzes the fascinating doubling around the Heine monument in "'Jetzt Wohin?' Das 'deutsche Gedächtnismal' für Heinrich Heine." See also *Der Spiegel* 19 (1982): 204–5 for coverage of ambivalence and controversy around the Heine monument.

18. *SS* (5: 227); translations of the French preface are modified, but follow closely Heine's *The Romantic School and Other Essays*, ed. Hermand and Holub.

19. Levine's text is unique and illuminating in its attention to the structure and nature of ambivalence and the exegetical ideology that wants to resolve ambiguities and obscurities. His reading of censorship through Freud allows an interesting focus on the processes of displacement. In "Der politische Schriftsteller und die (Selbst-) Zensur," Werner tends rather to read for decoding. Both Werner and Levine discuss the paradox of self-censorship, according to which style emerges as and through censorship. Both quote Heine, pointing out his strong identification with his censored style: "Ach! I can no longer write, I simply cannot, for we have no censorship. How should a person who has always lived under censorship be able to write without censorship? All style will end" (Werner, 44; Levine, 1). Gilman argues in "Heines Photographien" that Heine's use of "photography" serves "the Enlightenment purpose of entertainment and instruction" and that the sometimes obscure images are allegorical signs meant to reveal the hidden truths of his era. (23). Norbert Altenhofer examines in greater detail the allegorical aspect of Heine's texts in "Chiffre, Hieroglyphe, Palimpsest," as does Zantop in "Liberty Unbound: Heine's 'Historiography in Color'" in *Paintings on the Move*.

20. For important historical contextualization and an interpretation of Heine's writing as a kind of "photographing" of history, see Gilman, "Heines Photographien."

21. Zantop has similarly analyzed the relation between Heine's art criticism and the paintings he thematizes in "Liberty Unbound" and in her introduction to *Paintings on the Move*. Her analyses come close to my work here, focusing on the way that Heine's prose constructs the history it reports, and on the self-reflexive function of Heine's criticism. She concludes that "the paintings and his criticism metaphorically and literally represent his own aesthetic-political theory and practice" (44).

22. In *Lutetia*, Heine considers taking on French citizenship as a sort of monstrosity, which he describes in linguistic terms, contrasting the "natural meter" of

German poetry to the "parfümierte Quark," the "perfumed cottage cheese," of French alexandrines (*GS* 5: 479).

## Chapter 2. The Musical Alibi in Theories of Performativity

1. In his theorization of performative utterances, Austin, too, leaves open a similar space of "infelicities," the unavoidable flawed sphere of "ills" to which all historical acts are subject (*How to Do Things with Words*). His doctrine of infelicities delimits the sphere of actual individual performances from ideal structures as the conditions of possibility of performance; it marks a scission that, in Saussure's text, is covered over by the "symphony." The ambiguity of the term *performance* consists of its referring to the transcendental act of positing in the German Idealist tradition on the one hand, but on the other, constantly referring to actual particular performances as well. In "Toward a Theory of Reading in the Visual Arts," Marin articulates the problem of interpretation in the Chomskyan terms of competence and performance (294). Quoting this passage in *Narrative as Performance*, Maclean mistakenly allies "theory" with competence and "applications in individual readings" with performance. She thus misses precisely the simultaneous duality Marin indicates and elsewhere works out in terms of the temporal paradoxes of enunciation. On the analogy between competence/performance and *langue/parole*, see Ducrot and Todorov (120).

2. In *The Classical Style*, Rosen also expresses dismay at the interferences of performance that problematize the discernability—or even the existence—of the unity or unified pattern of "style" in which he is interested (104).

3. This is a central problem addressed by Butler's *Bodies That Matter* in response to Sedgwick. In their introduction to *Performativity and Performance*, Parker and Sedgwick give a good overview of the very broad range of the issues that have developed following Austin, as do the contributions in the same volume.

4. The presence or absence of these self-referential markers determines the distinction between *récit* and *discours* that Benveniste outlines in "Les Relations de temps dans le verbe français"; see also "La Nature des pronoms," both in *Problèmes de linguistique générale*, vol. 1. The tension he sets up between the "objective" grid provided by dates and the "subjective" time relations of *discours* would be interesting for the context here. Louis Marin has argued that the *récit* denies and represses (in the psychoanalytic sense), but cannot do without, the self-referential markers of *discours*, as outlined in *La Voix excommuniée*. See also Marin's "Sur un certain regard du sujet," "The Autobiographical Interruption," and "Toward a Theory of Reading in the Visual Arts."

5. Benveniste proceeds from Saussure's distinction between *langue* and *parole*. See Saussure's *Cours de linguistique générale* (esp. chapters 3–5), and the entry "Language and Speech" in Ducrot and Todorov, *Encyclopedic Dictionary of the Sciences of Language* (118–23).

6. This operation is inscribed as the "dialogic" dimension of enunciation; the

use of the word *I*, according to Benveniste, implies a *you* whose task it is to attribute the utterances of *I* to the speaker (see 1: 252–53; 2: 82).

7. I stress here that nowhere does Benveniste put forth a unified theory of enunciation, and that the various essays dealing with the topic present differing and sometimes contradictory perspectives. Kristeva rejects Benveniste's *sujet d'énonciation* as a transcendental ego existing separately from its discourse (*La Révolution du langage poétique*, 17–30). But despite the tone of his conclusions, Benveniste's emphasis on the discursive generation of the subject in his analysis of "cogito ergo sum" in "De la subjectivité dans le langage" is not reconcilable with a Cartesian interpretation of a transcendental subject. Similarly, one need not take his debate with Austin in "La Philosophie analytique et le langage" to be all that Benveniste has to say about performance in language, as Felman does in *Le Scandale du corps parlant*. His formal reduction of performative utterances in that essay does not, as she suggests, simply do away with the enunciative excess he allows elsewhere. Marin's characterization of enunciation and subjectivity in autobiography treats the paradoxes in Benveniste more subtly. The ambiguity in Benveniste is further supported by the interpretation of Meschonnic in *Critique du rythme*. Meschonnic believes that Benveniste, in his essay "La Notion de 'rythme' dans son expression linguistique," has "destabilized the theory of the sign itself." For Meschonnic, it is Benveniste who has made possible a theory of discursivity (69–70).

8. Ducrot puts this well in *Le Dire et le dit*, describing how enunciation institutes a "cleavage" within the observable given of an actual *énoncé* (68–69). Enunciation is a difficult concept because it attempts to generalize something always particular and thus differentiate it from a naive conception of an empirical singularity. The following formulation of Ducrot's approach to enunciation is helpful:

> With this term [*énonciation*] I will designate the event constituted by the appearance of the utterance [*énoncé*]. The actualization of an utterance is in fact an historical event: existence is given to something that did not exist before speaking and will not exist afterward. It is this momentary apparition that I call "enunciation" . . . I do not say that enunciation is the act of someone who produces an utterance: for me, it is the simple fact of an utterance appearing . . . it is not for me to decide whether there is an author and who it might be. (179)

Ducrot's discussion is interesting, though there are difficulties, especially in the problem of distinguishing the empirical and the formal subject of enunciation. Ducrot excludes from enunciation "the psycho-physiological activity implied by the production of the utterance (adding to it the play of social influence that conditions it)" (178). But these must be thought of as related to conditions of enunciation; the fact that they cannot be known is not sufficient reason to dismiss them.

9. On de Man's reading of performativity, see Hamacher, esp. "'Lectio': De Man's Imperative," in *Premises*. Lacour analyzes the intrusion of historicity into formal conceptualizations of rule theory, resulting in an aporia in the relation between convention and instance in "The Temporality of Convention."

10. Benveniste stresses this particularly: "The performative utterance, being an act, has the property of being *unique* . . . being an individual and historical act, a performative utterance cannot be repeated" (1: 273/236). While Felman criticizes Benveniste's attempts to formally delimit linguistic performatives, it seems to me that the recognition of the performative function of specific definable linguistic forms (e.g., question, imperative, etc.) does not per se exclude all nonformal linguistic performance or performance in excess of those forms. The formal restraints on performative utterances—that they are conventional structures—does not make them any less "performative." Though one may be interested in stressing the excess of performance, without formal and recognizable linguistic markers it would be impossible to discuss a "question" or a "promise" at all.

11. This is the point of Austin's distinction between illocutionary and perlocutionary force, which is in part the distinction between conventional and nonconventional acts; see *How to Do Things with Words* (120–21).

12. Ducrot includes within the definition of *langue* the "collection of sentences and utterances" that constitute the "given" explained by the theoretical construct "*langue*" (67–68). Such an extension of the meaning of *langue* includes the "synchronic" perspective on literary works viewed as a whole without regard to their production.

13. See Rowell, esp. chapter 4, and Warren Dwight Allen.

14. See Rousseau, *Oeuvres complètes*, vols. 13, 15.

15. For other discussions of this passage in de Man, see the Introduction, n. 7.

## Chapter 3. Instruments of Virtuosity

1. Mann discusses Heine's personal relationship to Meyerbeer (and others) in *Heinrich Heines Musikkritiken*, 101–13. In "Französische Quellen," Mann also discusses the problems of plagiarism and bribery. He argues that Heine's opinions of Meyerbeer are more French than German: "Along with the French, Heine held to be characteristically 'German' what in Germany was rather viewed as 'French'" (259). See also Werner on Heine's "Frenchness" in "Crossing Borders Between Cultures" in Hohendahl and Gilman's *Heinrich Heine and the Occident*.

2. Mann's terminology characterizing Heine's style in *Über die französische Bühne* invites comparisons when he points to "the virtuoso handling of anecdotes and portraits" in Heine's text (24). Mann also refers to "the spiritual affinity between Heine and Chopin" (69) precisely as another producer of "fairy-tale poetry." But one should be cautious in reading any simple identification of Heine with Chopin; in this passage, the identification is strategic.

3. Benjamin, "Die Aufgabe des Übersetzers" (*Gesammelte Schriften* 4: 1, 15).

4. The violence around musical performance also extended to the audience. Liszt was the first to be chased by fans who tried to tear off bits of his clothes. The destruction of instruments on stage, of course, later became a rock trademark, es-

pecially for The Who and for Jimi Hendrix, who set his guitar on fire at the Monterey Pop Festival.

5. See Derrida's reading of Rousseau in part 2, *De la grammatologie*.

6. In *Heinrich Heines Musikkritiken*, Mann notes Heine's participation in a Romantic interpretation of music, suggesting that his views on music might serve as a measuring stick for considering his relation to Romanticism: "Heine's view of music would be romantic, without its negative symptoms. But in its negative acception, we would call it rather a romantic critique of romanticism" (139).

7. It has been suggested that Heine used his negative reviews to bribe Liszt, and that this might also account for the positive change. See Mann (107–10).

8. While exclamations are generally explained as a sign of presence or expression, Ducrot supplements this function, adding to its significance the enunciative force by which the exclamation implies that it is a direct reaction to an object, as if compelled (185–88).

9. The *Klangfigur*, which has since served as the title for one of Adorno's works, was described by Chladni, who discovered the laws of the passage of sound through solid bodies, in *Entdeckungen über die Theorie des Klanges* (Leipzig, 1787). In *Die Akustik* (1802), the specific instructions for producing these figures indicate how popular such experiments had become. There were many efforts to translate sounds into images, for example in some of Rameau and d'Alembert's experiments with strings.

## Chapter 4. *Virtuosity, Rhapsody, and Romantic Philology*

1. Perrault's *Parallèle des anciens et des modernes* (1688–97), a major contribution to the "quarrel" between the ancients and the moderns, rejects the existence of the person Homer. In the mid-nineteenth century, debates about the relation of musical composition and performance were common in musical journals. Liszt was often criticized for failing to compose, most famously in a well-publicized debate with F.-J. Fétis, who is mocked by Heine and called "abominable" by Baudelaire. Fétis's best-known works are the *Biographie universelle des musiciens et bibliographie générale de la musique* and *La Musique mise à la portée de tout le monde*. Fétis's polemic against Liszt is also rendered in German in Liszt's *Gesammelte Schriften*.

2. For well-documented histories of Homer reception and discussions of the Homer question, see Simounsuuri; Adam Parry's introduction to Milman Parry; Anthony Grafton, Glenn W. Most, and James E. G. Zetzel's bibliographies and introduction to Wolf, *Prolegomena zu Homer*; and Latacz, "Tradition und Neuerung in der Homerforschung: Zur Geschichte der Oral Poesie-Theorie," in *Homer: Tradition und Neuerung*.

3. See Winckelmann, *Gedanken über die Nachahmung der griechischen Werke in der Malerey und Bildhauerkunst* (1756), and Schiller, *Über naive und sentimentalische Dichtung* (1795). Hegel theorizes the concept of Greek epic as the genre of a unified

world in *Vorlesungen über die Ästhetik*; this formulation continues to influence Lukács's presentation of lost epic totality and its ironic successor in the novel in *Theorie des Romanes*.

4. Milman Parry does challenge the domination of the concept of author as producer. His student Albert Lord also seems to do away with the opposition between composition and performance. In *The Singer of Tales*, Lord writes: "Singing, performing, composing are facets of the same act" (13). This might be seen as an idealized unity that cannot be conceptualized from the present; it clearly does not do away with the negative evaluation of repetition. "We must eliminate from the word 'performer' any notion that he is one who merely reproduces what someone else or even he himself has composed" (13). In *Poetry into Drama*, Herington argues more generally that Greek literature must be understood as a performing art.

5. The relation of dependency and doubling is underscored further by Wagner's dedication, inscribed only on the unpublished full score manuscript of *Lohengrin*, to Liszt, described as his "alter ego." Thanks to John Deathridge for bringing this to my attention; it is noted in the *Wagner Werk-Verzeichnis*. For a different reading of the "alter ego" problem, see Deathridge's "Wagner's Alter Ego" in the *English National Opera Guide*.

6. Especially in Lacoue-Labarthe's "Baudelaire *contra* Wagner." See also his *Musica ficta*.

7. Wagner's second wife, Cosima, was the daughter of Liszt and Marie d'Agoult.

8. Appendix 2 in Herington's *Poetry into Drama* assembles references to rhapsodes. The book also reproduces photographs of the vases that are a major source of evidence concerning rhapsodes, portraying, for example, the characteristic platform of his performance. On rhapsodes, see also Nancy, *Le Partage des voix*; Schadewaldt, *Von Homers Welt und Werk*; Sealey, "From Phemios to Ion"; and Havelock, *The Muse Learns to Write*.

9. Plato's *Ion* was largely responsible for delivering these notions of rhapsodic characteristics to later readers. In Plato's famous figure of poetic possession, Socrates explains to Ion:

> The spectator is the last of the rings I spoke of, which receive their force from one another by virtue of the loadstone. . . . You, the rhapsodist and the actor, are the middle ring, and the first one is the poet himself. But it is the deity who, through all the series, draws the spirit of men wherever he desires, transmitting the attractive force from one into another. And so, as from the loadstone, a mighty chain hangs down . . . we call it being "possessed" . . . from these primary rings, the poets . . . are filled with inspiration. (*Ion*, 536a–b)

10. In "Über epische und dramatische Dichtung" (On epic and dramatic poetry), Goethe and Schiller define the epic as a presentation of the past that eclipses the presence of the performer, who literally should not appear at all: "The rhapsode himself should not appear as a higher being within his poem; at best, he should read from behind a curtain so that one might abstract from all personality and believe to

be hearing only the voice of the Muses in general" (12: 251). Hegel is more precise about the relationship between the "objectivity" of the narration of past events and the effacement of the rhapsode: "Epic, in which the poet wants to unfold for us an objective world of events and ways of action, leaves nothing remaining to the performing rhapsode but to make his individual subjectivity retreat in the face of the deeds and events which he is reporting. The less he himself intrudes, the better; indeed, he can even be monotonous and soulless without much damage. What should have effect is the matter itself, the poetic treatment, the narration, not his real resounding, speaking and narrating" (*Ästhetik* 2: 323–24 / *Aesthetics* 2: 955–56).

11. Though this construction of *rhapsode* (*raptein*, "to sew or stitch" + *(h)odos*, "songs") is not universally accepted, it is clear that most of the tradition understood the word in this way. In Perrault's *Parallèle des anciens et des modernes*, one of the arguments offered against the unitarian interpretation of Homer refers to this etymology, suggesting that no author would choose to attach his name to a work stitched together, allying the rhapsodic with "bad style."

12. Foucault describes aptly the point at which the desire of commentary turns into the rhapsodic: "It must—and the paradox is ever-changing yet inescapable—say, for the first time, what has already been said, and repeat tirelessly what was, nevertheless, never said. The infinite rippling of commentary is agitated from within by the dream of masked repetition: the distance there, perhaps, nothing other than what was there at the point of departure: simple recitation" (*Archaeology of Knowledge and the Discourse on Language*, 221).

13. Sealey points out in "From Phemios to Ion" that by the time the rhapsodic art is represented in writing, the art has already entered into a state of degeneracy, implying an indeterminate margin of distortion between the art in its prime and its remnants in written representations. There can be no continuous progress from the oral to the written art. Sealey describes the discontinuity of the transition from orality to literacy as follows:

> Writing gives oral epics a rigidity which their composers never intended; to write an oral poem down is, in a sense, to misunderstand its nature. The conditions under which oral poems are written down can be defined with some precision. Two men, at least, must meet. One must be an oral poet, that is, a man who does not think of writing as the normal means of communicating poetry; the other must be a man who does regard writing as the normal means of communicating poetry. A public accustomed to written publication provides the only adequate motive for writing the Homeric poems down. (350)

This encounter cannot take place within a single historical continuum; it is not unlike the cultural time warp between Liszt and the Gypsies. A similar cultural time warp between illiteracy and writing is implied by Lord's notion of the Homeric epics as "oral dictated texts" (149). Compare Ong, *Orality and Literacy*.

14. Liszt published frequently in the *Revue et gazette musicale*, and also in *Le Monde*, *La France musicale*, *L'Artiste*, *Die neue Zeitschrift für Musik*, and the *Weimare*

*Zeitung*, for example. On Liszt's publication, see Haraszti; Waters's introduction to Liszt, *Chopin*; and Walker's bibliographies. Ramann, a musician and fan who met Liszt in 1859, not only edited the collection (1880–83) but also wrote the first extended biography of Liszt. A new bilingual edition (French and German) in nine volumes is currently in preparation by publisher Breitkopf and Härtel in Wiesbaden.

15. Liszt's compositions range from early piano music, often considered "show-pieces," including the *Hungarian Rhapsodies*, to symphonic poems, his most innovative form (*Dante Symphony, Prometheus, Faust*, e.g.), to religious works. He was also constantly engaged in writing instrumentations (in his capacity as conductor) and transcriptions of orchestral pieces for the piano. A complete list of his compositions can be found in the *Oxford Encyclopedia of Music*. Huneker provides an interesting and readable treatment on Liszt "as Composer"; Merrick gives a detailed account of Liszt's composition in terms of his religious interests; and Bartók makes interesting comments about Liszt's compositions in particular.

16. Hungary suffered from a severe flood of the Danube in 1838. It is told and retold how Liszt returned to Hungary for the first time since the age of ten, followed by a series of concerts in Vienna, the proceeds from which he donated to Hungary to repair damage from the flood. He raised "the colossal sum of 24,000 gulden, the largest single donation the Hungarians received from a private source" (Walker, 254). This anecdote points to the theme of "generosity," also an important character trait of virtuosity that comes up in Liszt's essay on Paganini as well. Like most things Liszt did, this act of charity had a mixed reception; many felt he did it only for publicity and as an attempt to conceal his blatant egotism.

17. See Chapter 5 for a discussion of Bartók's views on Liszt's nationality.

18. In *Des Bohémiens et de leur musique en Hongrie*, a book that demands a rigorous and sensitive study with respect to the treatment of the Jews as well as the Gypsies, Liszt claimed that Gypsy music was not Hungarian (i.e., Magyar). This theory was heatedly rejected by the Hungarians and opened a long-standing controversy; it was taken up again in the 1920's with twentieth-century sociological research methods by Bartók and Kodaly. Bartók defends Liszt but does not agree with his understanding of the popular origin of Gypsy music. Bartók writes:

> To start without preliminaries, I should like to state that what people (including Hungarians) call "gipsy music" is not gipsy music but Hungarian music; it is not old folk music but a fairly recent type of Hungarian popular art music composed, practically without exception, by Hungarians of the upper middle class. . . . It is futile to look for logic in the use of language. The living tongue puts out the most peculiar offshoots, which we simply have to accept as the consequence of a natural growth, even though they are illogical. Thus if we take the phrase "gipsy music" as an example of incorrect usage we should long since have acquiesced in its acceptance were it not for the continued ill effects of this false terminology. When Franz Liszt's well-known book on gipsy music appeared it created strong indignation at home. But why? Simply because Liszt dared to affirm in his book that what the

Hungarians call gipsy music *is really gipsy music!* It seems that Liszt fell innocent victim to this loose terminology. (206)

19. Brendel's jacket notes give a delightfully accurate and concise summary of the traditional objections to Liszt. He begins with the typical polemical questions: "Why is Liszt, that genius of a composer for the piano, the victim of so many misunderstandings and misjudgments? What hindrances lie in the way of a more dispassionate and less biased approach to his work?" He gives four reasons: his cosmopolitanism and eclecticism; his virtuosity, and the attendant vapidity of musical content; his unevenness; and his demands on the player. Brendel, a fellow virtuoso, comments:

> It may be seen in his works that Liszt was the greatest sovereign of the piano. Where is the pianist who can do justice to that production, to that range and directness of emotion? It would take some sort of superman to have at his command all the registers from religious submersion to raging self-destruction, from naive simplicity to intellectual venturesomeness, from grace to pathos, to be able to present the heights and depths of human character as well as the more sinister aspects, the no-man's-land of emotion. How many pianists would have to be fused together to obtain one Liszt? The public, for the most part, is of course far from demanding even half of a Liszt from Liszt players. It expects—and gets—speed, sentimentality, volume and endurance. (jacket notes)

Brendel also has many interesting things to say about Liszt in *Musical Thoughts and Afterthoughts*.

20. Walker attributes many of the "gaseous paragraphs" and the antisemitism to Sayn-Wittgenstein's 1881 edition. For his account of the text, see Walker, *Franz Liszt: The Weimar Years* (368–96). The English translation cross-referenced here is undated but appears to follow the 1881 edition, referring to both its French and German predecessors.

21. It is interesting that Liszt quotes Hegel here, as he often does. While Liszt apparently needs the words of others to articulate his theoretical standpoint, from Hegel's point of view it would not seem that the favor could be returned. Pointing to some deficiencies in his treatment of music, Hegel explains that one would have to have "a more exact knowledge of the rules of composition and a quite different acquaintance with the most perfect musical works of art than I possess or have been able to acquire, since from the real scholars and practising musicians—least of all from the latter, who are frequently the most unintelligent of men—we seldom hear anything definite and detailed on these matters" (*Ästhetik* 2: 299 / *Aesthetics* 2: 930).

## Chapter 5. Liszt's Bad Style

1. According to critical tradition, Liszt appears in one guise or another in many fictional works, among them George Eliot's *Daniel Deronda*, Balzac's *Béatrix*, George Sand's *Horace*, and Marie d'Agoult's *Nélida*, as well as in many "popular"

works unknown today (Liszt "zines"). My selection of "sources" here has been partly determined by circumstances, for many of the texts are difficult to obtain in the original or in a "reliable" form. I am using for the most part the German edition of Liszt's collected works, except for *Chopin*, of which I refer to the French edition. I have also taken the liberty of drawing on collected sources and citations in secondary works; these collections and secondary works often omit bibliographical references altogether. On the matter of Liszt's text, cf. Chapter 4, n. 21.

2. Liszt may well have affected the possibility of perceiving music today as much as the institution of temperament and Rameau's theory of harmony in the eighteenth century. Today's average piano performance is inconceivable without Liszt. Walker writes: "The modern piano recital was invented by Liszt. He was the first to play entire programmes from memory. He was the first to play the whole keyboard repertory (as it then existed), from Bach to Chopin. He was the first consistently to place the piano at right angles to the platform, its open lid reflecting the sound across the auditorium" (1: 285–86). Though we may take both the word and the practice of piano recitals for granted and never know that we are imitating Liszt, this was not the case at the time, as Seroff reports: "The term 'recital,' which Liszt gave to his concerts, bewildered the English. 'How can anyone recite upon a piano?' they asked" (65). Liszt also invented the concert tour and the performance "career."

3. The autonomy of the texture of the text here invokes Barthes's famous treatment in "The Death of the Author" in *Image - Music - Text*.

4. While Walker's massive biography seems definitive, I have also consulted Haraszti, Huneker, Ramann, Seroff, Waters, and Watson.

5. These attributes are characteristic, too, of the nineteenth-century dandy, a figure also strongly suggested by visual representations of the young Liszt, portrayed as handsome, with flowing hair and velvet jacket. But while the virtuoso and the dandy may share characteristics, the virtuoso is not grounded in ennui, an essential feature in Barbey d'Aurevilly's *Du dandysme et du George Brummell* and in most accounts of dandyism. Liszt is in no sense an idler, nor does he ever appear to be bored. Brummell, "dandyism itself," according to Barbey d'Aurevilly, also has impeccable judgment respected by all—a quality that is certainly never attributed to Liszt (673). But Liszt does have many of the characteristics that Barbey d'Aurevilly attributes to the dandy: the focus on effect, cold calculation, vanity, perfect timing, and the production of the unexpected. For analyses of dandyism, see Moers, Feldman, and Stanton.

6. For analyses of prosopopoeia ("giving a face or mask"), animation, and giving form as figuration, see especially de Man, *Rhetoric of Romanticism*, and the work of Johnson and Lacoue-Labarthe cited in the bibliography; see also Chapter 6, n. 2.

7. On style, see Chapter 1, n. 13. On the signature and authorship, see especially Derrida, "Signature evenément contexte" in *Marges de la philosophie*. On the association of "style," as well as the detail or ornament with "the feminine," see Derrida, *Éperons* and *La Vérité en peinture* (on the *parergon*); Schor, *Reading in Detail*; and Kamuf, "Writing Like a Woman." Schor, in *George Sand and Idealism*, and Miller, in

*Subject to Change*, also address the problematic consequences of the "death of the author" for feminism in view of the historical lack of recognition of female subjects. On the problems of the appropriation of the concept of "the feminine" as style in poststructuralist theory more generally, see Jardine, *Gynesis*, and Simpson, *The Academic Postmodern and the Rule of Literature* (92–110). See also Chapter 1, n. 13.

8. This quote, as well as those from the unnamed critics quoted in French in the following pages, are from the introduction to the 1941 French edition of *Chopin*.

9. This lack of a "mother tongue" reported by Seroff belongs to a legendary image of Liszt. Lina Mueller disagreed with this point at "Wagner and the Consequences," a conference held at Columbia University in October 1995. According to Mueller, Liszt's first language was German.

10. Cf. the following passage in Hegel's *Die Phänomenologie des Geistes* describing the emergence of self-consciousness: "The two extremes—that of the pure inner, the other of the inner that gazes into this pure inner—have now collapsed into one. . . . This curtain [appearance as a middle] is thus drawn away from the inner, and the look into the inner is present. . . . It becomes clear that, behind the so-called curtain that is supposed to hide the inner from view, there is nothing to see if *we* ourselves do not go behind it to look" (135–36).

*Chapter 6. Poetic Originality and Musical Debt:*
*Paradoxes of Translation*

1. De Man, *Rhetoric of Romanticism* (75).

2. Culler works out this logic in his essay "Apostrophe" in *The Pursuit of Signs*. Prosopopoeia is crucial in most of de Man's *Rhetoric of Romanticism*, but especially in the essays "Anthropomorphism and Trope in the Lyric" and "Autobiography as De-Facement." Johnson, in *A World of Difference*, works further with the violence of rhetorical animation, particularly in "Disfiguring Poetic Language" and "Apostrophe, Animation, and Abortion."

3. In "Apostrophe, Animation, and Abortion," Johnson agrees that apostrophe is "almost synonymous with the lyric voice" (185). Note 2 cites Culler; see also de Man's similar statement in his essay "Lyrical Voice in Contemporary Theory" in the anthology *Lyric Poetry: Beyond New Criticism*.

4. The oscillation between identification and rivalry occasioned by the difference between the arts structures the "*agôn*" between subjects discussed by Lacoue-Labarthe in *Musica ficta* and "Baudelaire *contra* Wagner." Lacoue-Labarthe analyzes how the subject of Baudelaire's essay recognizes itself, or "demands *itself* of Wagner" (*se demande à Wagner*) (33) and thus becomes involved in the logic of gift and debt. I am indebted to these texts and to Lacoue-Labarthe's seminar on Baudelaire held at the University of California at Berkeley, fall 1983. As argued in *Musica ficta*, Baudelaire "refinds" his own poetics in Wagner's writings; moreover, he argues, music ends up being a kind of writing for Baudelaire (81–82). In *Resonant Gaps*, Miner also discusses the question of rivalry, concluding that Baudelaire ultimately

privileges writing over music, primarily because of its critical capacity (see her chapter 4).

5. Miner reads this "chance" as an allusion to gambling suggested by Benjamin's interpretation of empty time and "unproductive repetition of beginnings" (*Resonant Gaps*, 28) in the motif of gambling in Baudelaire.

6. *Translation* is the privileged term for accounts of Wagner's music; it is reserved especially for Baudelaire's own rendition of music in the form of "Correspondances." The alternate versions of the essay in the *Pléiade* notes stress the word *translation* in relation to "Correspondances" even more than the published text (*OC* 2: 1462). Of course, nothing guarantees this supposed rootedness of translation in its original experience. The journalistic simulation of a grounding in direct experience is evident, for example, in Nerval's "Souvenirs de Thuringe" in *Lorely 4*. In *Les Fêtes de Weimar: Le Prométhée*, for example, Nerval seems to report about the commemoration of the birthdays of Goethe and Herder from direct experience, though at the end he admits: "Since I did not arrive until the second day of the festival, because of the unforeseen delay on what passes for a railway from Frankfurt to Kassel, I was not able to attend the performance of *Prométhée délivré*. I have only the resource of translating a German analysis which I have every reason to believe exact" (*OC* 2: 299). He also gives accounts of Wagner, reporting details of the workings of the composer's mind to which he could not possibly have immediate access (*OC* 2: 897).

7. If writing itself emerges as an interruption of its historical context, this discontinuity problematizes the attempt to construct an "objective" "horizon of reception," as Jauss does in "The Poetic Text Within the Change of Horizons of Reading: The Example of Baudelaire's 'Spleen II,'" in *Toward an Aesthetics of Reception*. Referring to Gautier's foreword to *Les Fleurs du mal*, Jauss writes: "For the purposes of our investigation the procedure can be abbreviated by appealing to an eyewitness of particular competence who, from a distance of ten years, gave one of the first great appreciations of the work and accurate defenses of his friend, and recognized more clearly than other contemporaries just what kind of horizonal change had unexpectedly been introduced here by a scant volume of poems" (171). Baudelaire's techniques show the questionability of the very notions of abbreviation, of eyewitness authority, of competence and accuracy, and of a smooth transition from unmarked anonymity to the incision of a particular pen as a representative of its background.

8. In *Resonant Gaps*, Miner gives an elaborate reading of the process of italicization in Baudelaire's essay (54–60). She links them both to allegorical motion and to a strange *paralysis*. She argues that the italics immobilize the text to the degree that they remain bound to the meaning "emphasis" (58). See also 215, n. 43.

9. The notion that music is a pedagogical tool used on children (or other "incompetents," such as slaves, women, etc.) who do not yet have the capacity to reason is a very old one in the Western tradition. Music is associated with the "proto-education" and formation delivered by mothers and nurses in the *Republic*; Plato describes how music, including tales, constitutes the first education of the soul as that

medium best suited to shape and mold the "young and tender" (2.376e–77c). Though this music is "false as a whole," when properly controlled it prepares the soul to recognize and conform with "harmony," predisposing character for and prefiguring the future education of philosophy (3.401c–d). Music, however, ought to be surpassed with growth, according to Plato, for it softens the soul (3.411a), bearing with it the danger of self-abandonment. Finally, the restricted art of music is meant to be outgrown and replaced by the "true" musical art attuning body and soul (9.591c–d).

10. My remarks on translation are indebted to the following: Walter Benjamin, "Die Aufgabe des Übersetzers," which does not simply follow upon Baudelaire's interest in the topic but is surely deeply implicated in it, given Benjamin's intense preoccupation with Baudelaire; Derrida, "Des Tours de Babel" in Graham, ed.; Rodolphe Gasché, "Saturnine Vision and the Question of Difference"; and Carol Jacobs, "The Monstrosity of Translation."

11. The deliberate critical insertion of the term *translation* seems necessary to open a vertical axis. In contrast, Bersani argues in *Baudelaire and Freud* that synaesthesia is self-transcending: "Sensuality spiritualizes. . . . It is as if a maximal sensual intensity passed over into the opposite of sensuality. Somehow that maximal point begins to create space; there is an 'expansion' like that of 'infinite things,' and perhaps a certain emptiness insinuates itself into the plenitude of the senses" (33–34).

12. Ion talks about the noncongruity between rhetorical devices and their effects as a professional problem in Plato's *Ion*:

> *Socrates.* Now then, are you aware that you produce the same effects in most of the spectators too?
>
> *Ion.* Yes, indeed, I know it very well. As I look down at them from the stage above, I see them, every time, weeping, casting terrible glances, stricken with amazement at the deeds recounted. In fact, I have to give them very close attention, for if I set them weeping, I myself shall laugh when I get my money, but if they laugh, it is I who have to weep at losing it. (535d–e)

## Chapter 7. *Rivalry Among the Arts and Professional Limitations*

1. While Baudelaire was plainly familiar with Liszt's texts, it appears that he did not know Liszt personally. The encounter over lunch Wagner describes in his autobiography is the only known mention of any actual contact between Liszt and Baudelaire. The *Pléiade* notes inform us that Baudelaire dedicated a copy of *Paradis artificiels* to Liszt (*OC* 1: 1341). But: "There is no mention of Liszt in any of Baudelaire's published letters nor any reference to Baudelaire in those of Liszt" (Bandy, 585). See also Patty.

2. Wagner outlines this theory in the text to which Baudelaire refers. See also the essay, "Zukunftsmusik" (*GS*, vol. 7). He specifically draws the analogy between the division of the arts and the differentiation of European national languages (95).

3. Baudelaire's repeated use of the word *méthode* evokes Cartesian overtones; Descartes, too, uses an elaborate metaphorics of architecture to present the logic of the subject's control over its discourse through method. See *Discours de la méthode* (for example, 41–43, 67–68).

4. The passage just quoted from Baudelaire is in fact almost directly lifted from Liszt, but with the essential difference that Baudelaire elides a paragraph of Liszt's technical analysis. Baudelaire also omits a page of the score that Liszt includes in his text to support his analysis.

5. The discursive function is part of the general definition of *poièsis*; see Lacoue-Labarthe, *Musica ficta* (87–88).

6. For example, in "Über musikalische Kritik," *GS* 5: 54–55.

7. Adorno gives an interesting analysis of the technology of the Wagnerian leit-motiv, both in a musical sense and in its broader theoretical and sociohistorical ramifications in his early work, *Versuch über Wagner* (*Gesammelte Schriften*, vol. 13).

8. Miner finds more significance in this passage and ties together a network of "knot" metaphors; for example: "Their way of 'binding and interlacing them-selves' . . . could signal either bonds of friendship or erotic intertwining, and the *'knot'* could refer either to dramatic tension built up in the opera's plot or to melodic curlicues that adorn the music like ribbons" (*Resonant Gaps*, 82).

While this reading has a certain strength, the "could" betrays itself. Miner finds allegorical success in Liszt's writing; what I read as the deferral of significance Miner reads as allegory: "For Liszt, it is the prelude's motif that makes the temple visible as both a monumental model and an ephemeral image of eternity. . . . In either case, Liszt's program functions simultaneously at two levels: it is at once a program and an allegory of how programs work" (46–47).

It is difficult to linger over the senselessness of digression. This is, of course, a characteristic of Liszt's writing that was both condemned and ridiculed by contem-porary critical reception and surely has much to do with why his texts are in no sense "canonical." The same epithets are also applied to his music. In contrast, Wag-ner's texts, which present a coherent and systematic theory, are widely read. Wag-ner is as much a part of literary as of musical history. There is also an enormous amount of literary material about Liszt; but with the exception of George Eliot's *Daniel Deronda*, much of this "popular" literature is largely unknown today.

9. The issues of expansion and compression are important in readings of the re-lation of Baudelaire's prose poems to their lyric counterparts, especially in Johnson's earlier writings on Baudelaire. De Man, too, often ends up insisting that the lyric instance is a dangerous seduction from which prose should protect us. The end of "Anthropomorphism and Trope" is particularly dramatic in this respect: "The most *it* [true mourning] can do is to allow for non-comprehension and enumerate non-anthropomorphic, non-elegiac, non-celebratory, non-lyrical, non-poetic, that is to say, prosaic, or, better, *historical* modes of language power" (*Rhetoric of Romanticism*, 262).

10. This discussion of speed implies an interesting critique of the approach to

music in Goodman's *Languages of Art*. In this work, often referred to as an important authority in music aesthetics, Goodman develops a logical notion of the "score" as that which defines the identity of a work, and concomitantly, "performance" as the compliance-class of the score. He excludes verbal indications of tempo and mood (e.g., "allegro," "andante" ) from the formal apparatus of the score because of their "ambiguity" and lack of precision. He writes: "Thus the verbal language of tempos is not notational. The tempo words cannot be integral parts of a score insofar as the score serves the function of identifying a work from performance to performance. No departure from the indicated tempo disqualifies a performance as an instance—however wretched—of the work defined by the score. For these tempo specifications cannot be accounted integral parts of the defining score, but are rather auxiliary directions whose observance or nonobservance affects the quality of a performance but not the identity of the work" (185).

While this attitude may satisfy a certain logical appetite, it is thoroughly inadequate for an aesthetics of music. This is why composers include such verbal indications in the first place. Liszt's verbal indication in his *Dante Symphony* is a case in point: "This passage shall be interpreted as a sacrilegious, derisive laughter." The question of the score and its relation to time is pertinent to Lévi-Strauss's use of the term and the role it plays in establishing the synchrony of myth (see esp. section 4.1, "The Structural Study of Myth"). In 4.4 he writes, for example: "The myth will be treated as would be an orchestra score perversely presented as a unilinear series and where our task is to re-establish the correct disposition" (177).

## Chapter 8. Music, Painting, and Writing in Baudelaire's 'Petits poëmes en prose'

1. Cf. the *Pléiade* notes (1: 1339), which also point out that the dedication was omitted in the version of the poem published in *L'Artiste* in 1864.

2. For example, Eigeldinger's "*Le Thyrse*, lecture thématique," stresses the poetic power of unification and reconciliation of "Le Thyrse." This interpretation entails (1) a privileging of the final statements over those preceding (178–79); (2) the reinforcement of authorial center and originality (174); and (3) the equivalence of music and poetry, thus the erasure and sublation of the syntactical extension of "Le Thyrse" (180–81). I have been demonstrating throughout how these conceptual directions systematically work together. An opposed critical tendency, with Johnson at the forefront, works to destabilize the reconciliatory ending and points instead to the infinite periphery surrounding an empty center. Johnson's work in *Défigurations du langage poétique* and her later work on Baudelaire are indispensable. In "Straight Lines and Arabesques," Klein also does a great deal to work against a traditional reading of unification, putting forth the hypothesis that "metaphor of metaphor is not, finally, a sub-category but that all metaphor, if sufficiently extended, tends constantly to displace its center and to lose itself in the self-generating play of its spinning periphery" (68). He also shows that a traditional concept of unity is inopera-

tive in Baudelaire's poem: "The ironic questions seem to point at a unity which is at the same time and paradoxically a duality, or, more accurately perhaps, to a unity structured by a difference which makes it neither dual nor self-identical" (81–82). However, he does not really explore the strange oscillation between reference and linguistic self-reference implied by the presence of Liszt and the problems of address that go along with it.

3. See esp. Klein on the copula (80–84).

4. The only actual contact recorded between Liszt and Baudelaire is the anecdote in Wagner's autobiography. The only correspondence is a short letter from Baudelaire to which there was apparently no reply. This note in the Liszt Museum in Weimar, published by Bandy for the first time, reads: "Dear Sir, I met Madame Wagner today, who informed me that you had received my brochure on Wagner, and that you would be able to see me. I wished to anticipate your visit, fearing that you would not find me at home, for I am very busy. I know that you are leaving on the 20th. I will come back to see you. For years I have desired to find the occasion to give you testimony of all the sympathy your character and your talent inspire in me. Ch. Baudelaire." Bandy explains: "This letter bears only the address: 'Monsieur Liszt,' which leads me to think that it must have been written at Liszt's residence where Baudelaire had called and found him not at home" (585).

5. I borrow the term *sonorous texture* from Abbate.

6. Sources are traced thoroughly in Zimmerman, "La Genèse du symbole du thyrse chez Baudelaire." Eigeldinger privileges Baudelaire's "originality" (174).

7. Thanks to Guerlac, who has worked extensively on this topic, for discussions, for sharing the manuscript of her book *The Impersonal Sublime: Hugo, Baudelaire, Lautréamont*, and for referring me to Wilner's essay.

8. This is notable, since there is a French word *caducée*, defined in *Le Grand Robert* as follows: "Attribute of Mercury, constituted of a rod surrounded by two interlaced snakes topped by two short wings. The caduceus is the symbol of peace, of eloquence and of commerce" (2: 262). Compare to *thyrse*: "Antiq. Attribute of Bacchus, a stick surrounded by leaves of ivy or vines, topped with a pine-cone, which was carried by the Bacchantes" (9: 299). Thus, Baudelaire translates an attribute of the messenger into one of the god of frenzy and intoxication. For more extensive histories of these terms, see Pauly and Wissowa. The thyrsus is carried by both Bacchus and his followers, uniting them in the communal frenzy Baudelaire invokes in his poem. In its many historical representations, the thyrsus remains primarily decorative, according to Pauly and Wissowa. The caduceus, an emblem of Mercury, appeared most often on coins and came to stand as a symbol of peace, implying negotiation, linguistic exchange, and mediation. The thyrsus, on the other hand, clings to the hand of Bacchus and fuses the followers with each other and with the divine intoxicant.

9. Feldman calls this equivocality androgyny; this dissolution of binary difference would also induce the collapse of gender difference (118). She pursues this logic

in arguing that Baudelaire's concept of similarity and analogy is "feminine" (120–26).

10. Like Little Hans in Freud's *Jenseits des Lustprinzips*, Baudelaire repetitively throws his own identity away in order to pull it back. The literary relations to Poe, Delacroix, and de Quincey, for example, are analogous to the substitution of the top for the mother in Freud's anecdote (see Freud 3: 224–27).

# Bibliography

Abbate, Carolyn. *Unsung Voices: Opera and Musical Narrative in the Nineteenth Century.* Princeton: Princeton University Press, 1991.

Abraham, Nicolas. *Rhythmes: De l'oeuvre, de la traduction et de la psychoanalyse.* Ed. Nicholas T. Rand and Maria Torok. Paris: Flammarion, 1985.

Adorno, Theodor W. "Die Wunde Heine." In *Noten zur Literatur.* Frankfurt am Main: Suhrkamp Verlag, 1981.

———. *Gesammelte Schriften.* Ed. Rolf Tiedemann. Frankfurt am Main: Suhrkamp, 1978.

———. "Heine the Wound." In *Notes to Literature.* 2 vols. Ed. Rolf Tiedemann, trans. Shierry Weber Nicholson. New York: Columbia University Press, 1991.

———. *Introduction to the Sociology of Music.* Trans. E. B. Ashton. New York: Continuum, 1989.

Adorno, Theodor W., and Max Horkheimer. *Dialektik der Aufklärung: Philosophische Fragmente.* Frankfurt am Main: Fischer Taschenbuch Verlag, 1979.

Allen, James Smith. *Popular French Romanticism: Authors, Readers, and Books in the Nineteenth Century.* Syracuse: Syracuse University Press, 1981.

Allen, Warren Dwight. *Philosophies of Music History: A Study of General Histories of Music, 1600–1960.* New York: Dover, 1932.

Altenhofer, Norbert. "Chiffre, Hieroglyphe, Palimpsest: Vorformen tiefenhermeneutischer und intertextueller Interpretation im Werk Heines." In *Texthermeneutik: Aktualität, Geschichte, Kritik.* Ed. Ulrich Nassen. Paderborn: Ferdinand Schönigh, 1979: 149–93.

Anderson, Benedict. *Imagined Communities: Reflections on the Origin and Spread of Nationalism.* London and New York: Verso, 1983.

Arendt, Hannah. "Heinrich Heine: Schlemihl und Traumweltherrscher." In *Die verborgene Tradition.* Frankfurt am Main: Suhrkamp Verlag, 1976.

*Aristotle's Theory of Poetry and Fine Art*. Trans. S. H. Butcher, intro. John Gassner. New York: Dover, 1951.

Auerbach, Erich. *Mimesis: The Representation of Reality in Western Literature*. Trans. Willard R. Trask. Princeton: Princeton University Press, 1974.

Austin, J. L. *How to Do Things with Words*. Cambridge, Mass.: Harvard University Press, 1962.

Balzac, Honoré de. *La Comédie humaine*. Paris: Bibliothèque de la Pléiade, 1950.

——. *Lost Illusions*. Trans. Herbert J. Hunt. London: Penguin, 1971.

——. *Illusions perdues*. Paris: Flammarion, 1990.

——. *Oeuvres complètes*. Paris, 1872.

Bandy, W. T. "Baudelaire and Liszt." *Modern Language Notes* (December 1938): 584–85.

Barbey d'Aurevilly, Jules-Amédée. *Oeuvres romanesques complètes*. 2 vols. Ed. Jacques Petit. Paris: Editions Gallimard, 1966.

Baricelli, Jean-Pierre. *Melopoiesis: Approaches to the Study of Literature and Music*. New York: New York University Press, 1988.

Barry, Kevin. *Language, Music, and the Sign: A Study in Aesthetics, Poetics and Poetic Practice from Collins to Coleridge*. Cambridge: Cambridge University Press, 1987.

Barthes, Roland. *Image - Music - Text*. Trans. Stephen Heath. New York: Hill and Wang, 1977.

——. *L'Obvie et l'obtus: Essais critiques III*. Paris: Editions du Seuil, 1982.

Bartók, Béla. *Essays*. Ed. Benjamin Suchoff. The New York Bartók Archive Studies in Musicology. London: Faber and Faber, 1976.

Barzun, Jacques, ed. *Pleasures of Music: An Anthology of Writing About Music and Musicians from Cellini to Bernard Shaw*. Chicago: University of Chicago Press, 1977.

Bataille, Georges. *La Littérature et le mal*. Vol. 9 of *Oeuvres complètes*. Paris: Editions Gallimard, 1970.

Baudelaire, Charles. *Art in Paris, 1845–1862: Salons and Other Exhibitions*. Trans. and ed. Jonathan Mayne. London: Phaidon Press, 1965; Ithaca, New York: Cornell University Press, 1981.

——. *Oeuvres complètes*. 2 vols. Ed. Claude Pichois. Paris: Bibliothèque de la Pléiade, 1975.

——. *Oeuvres complètes. Nouvelles histoires extraordinaires traduites d'Edgar A. Poe*. Ed. F.-F. Gautier. Paris: Editions de la Nouvelle Revue Française, 1928.

——. *Oeuvres complètes: Les Paradis artificiels*. Ed. Jacques Crépet. Paris: Louis Conrad, 1928 [1965].

——. *The Painter of Modern Life and Other Essays*. Trans. and ed. Jonathan Mayne. London: Phaidon Press, 1964; New York: Da Capo Press, 1986.

——. *Paris Spleen*. Trans. Louise Varèse. New York: New Directions, 1947.

Beaujour, Michel. "Short Epiphanies: Two Contextual Approaches to the French Prose Poem." In *The Prose Poem in France: Theory and Practice*. Ed. Mary

Ann Caws and Hermine Riffaterre. New York: Columbia University Press, 1983.

Bellet, Roger, ed. *Paris au 19e siècle: Aspects d'un mythe littéraire*. Lyon: Presses Universitaires de Lyon, 1984.

Benjamin, Walter. *Gesammelte Schriften*. 7 vols. Ed. Rolf Tiedemann and Herrmann Schweppenhäuser. Frankfurt am Main: Suhrkamp, 1974.

Benveniste, Emile. *Problèmes de linguistique générale*. 2 vols. Paris: Editions Gallimard, 1966.

——. *Problems in General Linguistics*. Trans. Mary Elizabeth Meek. Florida: University of Miami Press, 1971.

Berlioz, Hector. *Oeuvres littéraires: A travers chants*. Ed. Léon Guichard. Paris: Librairie Gründ, 1971.

——. *The Art of Music and Other Essays (A travers chants)*. Trans. and ed. Elizabeth Csicsery-Rónay. Bloomington and Indianapolis: Indiana University Press, 1994.

Bernstein, Susan. "Fear of Music? Nietzsche's Double Vision of the 'Musical-Feminine.'" In *Nietzsche and the Feminine*. Ed. Peter Burgard. Charlottesville: University Press of Virginia, 1994.

——. "Journalism and German Identity: Communiqués from Heine, Wagner, and Adorno." *New German Critique* 66 (fall 1995): 65–93.

Bersani, Leo. *Baudelaire and Freud*. Berkeley: University of California Press, 1977.

Bloom, Harold. *The Anxiety of Influence: A Theory of Poetry*. Oxford: Oxford University Press, 1973.

Bourdieu, Pierre. *Le Sens pratique*. Paris: Editions de Minuit, 1980.

Brendel, Alfred. Jacket notes for Franz Liszt, *Hungarian Rhapsodies*. Philips VSL11070. Record album.

——. *Musical Thoughts and Afterthoughts*. Princeton: Princeton University Press, 1976.

Briegleb, Klaus. *Opfer Heine? Versuche über Schriftzüge der Revolution*. Frankfurt am Main: Suhrkamp Verlag, 1986.

Butler, Judith. *Bodies That Matter: On the Discursive Limits of "Sex."* New York: Routledge, 1993.

Cage, John. *For the Birds*. New York: Boyars, 1981.

——. *Silence: Lectures and Writings by John Cage*. Middletown, Conn.: Wesleyan University Press, 1973.

Chladni, Ernst F. *Entdeckungen über die Theorie des Klanges*. Leipzig, 1787.

——. *Die Akustik*. Leipzig: Breitkopf und Härtel, 1802.

Chorley, Henry F. *Music and Manners in France and Germany*. 3 vols. 1841. Reprint, New York: Da Capo, 1984.

Chotzinoff, Samuel. Jacket notes for *Vladimir Horowitz: Homage to Liszt*. RCA LM-2584. Record album.

Culler, Jonathan. *The Pursuit of Signs: Semiotics, Literature, Deconstruction*. Ithaca, New York: Cornell University Press, 1981.

Dahlhaus, Carl. *Between Romanticism and Modernism: Four Studies in the Music of the Later Nineteenth Century*. Trans. Mary Whittall, with trans. of Friedrich Nietzsche's "On Music and Words" by Walter Kaufmann. Berkeley: University of California Press, 1980.

——. *Esthetics of Music*. Trans. William Austin. Cambridge: Cambridge University Press, 1983.

——. *Die Idee der absoluten Musik*. Kassel: Bärenreiter-Verlag, 1978.

Deathridge, John. "Lohengrin." In *The English National Opera Guide*. London: John Calder; New York: Riverrun Press, n.d.

Deathridge, John, Martin Geck, and Egon Voss, eds. *Wagner Werk-Verzeichnis: Verzeichnis der musikalischen Werke Richard Wagners und ihrer Quellen*. Mainz: Schott's Söhne, 1985.

Debussy, Claude. *Debussy on Music*. New York: Alfred A. Knopf, 1977.

Delacroix, Eugène. *The Journal of Eugène Delacroix*. Ed. Hubert Wellington, trans. Lucy Norton. Ithaca, New York: Cornell University Press, 1980.

——. *Oeuvres littéraires, 1: Etudes esthétiques*. Paris: Editions G. Crès, 1923.

de Man, Paul. *Allegories of Reading: Figural Language in Rousseau, Nietzsche, Rilke, and Proust*. New Haven, Conn.: Yale University Press, 1979.

——. *Blindness and Insight: Studies in the Rhetoric of Contemporary Criticism*. Minneapolis: University of Minnesota Press, 1983.

——. *The Rhetoric of Romanticism*. New York: Columbia University Press, 1984.

de Quincey, Thomas. *Confessions of an English Opium-Eater* and *Suspiria de Profundis*. Garden City, New York: Doubleday, n.d.

Derrida, Jacques. *De la grammatologie*. Paris: Editions de Minuit, 1967.

——. *The Ear of the Other: Texts and Discussions with Jacques Derrida: Otobiography, Transference, Translation*. Ed. Christie McDonald, trans. Peggy Kamuf and Avital Ronell. Lincoln: University of Nebraska Press, 1985.

——. *L'Ecriture et la différence*. Paris: Editions du Seuil, 1969.

——. *Marges de la philosophie*. Paris: Editions de Minuit, 1972.

——. *Margins of Philosophy*. Trans. Alan Bass. Chicago: University of Chicago Press, 1982.

——. *Of Grammatology*. Trans. Gayatri Chakravorty Spivak. Baltimore: Johns Hopkins University Press, 1976.

——. *Spurs: Nietzsche's Styles (Eperons: Les Styles de Nietzsche)*. Trans. Barbara Harlow. Chicago: University of Chicago Press, 1979.

——. *La Vérité en peinture*. Paris: Flammarion, 1978.

Descartes, René. *Discours de la méthode*. Paris: Garnier-Flammarion, 1966.

——. *Oeuvres*. Ed. Victor Cousin. Paris: F. G. Levrault, 1824–26.

*Dictionnaire alphabétique et analogique de la langue française*. 6 vols. Paul Robert. Paris: Société du Nouveau Littré, 1964.

*Dictionnaire de la langue française*. 4 vols. E. Littré. Paris: Librairie Hachette, 1881.

Dilthey, Wilhelm. *Einleitung in die Geisteswissenschaften*. Vol. 1 of *Gesammelte Schriften*. Leipzig: Teubner, 1922.

Ducrot, Oswald. *Le Dire et le dit*. Paris: Editions de Minuit, 1984.

Ducrot, Oswald, and Tzetan Todorov. *Encyclopedic Dictionary of the Sciences of Language*. Trans. Catherine Porter. Baltimore: Johns Hopkins University Press, 1979.

Eigeldinger, Marc. "*Le Thyrse*, lecture thèmatique." *Études baudelairiennes* 8.

———. *Lumières du mythe*. Paris: PUF, 1983.

Einstein, Alfred. *Music in the Romantic Era*. New York: Norton, 1947.

Eliot, George. *Works: Essays and Leaves from a Notebook*. Vol. 6. Edinburgh and London: William Blackwood, 1883.

Eliot, T. S. *The Music of Poetry*. Glasgow: Jackson, Son, 1942.

———. *To Criticize the Critic, and Other Writings*. London: Faber, 1964.

Engelsing, Rolf. *Der Bürger als Leser: Lesergeschichte in Deutschland 1500–1800*. Stuttgart: J. B. Metzlersche Verlagsbuchhandlung, 1974.

Febvre, Lucien, and H. J. Martin. *L'Apparition du livre*. Paris: Editions Albin Michel, 1958.

Feldman, Jessica. *Gender on the Divide: The Dandy in Modernist Literature*. Ithaca, New York: Cornell University Press, 1993.

Felman, Shoshana. *Le Scandale du corps parlant: Don Juan avec Austin ou la séduction en deux langues*. Paris: Editions du Seuil, 1980.

Fenves, Peter D. *A Peculiar Fate: Metaphysics and World-History in Kant*. Ithaca, New York: Cornell University Press, 1991.

Fétis, F.-J. *Biographie universelle des musiciens et bibliographie générale de la musique*. Brussels, 1835–44.

———. *La Musique mise à la portée de tout le monde*. Paris, 1847.

Foucault, Michel. *The Archaeology of Knowledge and the Discourse on Language*. Trans. A. M. Sheridan Smith. New York: Pantheon, 1972.

———. "What Is an Author?" In *Textual Strategies: Perspectives in Post-Structuralist Criticism*. Ed. Josué Harari. Ithaca, New York: Cornell University Press, 1979.

Freud, Sigmund. *Psychologie des Unbewußten*. Studienausgabe. Vol. 3. Frankfurt am Main: Fischer Taschenbuchverlag, 1982.

Fried, Michael. "Painting Memories: On the Containment of the Past in Baudelaire and Manet." *Critical Inquiry* 10 (March 1984): 510–42.

Gasché, Rodolphe. "Saturnine Vision and the Question of Difference: Reflections on Walter Benjamin's Theory of Language." *Studies in the Twentieth Century* 11.1 (fall 1986): 69–90.

Gautier, Théophile. *Baudelaire par Gautier*. Ed. Claude-Marie Senninger. Paris: Klincksieck, 1986.

———. *La Musique*. Paris: Bibliothèque-Charpentier, 1911.

Gilman, Sander L. "Heines Photographien." In *Heine Jahrbuch*. Hamburg: Hoffmann und Campe Verlag, 1988: 9–31.

———. *Jewish Self-Hatred: Anti-Semitism and the Hidden Language of the Jews*. Baltimore: Johns Hopkins University Press, 1986.

Goethe, Johann Wolfgang von, and Friedrich Schiller. "Über epische und dramatis- che Dichtung." In *Goethes Werke*. Vol. 12. Hamburg: Christian Wegner Verlag, 1953: 249–51.

Goodman, Nelson. *Languages of Art: An Approach to a Theory of Symbols*. Indianapo- lis and New York: Bobbs-Merill, 1968.

Graham, Joseph F., ed. *Difference in Translation*. Ithaca: Cornell University Press, 1985.

Grimm, Jacob, and Wilhelm Grimm. *Deutsches Wörterbuch*. Vol. 12, II. Abteilung: Verlag S. Hirzel, 1951.

Guerlac, Suzanne. *The Impersonal Sublime: Hugo, Baudelaire, Lautréament*. Stan- ford, Calif: Stanford University Press, 1990.

Habermas, Jürgen. *Strukturwandel der Öffentlichkeit: Untersuchungen zu einer Kate- gorie der bürgerlichen Gesellschaft*. Frankfurt am Main: Suhrkamp Verlag, 1990.

Hamacher, Werner. *Pleroma: Zu Genesis und Struktur einer dialektischen Hermeneutik bei Hegel*. In *Der Geist des Christentums*. Ed. W. Hamacher. Frankfurt am Main: Ullstein, 1978.

——. *Premises: Essays on Philosophy and Literature from Kant to Celan*. Trans. Peter Fenves. Cambridge, Mass.: Harvard University Press, 1996.

Haraszti, Emil. "Die Autorschaft der literarischen Werke Franz Liszts." *Ungarische Jahrbücher* 21 (1938): 173–236.

Havelock, Eric A. *The Muse Learns to Write: Reflections on Orality and Literacy from Antiquity to the Present*. New Haven: Yale University Press, 1986.

Havelock, Eric A., and Jackson P. Hershbell, eds. *Communication Arts in the Ancient World*. New York: Hastings House, 1978.

Hegel, Georg Wilhelm Friedrich. *Ästhetik*. 2 vols. Ed. Friedrich Bassenge. Berlin: Aufbau-Verlag, 1985.

——. *Aesthetics: Lectures on Fine Arts*. 2 vols. Trans. T. M. Knox. New York: Oxford University Press, 1975.

——. *Phänomenologie des Geistes*. Frankfurt am Main: Suhrkamp Verlag, 1976.

Heine, Heinrich. *Confessio Judaica*. Ed. Hugo Bieber. Berlin: Welt-Verlag, 1925.

——. *Historisch-kritische Gesamtausgabe der Werke*. Ed. Manfred Windfuhr. Ham- burg: Hoffmann und Campe Verlag, 1973.

——. *The Romantic School and Other Essays*. Ed. Jost Hermand and Robert C. Holub. New York: Continuum, 1985.

——. *Sämtliche Schriften*. 6 vols. Ed. Klaus Briegleb. Munich: Carl Hanser Verlag, 1971.

Herington, John. *Poetry into Drama: Early Tragedy and the Greek Poetic Tradition*. Berkeley: University of California Press, 1985.

Herwegh, Marcel. *Au soir des dieux: Des derniers reflets wagneriens à la mort de Liszt (1847. 1883–1886). Franz Liszt, Richard et Cosima Wagner, Princesse Carolyne Sayn-Wittgenstein, Georges et Emma Herwegh*. Paris: J. Peyronnet, 1933.

Hocks, Paul, and Peter Schmidt. *Literarische und politische Zeitschriften, 1789–1805.* Stuttgart: J. B. Metzlersche Verlagsbuchhandlung, 1975.

Hoffmann, E. T. A. *Kreisleriana.* Stuttgart: Reclam, 1983.

——. *E. T. A. Hoffmann's Musical Writings: "Kreisleriana," "The Poet and the Composer," Music Criticism.* Ed. David Charlton, trans. Martyn Clarke. Cambridge: Cambridge University Press, 1989.

Hohendahl, Peter Uwe. *The Institution of Criticism.* Ithaca, New York: Cornell University Press, 1982.

Hohendahl, Peter Uwe, and Sander L. Gilman, eds. *Heinrich Heine and the Occident: Multiple Identities, Multiple Receptions.* Lincoln: University of Nebraska Press, 1991.

Hosek, Chaviva, and Patricia Parker, eds. *Lyric Poetry: Beyond New Criticism.* Ithaca, New York: Cornell University Press, 1985.

Huneker, James. *Franz Liszt.* New York: Charles Scribner's Sons, 1911.

Jacobs, Arthur. *The New Penguin Dictionary of Music.* Harmondsworth, England: Penguin, 1983.

Jacobs, Carol. "The Monstrosity of Translation." *Modern Language Notes* 90 (1976): 755–66.

——. *Uncontainable Romanticism: Shelley, Brontë, Kleist.* Baltimore: Johns Hopkins University Press, 1989.

Jakobson, Roman. *Language in Literature.* Ed. Krystyna Pomorska and Stephen Rudy. Cambridge, Mass.: Harvard University Press, 1987.

James, Henry. "Charles Baudelaire." In *Literary Criticism: French Writers.* New York: Literary Classics of the United States, 1984.

Jankelevitch, Vladimir. *La Musique et l'ineffable.* Paris: Editions du Seuil, 1983.

——. *Liszt et la rhapsodie: Essai sur la virtuosité.* Paris: Plon, 1979.

Jardine, Alice A. *Gynesis: Configurations of Woman and Modernity.* Ithaca, New York: Cornell University Press, 1985.

Jauss, Hans Robert. *Toward an Aesthetics of Reception.* Trans. Timothy Bahti, intro. Paul de Man. Minneapolis: University of Minnesota Press, 1982.

Johnson, Barbara. "Apostrophe, Animation, and Abortion." *Diacritics* 16.1 (spring 1986): 29–39.

——. *The Critical Difference.* Baltimore: Johns Hopkins University Press, 1980.

——. *Défigurations du langage poétique: La Seconde Révolution baudelairienne.* Paris: Flammarion, 1970.

——. *A World of Difference.* Baltimore: Johns Hopkins University Press, 1987.

Kaiser, Gerhard R. "Baudelaire pro Heine contra Janin: Text - Kommentar - Analyse." In *Heine Jahrbuch.* Ed. Joseph A. Kruse. Hamburg: Hoffmann und Campe Verlag, 1983: 135–78.

Kamuf, Peggy. "Writing Like a Woman." In *Women and Language in Literature and Society,* ed. Sally McConnell-Ginet, Ruth Brocker, and Nelly Furman. New York: Praeger, 1980.

Kant, Immanuel. *Critique of Judgement*. Trans. J. H. Bernard. New York: Hafner Press, 1951.

——. *Critique of Pure Reason*. Trans. Norman Kemp Smith. New York: St. Martin's Press, 1965.

——. *Kritik der reinen Vernunft*. Berlin: Walter de Gruyter, 1968.

——. *Kritik der Urteilskraft*. Ed. Wilhelm Weischedel. Frankfurt am Main: Suhrkamp Verlag, 1981.

Kepler, Johannes. "The Harmonies of the World." Trans. Charles Glenn Wallis. In *Great Books of the Western World*. Vol. 16. Ed. Robert Maynard Hutchins. Chicago: Encyclopedia Britannica, 1952.

Kierkegaard, Søren. *Either/Or*. Trans. David F. Swenson. Garden City, New York: Anchor, 1959.

——. *Either/Or*. Trans. Howard V. Hong and Edna H. Hong. Princeton: Princeton University Press, 1987.

——. *Om Mozarts Don Juan*. Ed. Carl Johan Elmquist. Copenhagen: Jespersen of Pios Forlag, 1968.

Kirchner, Joachim. *Das deutsche Zeitschriftenwesen: Seine Geschichte und seine Probleme*. 2 vols. Wiesbaden: Otto Harrassowitz, 1958.

Klein, Richard. "Straight Lines and Arabesques: Metaphors of Metaphor." *Yale French Studies* 45 (1970).

Kleinknecht, Karl Theodor, ed. *Heine in Deutschland: Dokumente seiner Rezeption, 1834–1956*. Tübingen: Max Niemeyer Verlag, 1976.

Knaus, Jakob, ed. *Sprache - Dichtung - Musik*. Tübingen: Max Niemeyer Verlag, 1973.

Kontje, Todd. *Private Lives in the Public Sphere: The German Bildungsroman as Metafiction*. Pennsylvania: Pennsylvania State University Press, 1992.

Koopmann, Helmut, ed. *Heinrich Heine*. Darmstadt: Wissenschaftliche Buchgesellschaft, 1975.

Kracauer, Sigfried. *Jacques Offenbach und das Paris seiner Zeit*. In *Schriften*. Vol. 8. Ed. Inka Mülder-Bach. Frankfurt am Main: Suhrkamp, 1971.

Kramer, Lawrence. *Music as Cultural Practice, 1800–1900*. Berkeley: University of California Press, 1990.

Kraus, Karl. *Heine und die Folgen*. Munich: Albert Langen, 1910.

Kristeva, Julia. *Le Langage, cet inconnu: Une Initiation à la linguistique*. Paris: Editions du Seuil, 1981.

——. *Polylogue*. Paris: Seuil, 1977.

——. *La Révolution du langage poétique*. Paris: Editions du Seuil, 1974.

——. *Revolution in Poetic Language*. Trans. Margaret Waller. New York: Columbia University Press, 1984.

Kruse, Joseph A., and Michael Werner, eds. *Heine in Paris, 1831–1856*. Düsseldorf: Droste Verlag, 1981.

Lacoue-Labarthe, Philippe. "Baudelaire *contra* Wagner." *Etudes françaises* 17.3–4 (1981): 23–52.

——. *Musica ficta (Figures de Wagner)*. Paris: Christian Bourgois Editeur, 1991.

——. *Musica Ficta (Figures of Wagner)*. Trans. Felicia McCarren. Stanford, Calif.: Stanford University Press, 1994.

——. *Le Sujet de la philosophie: Typographies 1*. Paris: Aubier-Flammarion, 1979.

——. "Typographie." In *Mimesis des articulations*. Paris: Flammarion, 1975.

——. *Typography: Mimesis, Philosophy, Politics*. Ed. Christopher Fynsk. Cambridge, Mass.: Harvard University Press, 1989.

Lacoue-Labarthe, Philippe, and Jean-Luc Nancy. *L'Absolu littéraire: Théorie de la littérature de romantisme Allemand*. Paris: Editions du Seuil, 1978.

——. *The Literary Absolute: The Theory of Literature in German Romanticism*. Trans. Philip Barnard and Cheryl Lester. Albany: State University of New York Press, 1988.

Lacour, Claudia Brodsky. "The Temporality of Convention: Convention Theory and Romanticism." In *Rules and Conventions*, ed. Mette Hjort. Baltimore: Johns Hopkins University Press, 1992: 274–93.

Latacz, Joachim, ed. *Homer: Tradition und Neuerung*. Darmstadt: Wissenschaftliche Buchgesellschaft, 1979.

Ledré, Charles. *Histoire de la presse*. Paris: Librairie Arthème Rayard, 1958.

Lefebvre, Jean-Pierre. *Der gute Trommler: Heines Beziehung zu Hegel*. Trans. Peter Schöttler. Heine-Studien. Hamburg: Hoffmann und Campe, Heinrich Heine Verlag, 1986.

Leibniz, Gottfried. *De la monadologie*. Ed. D. Nolen. Paris: Felix Alcan, 1893.

——. *Nouveaux essais*. Vol. 1 of *Oeuvres philosophiques*. Ed. Paul Janet. Paris: Librairie Philosophique Ladrange, 1866.

Levine, Michael G. "Heines Ghost Writer: Zum Problem der Selbstzensur im 'Schnabelewopski.'" In *Heine Jahrbuch*. Hamburg: Hoffmann und Campe Verlag, 1987.

——. "Struggles with (Self)Censorship from Heine to Freud." Ph.D. diss., Johns Hopkins University, 1987.

——. *Writing Through Repression: Literature, Censorship, Psychoanalysis*. Baltimore: Johns Hopkins University Press, 1994.

Lévi-Strauss, Claude. "The Structural Study of Myth." In *The Structuralists from Marx to Lévi-Strauss*. Ed. Richard and Fernande DeGeorge. New York: Anchor, 1972. 169–94.

Lippmann, Edward A., ed. *From Antiquity to the Eighteenth Century*. Vol. 1 of *Musical Aesthetics: A Historical Reader*. New York: Pendragon Press, 1986.

Liszt, Franz. *An Artist's Journey: Lettres d'un bachelier ès musique, 1835–1841*. Trans. Charles Suttonie. Chicago: University of Chicago Press, 1989.

——. *Des Bohémiens et de leur musique en Hongrie*. Leipzig: Breitkopf und Härtel, 1881.

——. *Chopin*. Trans. and intro. Edward N. Waters. London: Free Press of Glencoe, 1963.

——. *F. Chopin*. Ed. Alfred Cortot and J. G. Prod'homme. Paris: Corréa, 1941.

——. *Gesammelte Schriften*. 6 vols. Ed. Lina Ramann. Leipzig: Breitkopf und Härtel, 1881.

——. *The Gipsy in Music*. Trans. Edwin Evans. London: William Reeves.

——. *Sämtliche Schriften*. Ed. Rainer Kleinertz and Gerhard J. Winkler. Wiesbaden: Breitkopf und Härtel, 1989.

——. *Unbekannte Presse und Briefe aus Wien, 1822–1886*. Ed. Dezso Legny. Wien-Köln-Graz: Verlag Hermann Böhlaus Nachf., 1984.

Liszt, Franz, and Richard Wagner. *Correspondence*. Vol. 1. Trans. Francis Hueffer. London: H. Grevel, 1897.

Lord, Albert B. *The Singer of Tales*. New York: Atheneum, 1974.

Lukács, Georg. "Heinrich Heine als nationaler Dichter." In *Deutsche Realisten des 19. Jahrhunderts*. Berlin: Aufbau-Verlag, 1950.

——. "Narrate or Describe?" In *Writer and Critic and Other Essays*. Ed. and trans. Arthur D. Kahn. New York: Grosset and Dunlap, 1974.

Maclean, Marie. *Narrative as Performance: The Baudelairean Experiment*. London: Routledge, 1988.

Maierhofer, Waltraud. "'Die Sprödigkeit des Stoffes': Heinrich Heine als Erzähler." *Heine Jahrbuch* 31 (1992): 92–105.

Mallarmé, Stéphane. *Oeuvres complètes*. Paris: Bibliothèque de la Pléiade, 1966.

Mann, Michael. "Französische Quellen für Heinrich Heines Berichte über 'Die Musikalische Saison.'" *Germanisch-Romanische Monatsschrift* 12 (1962): 253–67.

——. *Heinrich Heines Musikkritiken*. Hamburg: Hoffmann und Campe, Heinrich Heine Verlag, 1971.

Marin, Louis. "The Autobiographical Interruption: About Stendahl's *Life of Henry Brulard*." *Modern Language Notes* 93.4 (1978): 597–617.

——. "Toward a Theory of Reading in the Visual Arts: Poussin's *The Arcadian Shepherds*." In *The Reader in the Text: Essays on Audience and Interpretation*. Ed. Susan R. Suleiman and Inge Crossman. Princeton: Princeton University Press, 1980.

——. "Sur un certain regard du sujet." In *Les Sujets de l'écriture*. Ed. Jean Decottignies. Lille: Presses Universitaires de Lille, 1981: 41–62.

——. *La Voix excommuniée: Essais de mémoire*. Paris: Editions Galilée, 1981.

Marx, Karl, and Friedrich Engels. *Werke*. Berlin: Dietz Verlag, 1981.

McDonald, Christie V. "La Portée des notes." In *Les Fins de l'homme*. Ed. Philippe Lacoue-Labarthe and Jean-Luc Nancy. Paris: Editions Galilée, 1981: 597–617.

McLaughlin, Kevin. *Writing in Parts: Imitation and Exchange in Nineteenth-Century Literature*. Stanford, Calif.: Stanford University Press, 1995.

Mellers, Wilfred. *Romanticism and the Twentieth Century*. Part 4 of *Man and His Music: The Story of Musical Experience in the West*. New York: Schocken Books, 1969.

Merrick, Paul. *Revolution and Religion in the Music of Liszt*. Cambridge: Cambridge University Press, 1987.

Meschonnic, Henri. *Critique du rythme: Anthropologie historique du langage*. Paris: Editions Verdier, 1982.

———. *Pour la poétique II: Epistémologie de l'écriture. Poétique de la traduction*. Paris: Editions Gallimard, 1973.

Miller, Nancy K. *Subject to Change: Reading Feminist Writing*. New York: Columbia University Press, 1988.

Miner, Margaret. "Putting the Emphasis on Music: Baudelaire and the *Lohengrin* Prelude." In *Nineteenth-Century French Studies* 21: 3–4, 1993. 384–401.

———. *Resonant Gaps: Between Baudelaire and Wagner*. Athens: University of Georgia Press, 1995.

Moers, Ellen. *The Dandy: Brummell to Beerbohm*. New York: Viking Press, 1960.

Monroe, Jonathan. *A Poverty of Objects: The Prose Poem and the Politics of Genre*. Ithaca, New York: Cornell University Press, 1987.

Moss, Armand. *Baudelaire et Delacroix*. Paris: A. G. Nizet, n.d.

Nancy, Jean-Luc. *Le Discours de la syncope*. Paris: Flammarion, 1976.

———. *Le Partage des voix*. Paris: Editions Galilée, 1982.

———. *Le Sens du monde*. Paris: Editions Galilée, 1993.

Nattiez, Jean-Jacques. *Fondements d'une sémiologie de la musique*. Paris: Union Générale d'Editions, 1975.

Nerval, Gerard de. "Souvenirs de Thuringe." In *Lorely 4: Les Fêtes de Weimar: Le Prométhée*. Vol. 2 of *Oeuvres*. Paris: Bibliothèque de la Pléiade, Editions Gallimard, 1961.

Neubauer, John. *The Emancipation of Music from Language: Departure from Mimesis in Eighteenth-Century Aesthetics*. New Haven: Yale University Press, 1986.

Newcomb, Anthony. "Sound and Feeling." *Critical Inquiry* 10 (1984): 614–43.

Nietzsche, Friedrich. *The Birth of Tragedy and the Case of Wagner*. Trans. Walter Kaufmann. New York: Random House, 1967.

———. *Collected Works*. 18 vols. Trans. J. M. Kennedy. New York: Russell and Russell, 1964.

———. *Kritische Studienausgabe*. 15 vols. Ed. Giorgio Colli and Mazzino Montinari. Berlin and New York: de Gruyter, 1988.

———. *Werke*. 3 vols. Ed. Karl Schlechta. Frankfurt am Main: Verlag Ullstein, 1979.

Ong, Walter J. *Orality and Literacy: The Technology of the Work*. London and New York: Routledge, 1982.

Parker, Andrew, and Eve Kosofsky Sedgwick, eds. *Performativity and Performance*. New York: Routledge, 1995.

Parry, Milman. *The Making of Homeric Verse*. Ed. Adam Parry. Oxford: The Clarendon Press, 1971.

Patty, James T. "La Prèmiere Rencontre de Baudelaire avec Wagner (*Journal des debats, 18 mai 1849*)." *Bulletin baudelairien* 19.3 (1980): 71–84.

Patzer, H. "Rhapsodos." *Hermes* 80 (1952): 314–25.

Pauly, Augusta, and Georg Wissowa. *Real Enzyclopädie der classischen Altertumswissenschaft.* Ed. Wilhelm Kroll and Karl Mittelhaus. Stuttgart: J. B. Metzlersche Verlagsbuchhandlung, 1936.

Perényi, Eleanor. *Liszt: The Artist as Romantic Hero.* Boston: Little, Brown, 1974.

Perrault, Charles. *Parallèle des anciens et des modernes en ce qui regarde les arts et les sciences.* Intro. H. R. Jauss and M. Imdahl. Munich: Eidos Verlag, 1964.

Plato, *The Collected Dialogues.* Ed. Edith Hamilton and Huntington Cairns. Princeton: Princeton University Press, 1961.

Poe, Edgar Allan. *Great Short Works of Edgar Allan Poe.* Ed. G. R. Thompson. New York: Harper and Row, 1970.

Poulet, Georges. *Les Metamophoses du cercle.* Paris: Plon, 1961.

Pratt, Mary Louise. *Toward a Speech Act Theory of Literary Discourse.* Bloomington: Indiana University Press, 1977.

Preisendanz, Wolfgang. *Heinrich Heine: Werkstrukturen und Epochenbezug.* Munich: Wilhelm Fink Verlag, 1983.

Price, Kingsley, ed. *On Criticizing Music: Five Philosophical Perspectives.* Baltimore: Johns Hopkins University Press, 1981.

Prutz, Robert. *Geschichte des deutschen Journalismus.* Göttingen: Vandenhoeck und Ruprecht, 1971.

Raabe, Paul. *Bücherlust und Lesefreuden: Beiträge zur Geschichte des Buchwesens im 18. und frühen 19. Jahrhundert.* Stuttgart: J. B. Metzlersche Verlagsbuchhandlung, 1984.

Ramann, Lina. *Franz Liszt: Artist and Man.* 2 vols. London: W. H. Allen, 1882.

——. *Lisztiana: Erinnerungen an Franz Liszt (1873–1886/87).* Ed. Arthur Seidl. Mainz: Schott, 1983.

Rarisch, Ilsedore. *Industrialisierung und Literatur.* Berlin: Colloquium Verlag Berlin, 1976.

Ronell, Avital. *Dictations: On Haunted Writing.* Bloomington: Indiana University Press, 1986.

——. *Finitude's Score: Essays for the End of the Millennium.* Lincoln: University of Nebraska Press, 1994.

——. *The Telephone Book: Technology, Schizophrenia, Electric Speech.* Lincoln: University of Nebraska Press, 1989.

Rosen, Charles. *The Classical Style.* New York: W. W. Norton, 1971.

——. *The Romantic Generation.* Cambridge, Mass.: Harvard University Press, 1995.

Rostand, Claude. *Liszt.* Trans. John Victor. New York: Grossman Publishers, 1972.

Rousseau, Jean-Jacques. *Les Confessions.* 2 vols. Paris: Garnier-Flammarion, 1968.

——. *Oeuvres complètes.* Paris: Dalibon, 1825.

Rowell, Lewis. *Thinking About Music: An Introduction to the Philosophy of Music.* Amherst: University of Massachusetts Press, 1983.

Rubinstein, Arthur. *My Young Years.* New York: Alfred A. Knopf, 1973.

Ruwet, Nicolas. *Langage, musique, poésie*. Paris: Editions du Seuil, 1972.

Said, Edward W. *Musical Elaborations*. New York: Columbia University Press, 1991.

Sammons, Jeffrey L. *Heinrich Heine: The Elusive Poet*. New Haven: Yale University Press, 1969.

——. *Heinrich Heine: A Modern Biography*. Princeton: Princeton University Press, 1979.

Sartre, Jean-Paul. *Baudelaire*. Trans. Martin Turnell. New York: New Directions, 1950.

Saussure, Ferdinand de. *Cours de linguistique générale*. Paris: Payot, 1931.

——. *Course in General Linguistics*. Trans. Wade Baskin. New York: McGraw-Hill, 1966.

Schadewalt, Wolfgang. *Von Homers Welt und Werk*. Stuttgart: K. F. Koehler Verlag, 1944.

Scher, Steven Paul. *Verbal Music in German Literature*. New Haven: Yale University Press, 1968.

Schiller, Friedrich. *Sämtliche Werke*. 5 vols. Munich: Winkler-Verlag, 1968.

Schlegel, Friedrich. *Kritische Friedrich-Schlegel-Ausgabe*. Ed. Ernst Behler. Paderborn: Ferdinand Schönigh, 1963.

Schonberg, Harold C. *The Virtuosi: Classical Music's Great Performers from Paganini to Pavarotti*. New York: Vintage Books, 1988.

Schor, Naomi. *George Sand and Idealism*. New York: Columbia University Press, 1993.

——. *Reading in Detail: Aesthetics and the Feminine*. New York: Methuen, 1987.

Schottenloher, Karl. *Flugblatt und Zeitung*. Berlin: Richard Carl Schmidt, 1922.

Schubert, Dietrich. "'Jetzt Wohin?' Das 'deutsche Gedächtnismal' für Heinrich Heine." *Heine Jahrbuch* 28 (1989): 43–71.

Sealey, Raphael. "From Phemios to Ion." *Revue des études grecques* 70 (1957): 312–51.

Searle, John. "Reiterating the Differences: A Reply to Derrida." *Glyph* 1 (1977): 198–208.

Searle, John, Ferenc Kiefer, and Manfred Bierwisch, eds. *Speech Act Theory and Pragmatics*. Dordrecht, Holland: D. Reidel, 1980.

Seroff, Victor. *Franz Liszt*. New York: The Macmillan Company, 1966.

Sheppard, Leslie, and Herbert R. Axelrod. *Paganini*. New Jersey: Paganiniana Publications, 1979.

Simonsuuri, Kirstie. *Homer's Original Genius: Eighteenth-Century Notions of the Early Greek Epic*. Cambridge: Cambridge University Press, 1979.

Simpson, David. *The Academic Postmodern and the Rule of Literature: A Report on Half-Knowledge*. Chicago: University of Chicago Press, 1995.

Somfai, Laszlo, ed. *Documenta Bartokiana 5*. Mainz: Schott, 1977.

Smeed, John W. *German Song and Its Poetry, 1740–1900*. London: Croom Helm, 1987.

Stanton, Domna C. *The Aristocrat as Art: A Study of the* Honnête Homme *and the Dandy in Seventeenth- and Nineteenth-Century French Literature*. New York: Columbia University Press, 1980.

Subotnik, Rose Rosengard. *Developing Variations: Style and Ideology in Western Music*. Minneapolis: University of Minnesota Press, 1991.

Terdiman, Richard. *Discourse/Counter-Discourse: The Theory and Practice of Symbolic Resistance in Nineteenth-Century France*. Ithaca, New York: Cornell University Press, 1985.

Thomas, Downing A. *Music and the Origins of Language: Theories from the French Enlightenment*. Cambridge: Cambridge University Press, 1995.

Valéry, Paul. *Oeuvres*. Ed. Jean Hytier. Paris: Bibliothèque de la Pléiade, 1957.

———. *The Collected Works of Paul Valéry*. Vol. 8. Trans. Malcolm Cowley and James R. Lawler. Princeton: Princeton University Press, 1972.

Vico, Giambattista. *The New Science of Giambattista Vico*. Trans. Thomas Goddard Bergin and Max Harold Fisch. Ithaca, New York: Cornell University Press, 1968.

*Vocabolario della lingua italiana*. 5 vols. Ed. Aldo Duro. Rome: Istituto della Enciclopedia Italiana, 1994.

Wackenroder, Wilhelm Heinrich. *Dichtung, Schriften, Briefe*. Berlin: Union Verlag, 1984.

Wagner, Richard. *Dichtungen und Schriften*. 10 vols. Ed. Dieter Borchmeyer. Frankfurt am Main: Insel Verlag, 1983.

———. *Gesammelte Schriften und Dichtungen*. 10 vols. Leipzig: Fritsch, 1897.

———. *Mein Leben*. 2 vols. Munich: F. Brickmann, 1911.

———. *My Life*. Trans. Andrew Gray. New York: Tudor Publishing, 1936.

———. *Richard Wagner's Prose Works*. Trans. W. A. Ellis. New York: Boude Brothers, 1966.

———. *Wagner Writes from Paris: Stories, Essays, and Articles by the Young Composer*. Ed. and trans. Robert L. Jacobs and Geoffrey Skelton. New York: John Day Company, 1973.

Walker, Alan. *Franz Liszt: The Virtuoso Years, 1811–1847*. Vol 1. Ithaca, New York: Cornell University Press, 1983.

———. *Franz Liszt: The Weimar Years, 1848–1861*. Vol. 2. Ithaca, New York: Cornell University Press, 1989.

Watson, Derek. *Liszt*. New York: Schirmer, 1989.

Weber, Samuel. *Mass Mediauras: Form, Technics, Media*. Stanford, Calif.: Stanford University Press, 1996.

Werner, Michael. "Der politische Schriftsteller und die (Selbst-) Zensur: Zur Dialektik von Zensur und Selbstzensur in Heines Berichten aus Paris, 1840–1844 ('Lutezia')." In *Heine Jahrbuch*. Hamburg: Hoffmann und Campe Verlag, 1987.

Wilner, Joshua. Baudelaire's *Poeme du Hachich*: "Le Bonheur Vomitif."

Winckelmann, Johann Joachim. *Gedanken über die Nachahmung der griechischen Werke in der Malerei und Bildhauerkunst*. Trans. and intro. Elfriede Heyer and Roger C. Norton. La Salle, Illinois: Open Court, 1987.

Winn, James Anderson. *Unsuspected Eloquence: A History of the Relations Between Poetry and Music*. New Haven: Yale University Press, 1981.

Wolf, F. A. *Prolegomena to Homer: 1795*. Trans. and ed. Anthony Grafton, Glenn W. Most, and James E. G. Zetzel. Princeton: Princeton University Press, 1985.

Zantop, Susanne, ed. *Paintings on the Move: Heinrich Heine and the Visual Arts*. Lincoln: University of Nebraska Press, 1989.

Zimmerman, Melvin. "La Genèse du symbole du thyrse chez Baudelaire." *Bulletin baudelairien* 2: 1 (August 1966).

# Index

In this index an "f" after a number indicates a separate reference on the next page, and an "ff" indicates separate references on the next two pages. A continuous discussion over two or more pages is indicated by a span of page numbers, e.g., "57–59." *Passim* is used for a cluster of references in close but not consecutive sequence.

Library of Congress Cataloging-in-Publication Data

Bernstein, Susan
    Virtuosity of the nineteenth century : performing music and
language in Heine, Liszt, and Baudelaire / Susan Bernstein.
      p.    cm.
    Includes bibliographical references and index.
    ISBN 0-8047-3279-5 (cloth) — ISBN 0-8047-3505-0 (pbk.).
    1. Music and language.   2. Music and literature.   3. Music—
19th century.   4. Virtuosity in music.   5. Heine, Heinrich,
1797–1856.   6. Liszt, Franz, 1811–1886.   7. Baudelaire, Charles,
1821–1867.   I. Title.
ML3849.B37   1998
780'.08—dc21

                                      98-8654
                                        CIP
                                        MN

Original printing 1998
Last figure below indicates year of this printing:
07   06   05   04   03   02   01   00   99   98